PRAISE FOR *BLUE SKY KINGDOM*

"In *Blue Sky Kingdom,* Bruce Kirkby not only takes us far across the world and deep inside a rarely seen culture, but also allows us an intimate view of his family, all while writing with tender honesty, penetrating insight and a delightful lack of bravado. Kirkby gently reminds us to breathe, embrace the unfamiliar and celebrate even the smallest of moments."

—Jill Fredston, author of *Rowing to Latitude* and *Snowstruck*

"Bruce Kirkby has lived the dream of the modern globe-trotting adventurer: crossing Arabian sand seas, sea-kayaking Iceland and Borneo, traversing Northern Mongolia on horseback. In *Blue Sky Kingdom,* Kirkby's wife and two young sons join him for a different kind of journey—to an isolated Buddhist monastery, yes, but also to the elusive and fragile heart of wisdom that we all hope to glimpse in this lifetime. What a heartfelt, lovely and kind book this is."

—Daniel Duane, author of *Caught Inside*

"Insightful and adventurous, *Blue Sky Kingdom* offers a road map on how to learn from the world . . . There is wisdom in this book. Open it and let your imagination soar."

—Conrad Anker, acclaimed American alpinist

"In an era when countless demands make it increasingly easy to ignore people and engage instead with devices, *Blue Sky Kingdom* provides a much-needed call back to the physical world."

—Darcy Gaechter, author of *Amazon Woman*

"A rollicking journey, full of insights on cultivating a nourishing, fully present life amidst so much noise and distraction."

—Brad Stulberg, coauthor of *Peak Performance* and *The Passion Paradox*

"By any standards, it's a big adventure to travel the slow way across the world to a remote corner of the Himalaya and live there for months in a spartan Buddhist monastery—but taking young children along ramps it up to another level. Written with zest and clarity, Bruce's account is compelling, moving, funny and above all honest, sharing hardships and frustrations along with the joys and ultimate rewards."

—Maria Coffey, author of *Where The Mountain Casts Its Shadow*

BLUE SKY KINGDOM

BLUE SKY KINGDOM

AN EPIC FAMILY JOURNEY TO THE
HEART OF THE HIMALAYAS

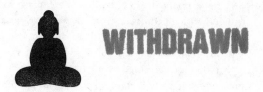

BRUCE KIRKBY

PEGASUS BOOKS
NEW YORK LONDON

BLUE SKY KINGDOM

Pegasus Books, Ltd.
148 W. 37th Street, 13th Floor
New York, NY 10018

First Pegasus Books edition October 2020

Interior design by Maria Fernandez

Library of Congress Cataloging-in-Publication Data is available.

ISBN: 978-1-64313-568-7

10 9 8 7 6 5 4 3 2 1

Printed in the United States of America
Distributed by Simon & Schuster
www.pegasusbooks.com

For the novice monks of Karsha Gompa,

Lama Wangyal,

and above all,

for Pitter, Big B and Tiny T.

CONTENTS

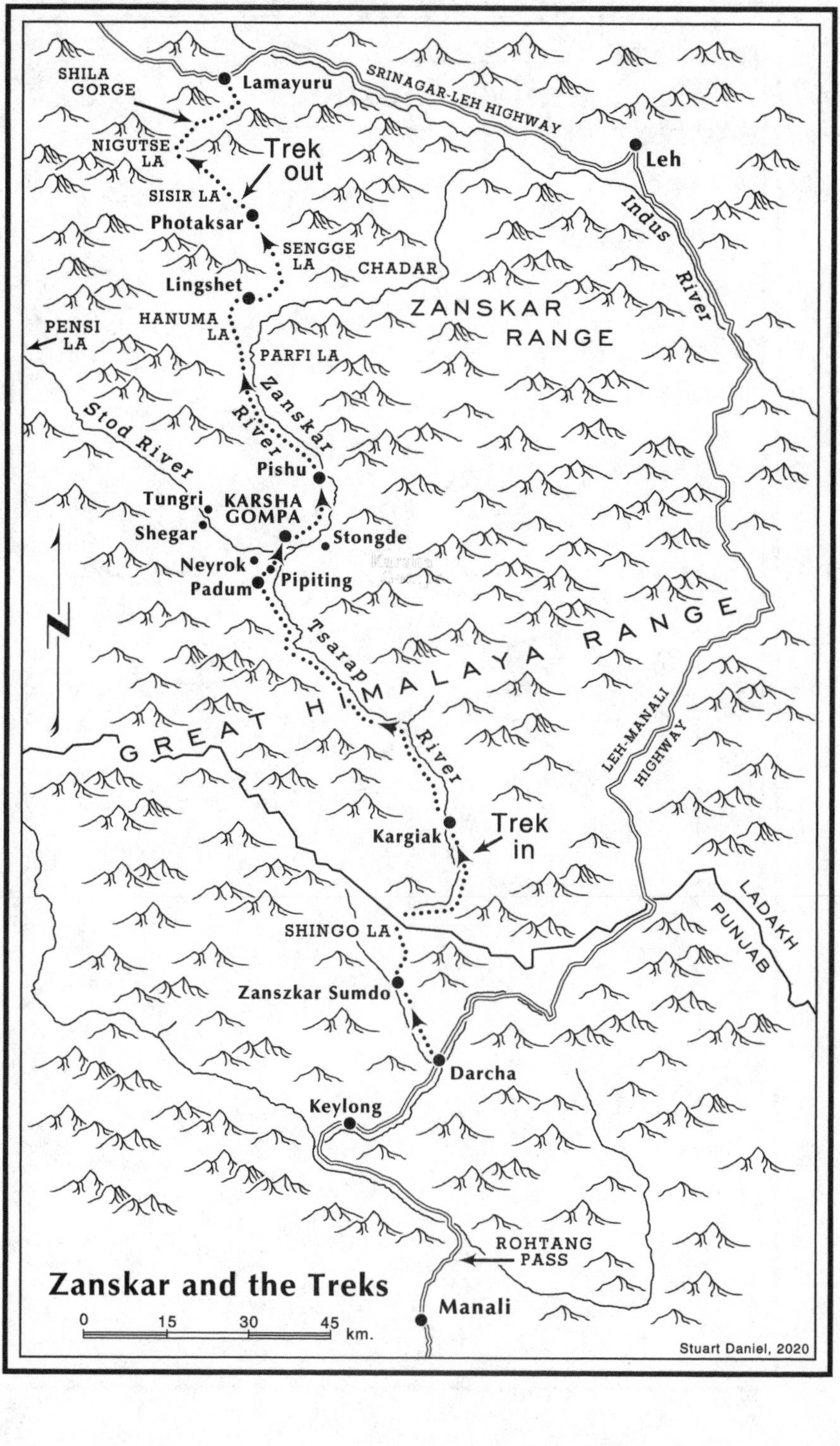

SHILA GORGE

Lamayuru

SRINAGAR-LEH HIGHWAY

Leh

NIGUTSE LA

Trek out

SISIR LA

Photaksar

SENGGE LA

CHADAR

ZANSKAR RANGE

Indus River

Lingshet

HANUMA LA

PARFI LA

Zanskar River

PENSI LA

Stod River

Pishu

Tungri

KARSHA GOMPA

Shegar

Stongde

Neyrok

Padum

Pipiting

N

Tsarap River

G R E A T   H I M A L A Y A   R A N G E

LEH-MANALI HIGHWAY

Kargiak

Trek in

LADAKH

PUNJAB

SHINGO LA

Zanszkar Sumdo

Darcha

Keylong

ROHTANG PASS

Manali

Zanskar and the Treks

0   15   30   45 km.

Stuart Daniel, 2020

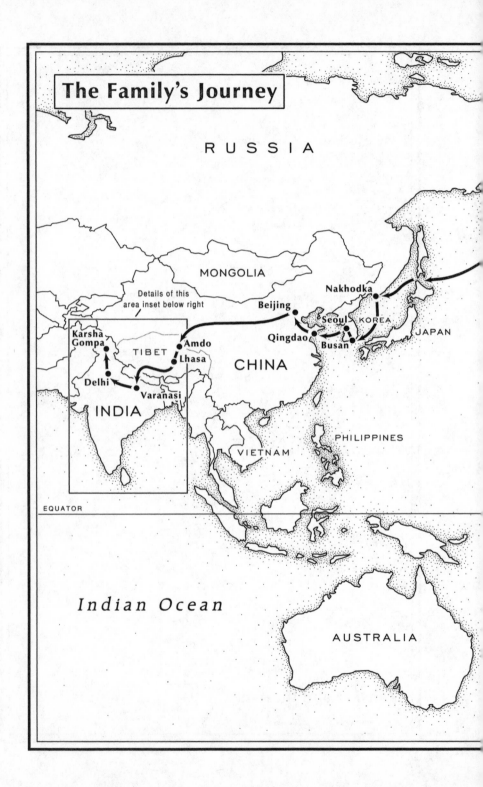

The Family's Journey

RUSSIA

MONGOLIA

Nakhodka

Details of this
area inset below right

Beijing

Seoul KOREA

JAPAN

Karsha
Gompa

Amdo

TIBET

Lhasa

Qingdao

Busan

CHINA

Delhi

Varanasi

INDIA

PHILIPPINES

VIETNAM

EQUATOR

Indian Ocean

AUSTRALIA

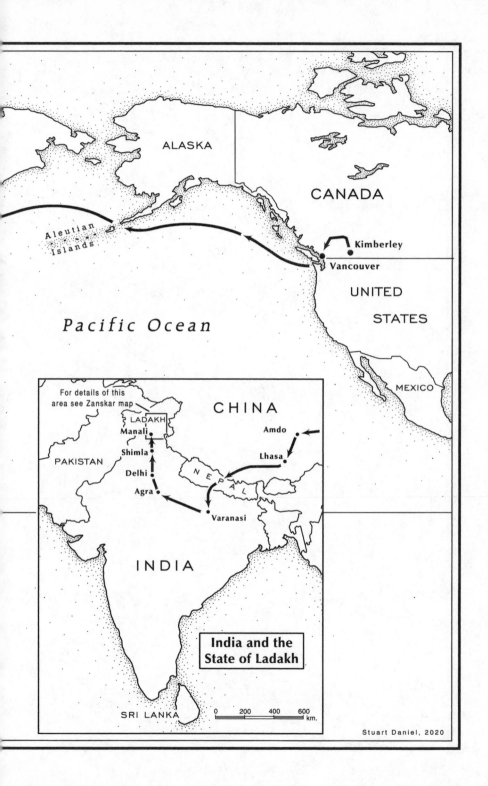

ALASKA

CANADA

Aleutian
Islands

Kimberley

Vancouver

UNITED

STATES

Pacific Ocean

MEXICO

For details of this
area see Zanskar map

CHINA

LADAKH

Manali

Amdo

PAKISTAN

Shimla

Lhasa

N E P A L

Delhi

Agra

Varanasi

INDIA

**India and the
State of Ladakh**

SRI LANKA

0   200   400   600
km.

Stuart Daniel, 2020

PROLOGUE

Attention is the rarest and purest form of generosity . . .
—Simone Weil,
Letter to Joë Bousquet,
April 13, 1942

Himachal Pradesh
Northern India

Lumbering trains carried our family westward across the Indian Plains. The terrific heat of summer had descended, and our days dissolved into a mirage of dust, tightly pressed bodies, greasy curry and children's storybooks.

"Way too smelly," our young boys would groan as the tang of perspiration and urine rose in unison with the thermometer.

So we surrendered our seats, choosing instead to stand before open carriage doors, braced together against the wind, watching the country race past: teeming streets, brick factories, rice paddies, water buffalo, egrets on the wing. And late each afternoon, just as the sun's final embers drifted from the sky, I spotted dark clouds gathering on the horizon—looming a little closer each day, as if pursuing us.

But it wasn't until we reached the foothills that the fever broke.

We were crammed into a dilapidated bus, bouncing up steep mountain roads scarred by rockfall, when a wave of cool air crashed over us. Moments later, heavy drops began hammering on the roof. With faces pressed against foggy windows, our boys watched as the surrounding hillsides were obscured behind silver monsoon curtains. In terraced fields, farmers scampered beneath umbrellas of oak and chestnut, and along roadside ditches, groves of head-high marijuana bowed to the deluge.

Inside the former British hill station of Manali, tarps were hastily yanked over market stalls. Horns beeped, dogs barked and foreigners in fluorescent jackets darted down cobblestone alleys, between trekking agencies, German-style bakeries and cybercafés. Overhead, thickets of hand-painted signs, satellite television dishes and tangled power lines obscured the hemorrhaging skies, so profuse they reminded me of rainforest foliage. Long before this deep valley became lionized as a stoners' paradise, it was known among Hindus simply as Kulantapith—or "the end of the habitable world."

It certainly wasn't that anymore.

Exhausted and fighting the flu, the four of us took refuge in a stone cottage tucked amid the crooked temples and stooped shanties of Old Town, where orchards of apple and plum gave way to mountainsides of cedar and mist. Packed together into one small bed, we read aloud *The Berenstain Bears and Too Much TV* while sipping ginger tea. Then Richard Scarry's *Busy, Busy World*. Then Bill Peet's *Wump World*. Outside an open window, the downpour intensified.

Long after our boys had drifted off to sleep, my wife and I worked beneath a bare lightbulb. Slowly and steadily we sorted a tangle of gear and supplies into two piles. The bigger mound—things we once thought we needed but actually didn't—would be abandoned. The smaller pile held just the essentials: everything required to survive three months amongst the world's highest peaks.

The next day, a minivan would carry us north, over soaring passes, toward an unmarked trailhead. From there, we would set out by foot, crossing the spine of the Great Himalaya Range and plunging into that swirl of summits and contested borders where China, Pakistan and India collide. Our destination was Karsha Gompa, a thousand-year-old Buddhist monastery barnacled to cliffs above the union of two great rivers—our home until winter.

In an adjacent room, door slightly ajar, both boys slept soundly with a fan blowing on them, cheeks flushed and sheets cast aside. Chestnut-haired Bodi was seven. Angular and lanky like a caribou, he was a thoughtful boy and exceptionally bright—hesitant around strangers and a stickler for routine. Three-year-old Taj was Bodi's foil—blond, carefree and giggly. His easy manner had drawn others to him from the earliest days.

As I gazed at our sleeping boys—mouths open, dried drool on their cheeks, so perfect, so trusting, so fragile—a fleeting shadow passed inside me. Tomorrow would mark the point of no return. *What dangers lay ahead? Was this journey really in their best interests? Or was it fuelled by my own ambitions?* I glanced at Christine, but said nothing. I knew she worried too, in her own ways.

Wearing a sweat-dampened tank top, blonde hair tousled, my wife was trying to coerce toothbrushes, baby wipes and hotel shampoo bottles into an uncooperative stuff sack. Sensing my pause, she pointed to the jumble of filmmaking equipment at my feet.

"I really don't think you need that stuff. We are already overloaded. And making a film is just going to be another distraction."

"Yeah, yeah, I know, but . . ."

I wasn't about to ditch the film project now. I'd already invested thousands in new equipment—Steadicam, slider rails, wireless microphones—and after training myself to use it, I'd shipped it all to Manali at great effort, with plans to make a documentary about our time at the monastery. Stubbornly, I tried to cram a bulky tripod into an overstuffed duffel, without success.

"Seriously, you should just ship it back home," Christine said. Then she added with a sigh, "I'm sick and tired of cameras."

"This will be different," I promised. "It's only me."

But even as I said it, I knew I'd already asked too much of her.

A crew from the Travel Channel had been following our family since the day we'd left home in Canada twelve weeks earlier, filming us from dusk till dawn.* Most were kids in their twenties with tattoos and nose rings, wearing flat-brimmed ball caps and skateboarding shoes. Selfishly, I had agreed to the television project at the last minute, viewing it as a way to advance my freelance writing and photography career—as well as an opportunity to pay bills during our six-month absence. An introvert by nature, Christine had been lukewarm about the idea from the start. Her greatest concern remained how it might affect our boys.

---

* The resulting series, *Big Crazy Family Adventure*, aired on the Travel Channel.

But the end was nigh. The next day most of the entourage would jet back to Los Angeles, leaving just a skeleton crew to accompany us on foot across the Himalaya. Those stragglers would leave us in peace upon reaching the monastery.

"It's your choice," Christine eventually shrugged. "But I think you should scrap the film stuff and concentrate on our boys."

❧

Half a year earlier and half a world away, in the stillness of a December dawn, I sat between Bodi and Taj at our kitchen table in Kimberley, British Columbia. A scattering of cereal boxes and an empty milk jug lay before us. In the wood stove nearby, a fire crackled to life, and as the house warmed, timbers popped and groaned. Upstairs, Christine remained in bed, exhausted and puffy-eyed—an over-stretched mother clinging to a rare moment of reprieve. Outside, snowflakes the size of butterfly wings spiralled down in darkness.

Absently spooning granola to my mouth, I scrolled through Facebook, my phone casting an eerie blue light over the boys. Of course everything that floated across the screen was trivial, mindless crap. But I kept on digging, driven by the same urge that draws the beachcomber to the ocean, or the gold panner to the river; the eternal hope that somewhere amongst all that crap might lie a treasure.

"DAD!" Bodi screamed, interrupting my trance. "Did you hear a single word I just said?"

"Bo-Bee!" Tiny Taj shouted, stabbing a rubber spoon overhead and spilling Cheerios across fuzzy pyjamas, celebrating fathomless love for an older brother who increasingly ignored him.

Pushing the phone aside, I tucked a strand of hair behind Bodi's ear and kissed his silken cheek. "Tell me again," I whispered.

Painstakingly, Bodi enumerated the distance to every planet in our solar system. The numbers were almost certainly accurate, as Bodi has a mind for such details, but as I listened, I grew aware of a deeper truth—I hadn't heard a word he'd previously said, despite the fact that he was sitting right beside me and despite the fact that he stood among the most precious things in my life.

With unsettling frequency, I seemed to be drifting through life with my consciousness untethered. I lost track of conversations. It was not uncommon to drive somewhere, only to find myself unable to recall anything of the journey. In the supermarket, I wandered the aisles, unsure what I had come for. I had even lost the ability to read several consecutive pages of a book without Googling something. My brain felt constantly ravenous, its capacity for concentration and contemplation gone. The result was a state of never quite feeling caught up, of permanently fractured awareness.

The situation had worsened following the purchase of an iPhone. Now instead of reaching for my wife at dawn, I reached for the bedside table. Ungodly stretches were passed in the privacy of the bathroom, scrolling through Twitter in private, while large portions of my work days vanished into email and Internet wanderings. At the playground, I flicked through Instagram in the company of other preoccupied parents while my boys dangled hopelessly in swings.

On top of that, since the birth of our children, both Christine and I had grown increasingly socially isolated. Between sleepless nights, runny noses, emails, business trips, mortgage payments and all the other tiny, imperceptible assaults of modern life, it felt like we were slipping underwater. And while our marriage itself wasn't in threat of capsizing, it wasn't all smooth sailing either. We bickered, went to counselling, and then bickered some more.

"How we spend our days is, of course, how we spend our lives," Annie Dillard famously noted, and while I worried about our deteriorating situation, modern malaise is unremarkable. Inescapable, some might suggest. And we had more immediate concerns.

Three years earlier, on a blustery November afternoon, Christine and I had taken Bodi to a child development center in a neighboring town, where in a cinder-block basement, behind a soundproof window, we watched our son endure a battery of tests. Later, a hushed team of specialists gathered to deliver an opaque diagnosis of PDD-NOS, pervasive developmental disorder, not otherwise specified. It would take years for me to grasp the full implications, but the synopsis was clear—Bodi experienced the world differently than most.

In the intervening years, Christine and I had tried everything we could, enrolling him in a palette of interventions, including social skills coaching, behavioral therapy, speech pathology, counseling and occupational therapy. Like all parents, we wanted to provide our son with every opportunity and possibility we could, helping him grow into everything he was capable of being. But despite these relentless efforts, I remained haunted by a vague sense we were somehow losing ground.

But it wasn't until that quiet winter morning, as Bodi bawled and Taj sprayed Cheerios across the table, that I saw the years slipping past and our boys growing older. I sensed a million opportunities lost and I recognized the role my own lack of attention was playing. And I understood that if there was to be any hope of truly connecting with my eldest son, of deciphering all the opaque messages he left scattered in his wake and bringing to light all the beauty concealed within, I needed to be goddamned present.

Something had to change.

For years, Christine and I had batted around the idea of taking our family to live in a Himalayan Buddhist monastery—we envisaged somewhere far from the tentacles of modernity. But it had always been a sort of fantasy, something that might happen *someday*.

Well, on that midwinter morning, as butterfly wings fluttered against the dark windows, I sensed that *someday* had arrived.

Christine—a truly amazing woman—required almost no convincing. She once spent an entire winter in the basement of a Calgary community hall, studying the complex rituals and iconography of Tibetan Buddhism, and ever since had harbored a desire to experience the ancient tradition first-hand. Within days, plans began taking shape.

Friends and family suggested we were overreacting. Dragging two young children halfway around the world, to live in uncertain (but certainly rudimentary) conditions, because of a vague notion that we all might be better off for it? Why not something slightly more *normal*? A cruise? A few weeks at a Mexican all-inclusive? If it was adventure we sought, what about a month in Costa Rica, where we could recharge in comfort and safety. Fair enough; I saw their point.

But our journey was never meant to be an escape. Nor for that matter was it a search for enlightenment. Our plans were simply driven by instinct, by self-preservation. It felt as if we had slipped into the ocean's depths, and our only choice was to swim for all we were worth toward a distant, obscure light—something we hoped was the surface.

❧

It was past midnight when Christine finally clicked off the bulb in our Manali cottage, and we crawled together beneath the thin sheets of a hard bed. I held her for a time, before humidity and heat drove us apart. In the stillness that followed, wind rattled panes. A gecko darted across cinder blocks. When sleep came it was fitful and plagued by the recurring sensation that I was falling. At some point Bodi screamed in the darkness and Christine leapt up to comfort him.

Two duffel bags sat beside the cottage door. Inside we'd stuffed a few warm clothes, a tent and sleeping bags, headlamps, toiletries, a first aid kit, two small stuff sacks crammed with Lego, two child carrier backpacks, a bag of school supplies, a handful of books, one small camera and our journals.

Everything else we left behind.

7

THE SHALLOWS

As we embrace technology's gifts, we usually fail to consider what they ask from us in return—the subtle, hardly noticeable payments we make in exchange for their marvelous service.

—Michael Harris,
The End of Absence

1

UNTETHERING

Kimberley
British Columbia

Like a tiger stalking prey, three-year-old Taj slipped into our bedroom before dawn, stealthily crossing the squeaky floor without a sound. Then he pounced. Christine's yelp raised Bodi, who appeared softly at the door, like a mouse.

"Can we do our screen time?" he pleaded, referring to the pair's daily thirty-minute allotment.

"Puh-leeze?" begged Taj.

"You know this is the last time, right?" Christine demanded. "We are leaving in a few hours. And I don't want any arguments when I say it's time to turn the TV off."

"OK, Mom. Thanks."

Christine clicked on the television, and the pair settled in our bed—a sea of duvet separating them, because Bodi couldn't abide Taj's fidgeting. As I hurried downstairs to brew coffee, I was aware that neither had any idea what was coming. How could they?

Of course Christine and I had discussed our approaching journey with them, but comprehension of such distance and time remained beyond their grasp. Their only foundation in the months ahead would be us.

The television crew soon arrived, paper coffee cups in hand, frustrated they'd missed our rising. They'd landed in Kimberley three days earlier, alongside the first robins of spring, jetting up from Los Angeles as snow receded from the local Purcell Mountains. Young and enthusiastic, they'd trampled purple crocuses behind our home while smoking cigarettes and drinking bottled water. For most, Canada represented their first trip abroad.

There were sixteen in total (a shocking number to us): three camera operators, two audio technicians, four producers ("Pro-douchers," an Aussie camera operator whispered during introductions), two production assistants, a data manager and four doing who-knows-what. Wes, a young Australian, was in charge. Although he looked like the front man for a boy band, with gelled hair and dashing looks, I genuinely liked him, for he radiated enthusiasm.

I gathered the crew members in our kitchen and draped silken *khata* scarves around their necks, a traditional Himalayan Buddhist gift bestowed upon arrival or departure. The scarves had been given to me decades earlier, by Sherpa companions on Everest, with wishes of safety and luck; I passed them on in the same spirit.

Then heavy cameras were hoisted. An audio technician taped wireless microphones inside our shirts while a drone hovered outside our house like a giant mosquito, flitting from window to window.

"Just pretend we're not here," said Wes.

Seriously?

Bodi and Taj orbited these cool TV cats, intrigued by their slouchy toques and Chuck Taylor sneakers. Christine and I were too damn busy to pay much attention and quickly returned to checking lists that stretched across palms and up forearms, all the supplies for a journey that would begin at the back door of our home in Kimberley and carry us north of the Arctic Circle, through semitropical Asia, and finally, high into the Himalaya.

Our packing strategy was simple. If we crammed everything we needed into two gigantic duffels, I could carry both—one on my back, and one in my arms—leaving Christine free to grasp the boys' hands, and allowing our family to navigate every situation we expected to encounter: train stations, markets, busy streets, crowded hostels.

Two hours later, after stuffing the boys' feet into tiny hiking boots, Christine herded them out the back door. The last thing I did before locking up was turn off my iPhone and toss it in a kitchen drawer. Anyone sending an email in the coming six months would receive an auto-response: *Back in November. Sorry for the inconvenience.*

Frost crunched underfoot and a dusting of late-season snow covered the two canoes strapped atop our rusty pickup. An hour's drive brought us to the headwaters of the Columbia River, where I chopped down a pair of saplings, using them as spars to lash the canoes together and form a stable catamaran. By the time we had our gear loaded and life jackets on, the early May sun was scorching.

"India, six miles!" Taj declared, thrusting an arm skyward.

"Any fish down there?" Bodi asked, peering over the gunwale as I struggled to spread sunscreen on his cheeks.

"Rainbow trout?" Christine guessed.

"Oh yeah!" Bodi leapt to his feet, grabbing for his fishing rod. "Get ready to eat rainbow trout."

We paddled north, following the sluggish river through wetlands, serenaded by red-winged blackbirds and the occasional shotgun crack of a beaver tail. The television crew orbited us in motorboats. Like dogs meeting for the first time in a park, we were still sniffing and testing boundaries.

Christine dug through her pack and handed the boys water bottles, urging both to drink. Ignoring her request, Bodi picked up his tiny paddle and splashed the water. Taj waved his fishing rod back and forth, as the lure—hook removed—rattled off hull and hats.

After lunch, storm clouds appeared on the horizon and the motorboats zoomed close. Cameras were raised, and a producer launched into a breathless OTF interview—"on the fly," in television parlance.

"Lightning!" she intoned earnestly. "Are the kids in danger?"

I found it hard to muster much concern—it was just a distant smattering of dark clouds—but the producer's obvious worry launched Bodi into hysterics. Christine tried to calm him. Taj swung his fishing rod and I paddled on in silence. All the while, cameras rolled.

That evening we camped on a vast sandy beach, exposed by low water. After recording us cooking a pasta dinner over a driftwood fire, the crew disappeared, whisked away by motorboat to a distant motel. In the stillness of their wake, Christine and I pitched our tent while stars whispered from an indigo sky. We were brushing the boys' teeth when howls erupted nearby.

"Wolves!" Christine whispered. "They're blessing our journey."

"Holy cow!" Bodi gasped.

"Bodi, they are not cows!" Taj said, clutching Christine's leg.

The pack passed close by, slipping like spirits through the lowland alder. I have always taken the fleeting appearance of *Canis lupus* as a good omen, like finding a heart-shaped rock or glimpsing the aurora borealis, and I nodded to the passing shadows.

❧

After five days on the Columbia River, we reached the lumber town of Golden, where we stashed the canoes, hauled our duffel bags to the Trans-Canada rail line, and caught a train for the coast.

In Vancouver, a taxi carried us to the industrial wharf, joining a long line of eighteen-wheel transport trucks delivering cargo containers. Christine gasped when she caught sight of the *Hanjin Ottawa*'s black hull, three football fields long and soaring skyward more than ten storeys. This vessel would carry five thousand containers—and us—across the Pacific, yet was small by modern standards.

A short man in a tan uniform and orange hard hat waited for us at the end of a frighteningly long gangplank. Four gold bars adorned his shoulder boards.

"Thank god you are not Swiss," he barked. "It's always the Swiss travelling by container ship these days. But I think Canadians are less picky, no?"

Peering at us over his reading glasses, he introduced himself as Captain Huth, but in the same breath insisted we call him Captain Klugscheisser, which he explained meant "clever person."* Stooping to shake our boys' hands, he added, "I think we may have two more *klugscheissers* here, no?" Then with a crisp salute, he waved us up the gangplank.

Just four members of the television crew (two camera operators, one audio technician, one producer) would accompany us. Wes and the rest would catch a plane across the Pacific, meeting us in Busan, South Korea, in two weeks.

As we climbed aboard, one of the camera operators whistled to get our attention. Klugscheisser was furious. "The only things that whistle aboard this ship are the wind and me," he barked. Whistling is considered bad luck amongst mariners, thought to change the winds and rumoured to have been the signal

---

* A more literal translation is "smart ass."

that launched mutiny aboard the *Bounty*. The camera operator promised not to whistle again aboard the boat.

"This is not a boat," Klugscheisser roared. "She's a ship."

An elevator carried us to the sixth level of the superstructure, and a door marked OWNER'S CABIN. Christine's face lit up as it swung open, revealing a carpeted suite complete with sofas, wood panelling and mood lighting.

"I did not expect such luxury," she admitted. "Somehow I'd always imagined we'd be sleeping on hard bunks. In a damp bilge. Infested with rats."

❧

The next morning the *Hanjin Ottawa* cast off. Bow thrusters nudged the towering hull from the wharf, then the ship's immense ten-cylinder engine—capable of powering a small town—settled into a deep, thunderous rhythm that would remain unchanged until we reached Asia.

A few hours later we plowed past the city of Victoria, and a small speedboat pulled alongside the *Hanjin*. A rope ladder was lowered toward it, and a man in naval uniform appeared on the deck beside us. After tousling our boys' hair, the harbour pilot hoisted himself over the railing and lowered himself arm over arm, bouncing against the hull as the ship pitched. Finally, in a James Bond–esque manoeuvre, he leapt into the waiting speedboat and was whisked away.

Land soon dropped behind us. The air grew colder. Sea, sky, mist and waves melded, and we steamed on into a kaleidoscope of blue and grey.

❧

A decade earlier, Christine and I had moved to Kimberley, a sleepy one-traffic-light town tucked into British Columbia's Interior Mountains, where homes are heated with firewood and freezers are crammed with elk meat. We bought a ramshackle miner's house, drove a rusting pickup and had no retirement savings. The pursuit of money was not central to our lives, and we certainly weren't rich—at least not by the standard measure of accountants.

After graduating with a degree in engineering physics in 1990, I quit my database programming job after four months, preferring the infinitely more rewarding task of guiding whitewater rafts on the nearby Ottawa River, unconcerned by the 95 percent slash in pay.

Glorious, carefree summers in the Arctic followed, where I led canoe and raft expeditions on Northern rivers. Winters were spent sea kayaking in the Caribbean, skiing in the Alps and biking through Asia. With time, I began migrating toward larger expeditions: crossing Arabia by camel; making a raft descent of Ethiopia's Blue Nile Gorge; and joining a Canadian team on Everest, where I was responsible for sending satellite updates to sponsors.

When I decided to write a book about these journeys, it seemed a dubious ambition, for I'd failed both English and typing in high school. But a publisher bought the manuscript, editors helped polish my words, reviewers offered praise, and to my surprise, people actually read it. A few years later I wrote another. Soon magazines were sending me on foreign assignments. I started writing a weekly travel column for *The Globe and Mail*. I returned to the Arctic to work as a guide every summer, but otherwise my income was sporadic and uncertain. I rarely knew where the next paycheck was coming from—and frankly, it didn't matter. I was happy.

I met Christine at a Calgary gym in 1999, where she worked as a personal trainer. Raised in a small Prairie town by a welder and a rodeo queen, she was a preternaturally talented athlete, something she demonstrated by jogging me into the ground on early dates. Despite wildly different childhoods—hers included snowmobile races, muscle cars, Wonder Bread and Spam while mine featured a mother growing alfalfa sprouts on the windowsills and a nuclear physicist father—it was clear we both valued experiences over money. From the start, being together was easy.

Christine had travelled widely before we met, backpacking through Australia, Fiji, Europe and Nepal. Although she had never slept in a tent, she dove into the deep end on our first trip, a twenty-four-day sea kayaking journey along Canada's West Coast. Increasingly challenging journeys followed: a forty-day coast-to-coast trek across Iceland, two months packing horses on the Mongolian steppe (neither of us had ridden a horse before), traversing the north coast of Borneo in a folding kayak, exploring the jungle-tufted islets of Myanmar's Mergui Archipelago (where we were briefly tossed in jail) and a three-month paddle through the iceberg-strewn fjords of Greenland's rugged east coast.

Many suggested it was unfair of me to drag Christine on such journeys. Or hinted I was a lucky man to have found a partner who tolerated my "vacations." The veiled insinuation—that Christine would never willingly choose to pursue such wilderness experiences of her own volition—always felt deeply insulting.

For her part, Christine regarded our journeys with remarkable humility. In contrast to the bravado and posturing common in today's world of outdoor athletes, none of our trips seemed like a big deal to Christine. If I ever caught her describing the events to her friends, it was as casually as one might talk of camping out in the backyard. To me it was clear she went to the wilderness for the purest of motives: because she loved being out there.

And I loved her all the more for it.

❧

The idea of taking our boys to live in a Himalayan Buddhist monastery had been kicking around for years—a vague, pie-in-the-sky type of plan, which Christine and I came at from wildly different perspectives.

As a long-time practitioner of meditation and yoga, Christine was an innately spiritual woman, with interests that spilled into psychics, seers, shamans, auras and the deleterious effects of Mercury in retrograde—all concepts somewhat disquieting to my scientific mind. Hermann Hesse's *Siddhartha* was her favorite undergraduate book. Crystals and dreamcatchers adorned her nightstand. Visits to ashrams and silent yogic retreats were not uncommon. When the weekend newspaper arrived, she flipped first to the horoscopes.

On the other hand, I was a lifelong skeptic with a reflexive resistance to all forms of otherworldliness, raised upon a steady diet of peer-reviewed, data-driven, journal-published science. At times I wished I could share Christine's unquestioning faith in the inexplicable, feeling somewhat inadequate for not being able to "let myself go," but the unvarnished truth, if I dug deep, was that I just didn't get it. Apart from an abstract feeling of divine wonderment in the face of nature, I remained a staunch non-believer.

So spirituality represented a divide between Christine and me, and one we occasionally squabbled over. I suggested reincarnation was not just improbable, but flat out illogical. The earth's population had increased by over five billion people in the last century. Where had all those new souls come from?

"Oh, Bruce. It's not like that. I can't explain, but it's just something I know inside to be true."

Such debates were unwinnable, and with time, we learned to accept our differences.

But curiously, I'd always felt open to Tibetan Buddhism. Over the space of a dozen Himalayan journeys I'd found comfort and camaraderie in the presence of Nepal's cheery Sherpas, the famed high-altitude porters and mountaineers of Tibetan Buddhist ethnicity. When things turned pear-shaped on an expedition, as they inevitably did, instead of shouting and worrying, the Sherpas laughed and carried on. Even in the face of terrible trials, their joy seemed irrepressible. Whatever their secret sauce was, I wanted a taste.

On a deeper level, Buddhism's core tenets—tolerance, compassion, non-attachment, impermanence—all sounded like common sense to me. I was unexpectedly drawn to Tibetan Buddhism's spiritual leader, the wildly popular fourteenth Dalai Lama, whose jolly persona disarmed me, while his oceanic compassion humbled me. And his words resonated with simple truth. "There is no need for temples. No need for complicated philosophy. Our own brain, our own heart is our temple; the philosophy is kindness."

I often found myself dreaming the aging monk would run for political office, instead of today's bitterly partisan leaders, for I'd support his platform of love and practicality in a heartbeat.

So Christine and I—each in our own way—were curious to know more about this ethereal religion. Or philosophy. Or whatever it was.* Neither of us had ambitions to create little Buddhists of our boys, but we both felt that immersing them in the uncluttered life of a Himalayan monastery could do no harm, and possibly a world of good.

Still, the idea of dropping everything and taking our family to live in a Buddhist monastery remained a distant dream, something that might happen *someday*.

Until the Cheerio Epiphany.

❧

But where in the Himalaya should we go? And how on earth could we arrange for our family to stay at a monastery?

---

* Whether Buddhism is a religion or philosophy remains a matter of ongoing debate, with convincing arguments on both sides. But the nontheistic tradition—without god or supreme creator—refuses to fit neatly in either category.

Christine and I were both drawn to Bhutan, a nation widely recognized for its policy of placing gross national happiness ahead of gross domestic product. I'd visited the reclusive country years earlier on a photography assignment and found myself enchanted by the gentle people and their firmly held traditions. But situated on the southern flanks of the Himalaya, Bhutan catches the brunt of the monsoon. My interest waned upon learning of thick forests that would limit opportunities for trekking and exploration. Stories of rampant leeches were enough to dissuade Christine.

Next we turned our eyes to Tibet, the fountainhead of Himalayan Buddhism. Following China's invasion some fifty years earlier, travel remained tightly regulated and foreigners required a government-assigned guide to stray anywhere beyond the capital of Lhasa. It was clear our family would never be permitted to live freely in a monastery.

We considered India's colorful hill stations of Sikkim and Darjeeling, and Nepal's ancient enclaves of Mustang and Dolpo, but nothing seemed quite right.

Then an old friend with decades of Himalayan mountaineering experience suggested Ladakh. The normally taciturn man described in reverential tones the ancient culture and warm-hearted residents. "Ladakhis might even outstrip Sherpas in terms of pure, genuine friendliness," he gushed. "They are 9.5 on a scale of 10. Seriously. You gotta go."

It was high praise for a land and people I knew nothing about.

❦

Ladakh—or *La dags* in Tibetan, meaning "land of the high passes"—is perched in the outermost reaches of northern India, on the very edge of the Tibetan plateau, shoehorned between the disputed borders of Pakistan and China. It is a severe and forbidding landscape of crumbling mountains, relentless wind and cruel sun—a high-altitude desert tucked in the rain shadow of the Himalaya.

Once a remote backwater on caravan routes criss-crossing Central Asia, Ladakh was closed to foreign tourists in 1947, following the partition of India and Pakistan, and only partially reopened in 1974.

A pair of hastily completed military highways brought the first whispers of change to the region. The first road, running east–west, connected the Ladakhi capital of Leh with the Kashmiri capital of Srinagar. It was carved out in 1963, following the discovery that Chinese forces had slipped across the murky borders a decade earlier and constructed infrastructure on Indian soil without detection, an act symbolic of how vast and unpeopled the western Himalaya remained. A second road was constructed in the 1980s, running north–south from Leh to Manali, allowing for the hasty transport of Indian troops and weaponry toward sensitive frontiers.

With the roads came the ineluctable creep of modernity—loss of traditions and erosion of social cohesion. Heaviest hit was the capital city, Leh, which now sees over a million tourists every year.

But vast swaths of central Ladakh remain beyond the reach of roadside Coke stands and smoke-belching trucks, and it was while studying maps that I first spotted Zanskar. For centuries this remote valley—tucked between the Great Himalaya and Zanskar Ranges—remained notoriously hard to access, and even today, continues to exist in relative isolation.* Home to some fifteen thousand souls, sprinkled between forty hamlets and a dozen monasteries, the ancient agrarian society has endured nearly unchanged for millennia.

By coincidence, friends from Kimberley had recently returned from trekking in the region. Caught by a freak blizzard while on the trail, they'd sought refuge at Karsha Gompa, the largest Buddhist monastery in Zanskar.† The Head Lama took the pair in, offering lodging and copious amounts of tea in exchange for a week of roof shovelling.‡

"Oh, he'd love your family to visit," our friends promised.

But with no phones or Internet at the monastery, how could we ask?

Eventually we tracked down the lama's nephew, a student in southern India, and inquired if our family might visit his uncle, perhaps stay for a few months and teach English.

Weeks later we received his cryptic reply: *Most generously. Problems are none.*

---

*   In 1976 a dirt track was constructed over the Pensi La pass, bringing the first whispers of modernity and waves of curious tourists. But lying near the Pakistan border, the track is difficult to access and closed for six months of every year by snow.

†   *Gom* is Tibetan for "meditation," and *gompa* refers to a place of meditation. Today the term is widely used by travellers to imply any Buddhist monastery, but it more precisely refers to a fortified Buddhist compound.

‡   The terms "monk" and "lama" are used without distinction in Zanskar—and in this work—although subtle differences do exist. A monk is one who practices religious asceticism while a lama, meaning "guru" in Sanskrit, is a Buddhist teacher of advanced spiritual attainment.

❦

And then there is the TV crew to explain.

In the years before Bodi was born, Christine returned to university, completing first a master's degree in counseling psychology, and later a doctorate. She defended her dissertation with Taj in her womb. She saw occasional clients in a private practice, but the vast majority of her energy was devoted to raising our boys—a shared decision I supported wholeheartedly.

Which meant my erratic income was responsible for feeding four hungry mouths. So I pursued every opportunity, saying yes to anything, no matter how unqualified I was, confident the details could be sorted out later. For years, I had been in touch with an ambitious young Australian television producer, tossing around ideas for an adventure-based television series. Nothing ever seemed to fit, but nonetheless, we stayed in contact.

Shortly after we started planning our journey, Wes called and I apologetically explained I'd be away for the remainder of the year, travelling to the Himalaya with my family, where we'd live amidst Buddhist monks in a remote monastery. I promised to give him a shout as soon as I returned to talk about other television ideas. There was a long pause on the line.

"Hold on, mate. Maybe that's it? The ultimate family relocation!"

After drafting a hasty proposal, Wes circulated it among Los Angeles television executives. Having seen television pitches fail before, I dismissed the possibility as outlandish and carried on with preparations—vaccinating our children, applying for visas, packing and repacking the lightest of gear.

Late one night, just months before departure, the phone rang. It was Wes.

"Better sit down, big guy. Travel Channel loves the idea. I think we are going to get the green light."

I sensed a world of opportunity opening before us, never pausing to consider the imposition of such a production on our family. Christine was lukewarm to the idea, worried the crew would destroy the very peace we sought. I suggested our family could still disconnect from screens and connect to each other—even while being filmed. Most importantly, Wes had promised we'd be left in peace upon reaching the monastery.

Ultimately, as is often the case, money was the deciding factor. Production fees could pay the bills in our absence. So with a mix of trepidation, excitement and some reluctance, we said yes.

Hoping to avoid an overproduced reality show, I suggested we engage just a single camera operator, embedded within our "travelling family," allowing us to capture a gritty, authentic vision of the experience.

"Sorry mate, but the network has a different vision," Wes explained. "They're after something cinematic. There's gonna be a crew of sixteen, minimum. There's even a budget for helicopters. It's gonna be epic, mate. Epic!"

For the first time, I sensed we might be in over our heads.

❧

The *Hanjin Ottawa* followed a great polar arc on its journey across the Pacific, tracing the same straight-line routes flown by aircraft, northward past Alaska and the Aleutian chain, across steely grey Arctic waters, then south down Russia's Kamchatka Peninsula, toward the busy ports of Asia. There were thirty-two souls aboard: eight German officers, sixteen Filipino deckhands, four television crew and our family. Together we faced two enormities: ocean and time.

Time was tamed by a strict schedule.

Breakfast was served at 7:30 sharp, then morning tea at 10:00, lunch at 12:00, afternoon tea at 15:30 and finally supper at 17:30. Officers ate European food in one mess while the deckhands were served Asian food in another, and we took turns visiting both. Bodi, a stickler for punctuality, thrived under this rigid marine protocol.

I could have happily passed the rest of the days reclining on deck chairs, watching the ever-changing colors and moods of the ocean. But that wasn't going to work with two boys who required constant attention, so we developed our own strict family routine as well.

Each and every day after breakfast, we donned life jackets and walked the perimeter of the ship together, a trek of more than a kilometer, always pausing to play hide-and-seek on the expansive bow. Afterward, we visited the karaoke room, where off-duty Filipinos cheered wildly as Bodi belted out K-pop anthems. Following lunch, we read stories to the boys. Then, as the pair drew in their journals, Christine and I spelled each other off for an hour of physical exercise, running laps of the ship or visiting a small gymnasium with weights, a punching bag and table tennis.

The ship's swimming pool was empty—sea water in northern latitudes is unconscionably cold—but the sauna worked and we visited it regularly. A small theatre held VHS movies from the 1980s. Library shelves were heavy with nautical tomes. Wine and beer were available in the commissary, to which Klugscheisser held the only key

Days before leaving home, we had purchased our family's first iPad. It was a concession, aimed at helping our boys pass the interminable hours aboard trains, buses and cars. Optimistically, we'd loaded it with educational games designed to improve math, spelling, social skills and eye contact, but within days, members of the television crew had exposed our boys to more nefarious possibilities: *Fruit Ninja, Cartoon Wars, Plants vs. Zombies*. Resistance proved futile.

The temptation on the *Hanjin*, with endless hours to fill, was to start using the tablet as some type of pediatric travel sedative, but driven by a mix of guilt and principle, Christine and I maintained our half-hour daily rations of screen time. This didn't prevent our two young negotiators from hammering us relentlessly in a quest for longer quotas, and soon it appeared their days were centered on the infernal device—an addiction eerily reminiscent of my own relationship to my smartphone.

❧

After a week at sea, a pig was skewered on a piece of rebar, stuffed with lemongrass, then roasted above a bed of charcoal. Deckhands took shifts rotating the browning animal by hand.

"I am so happy for the pig we are going to eat," Taj clapped as he watched.

That evening, colorful lights were strung across an upper deck, alongside flags representing every nationality aboard the *Hanjin*: Filipino, Polish, German, Czech and Canadian. Klugscheisser made the first ceremonial cut, and then dinner was served. Crates of San Miguel Beer appeared and house music thumped from tinny speakers. Our boys danced without restraint, encouraged by the cheers of the ship's crew.

Despite such joys, I remained constantly aware that we were interlopers in an industrial environment. Grease-covered wrenches the size of horses' legs hung in rows outside the engine room. Massive shipping containers groaned with each pitch of the ship. Steam hissed from hidden vents, heavy doors slammed, and through it all skipped our velvety boys.

The deck railings caused Christine and me the most dread, for they were all that stood between our boys and oblivion. Widely spaced and designed to prevent a full-grown man from pitching overboard, it appeared Bodi or Taj could easily slip through these barriers. And if they did—like tripping in front of a train—there would be no chance of survival.

"It can never happen," Klugscheisser replied when I asked if he'd witnessed anyone going overboard during his decades at sea.

The *Hanjin Ottawa* cruised at twenty-one knots (thirty-eight kilometers per hour), he explained, and required nine minutes to slow down and turn around. By that time, a full-sized life raft would disappear from view. A person floating in the frigid waters of the North Pacific would be lost forever.

So we insisted the boys don life jackets each and every time they passed through the storm-safe doors leading to outer decks—not so much for flotation as for the grab-loops on the collars, which Christine and I never let from our grasp.

❧

After twelve days at sea, a gale blew up and the volcanic summits of Russia's Kamchatka Peninsula wobbled on the horizon. Biting winds sent foam tumbling across black waters. Containers strained against lashings. Buckles screamed in protest. Flocks of shearwaters and petrels took shelter in the lee of the superstructure. In the mess hall, a wall calendar swung to and fro like a pendulum.

A piercing siren indicated an abandon-ship drill that afternoon, and we hurried to join the crew on a rain-swept deck, at the muster station. The first mate barked a roll call. Thirty-one of thirty-two souls replied "aye." Only Klugscheisser was absent. In marine tradition, he remained on the bridge. He would be the last to leave the ship in case of a disaster—if at all.

Then the first mate unlocked an orange survival pod (no larger than a rowboat) and everyone piled aboard. Bodi went first, complaining bitterly that it smelled stale inside. Taj followed, wide-eyed. The last thing I saw as I ducked inside was the *Hanjin*'s call sign stencilled on the roof, conveying an ironically misspelled message: DANM.

That evening Klugscheisser appeared at our cabin door. He looked tired, and instructed us to sleep sideways on the double beds. "That way you won't fall out if the ship pitches hard."

As I lay in darkness, listening to Taj's delicate snores while the storm shrieked outside, I wondered if the captain knew something we didn't.

❧

Hanjin's gargantuan anchor chain peeling from the windlass woke me. Peering from our portal, I discovered perfectly calm seas. Nearby, a grassy headland rose from black waters. Green! After two weeks of nothing but blue and grey, the color hit me like an electric shock, bringing unexpected joy. Life, again.

A late-night radio call had diverted us to Nakhodka, Russia, where fuel was wildly discounted. As customs officers boarded the ship, Klugscheisser warned me to hide any valuables, and I stashed a stack of Ben Franklins behind pipes in our cabin roof. (We'd brought four thousand US dollars in cash to see us through our time in Zanskar, a land beyond ATMs.) International maritime agreements waive visa requirements for a ship's crew while in port. But our family and television crew, lacking Russian visas, were taken ashore in a tugboat, fingerprinted and fined six hundred dollars. Three days later, her belly full again, the *Hanjin* chugged back into the endless blue.

On the seventeenth day, we plowed into the steamy air of Asia. Peeling off puffy jackets, we replaced them with shorts and T-shirts. An egret appeared, winging its way majestically toward us, landing with a squawk on the superstructure.

By nightfall, the spectral orange lights of modern Korea burned on the horizon, like a wildfire out of control.

2

THE LITTLE PROFESSOR

The *Hanjin Ottawa* made landfall after midnight at Busan, South Korea. Dawn revealed an army of spider-like cranes, plucking containers from the ship and dropping them atop lines of waiting trucks. Lights flashed and alarms shrieked, but there wasn't a living soul in sight. Like all great ports, what was once a hive of opium dens, bordellos, mercenaries and markets had become an industrial wasteland, sanitized by the advent of mass container transport.

After eating a final breakfast of eggs and sausage alone in the mess, we found the entire crew gathered on deck waiting to bid us farewell. Even the mechanics had emerged from the ship's belly, where the engine was being readied for passage to Shanghai. Klugscheisser escorted us down the gangplank, pulling us into an embrace, his eyes growing misty.

Then we stepped into Asia.

Wes and the rest of the television crew were waiting for us on the wharf, wearing hard hats and hi-vis vests. After hugs and high-fives, Christine and I submitted to a round of on-camera interviews. At Wes's urging, Bodi and Taj said a few cute things. Beyond Immigration, a taxi carried us toward a homestay arranged from Canada months earlier.

A hotel or hostel would have undoubtedly been easier, but such amenities are increasingly shaped by Western preferences. When we travel, Christine and I tend to seek differences, and we wanted to instill the same in our boys—the habit of adapting to the unfamiliar, rather than instinctively bending the unfamiliar toward ourselves.

Outside the cab windows we glimpsed a world of cement, plastic and glass, lit by neon and peopled by a citizenry glued to smartphones and selfie sticks. Rows of relentlessly uniform apartments sprouted from green hillsides like mushrooms. In the space of a generation, South Korea has risen from the ashes of a devastating civil war to become an economic powerhouse.

Caught in snarled traffic, we were at a standstill in the middle of a seven-kilometer-long suspension bridge when Bodi announced he had to go pee—immediately! He couldn't wait an instant. Christine looked at me, shrugged, and then handed him her water bottle. Tinkling followed, and the tang of urine filled the minivan. Our driver looked appalled and opened his window, but said nothing.

A cherubic teenage girl waited for us outside a soaring waterfront apartment, wearing a cardigan, despite crushing humidity, and Hello Kitty tennis shoes.

"Hello, family," Kim Na Young cooed, bowing low.

"*Ann yeong haseyo,*" Taj replied (with prompting from Christine), which means hello, or more literally, "Are you peaceful?"

Aboard the container ship, we'd taught both boys the essential Korean greetings, and now Kim Na Young blushed.

A silent elevator whisked our family and the television crew to the forty-fifth floor, where Kim lived with her middle-aged parents, Sunny and Nikki. Sunny was a professional windsurfer, and Nikki an investment broker. Kim explained her father had left work early to meet with us, a practice known as *kal toe*—"knife office"—and viewed with disdain in a country where sixty-hour work weeks remain common.

After dropping our duffels in a barren hardwood room beside sleeping mats and shelves crowded with porcelain cats, the family prepared a traditional lunch of seared beef, lotus roots and fiery kimchi.

Later they accompanied us to nearby Haeundae Beach, all wearing sunglasses the size of drink coasters. The heat was overwhelming, and our boys stripped to their underwear while Christine and I rolled up our pants, frolicking in breaking waves along with throngs of giddy locals. Amid the frivolity, I heard what I thought was a mosquito, but realized was a drone from the television crew, buzzing just feet over our heads.

We'd grown accustomed to the crew's presence, and despite how awful it probably sounds, being filmed from dawn to dusk was proving less intrusive than I'd feared. In some ways, it felt like we'd embarked on a (well-documented) road trip with a bunch of college kids—and our children.

Even Bodi, who finds the company of strangers vexing, had grown accepting of the crew. But that didn't mean he made their lives easy. He routinely turned his back on the cameras. And if a producer asked him to repeat a line, he would refuse to do so, fuming that he had already said it. Whenever the microphone battery pack clipped to his waist grew hot, as they were prone to do, he'd rip it off and toss it aside, leaving the audio technician frantically scrambling to retrieve the thousand-dollar piece of equipment. But Bodi was never once angry at the crew members themselves, for in him I have glimpsed the rarest of all human qualities: a complete absence of malice.

At a pungent market, we watched as eels were skinned alive, touched the sandpapery skin of sharks and held gelatinous sea cucumbers. Bodi and Taj sampled fried moth larvae, a roadside snack that smelled like musty gym socks and tasted no better, popular with drunken men. Later, Bodi paused before a display of beaded bracelets and quietly asked Christine if he could buy a pink one.

"Of course," she replied.

But we had no Korean cash, and a nearby ATM rejected my Canadian bank card. I tried five more bank machines without luck. By the time I returned, empty-handed, tears were cascading down Bodi's cheeks. Soon he was thrashing about on the sidewalk, gasping for breath. As Christine comforted our distraught son, I instinctively tried to block the view of the hovering television cameras.

The situation was soon resolved. Sunny lent us two thousand won (around two dollars US) and we bought the pink bracelet. Bodi rubbed his reddened eyes, and the emotional storm receded. Eventually I found a bank machine that accepted my card, spitting out a wad as thick as a paperback. But as we were swept on by rush-hour crowds, toward a *bulgogi* barbecue dinner, I found myself again agonizing over a decision Christine and I had made months earlier.

❦

Christine went into labour on a midwinter night. Our first child was two weeks overdue, and the midwife had planned to induce birth the next morning with a foul-smelling concoction of castor oil and lemon verbena. But for a Prairie girl raised in small-town arenas, the excitement of *Hockey Night in Canada* was enough.

The first contractions began during the third period, and by midnight, it was clear this was no false alarm. We set off for the hospital in neighbouring Cranbrook, and as our rusty Toyota raced through darkness, snowflakes streaking toward the windshield made it appear as if we were travelling at light speed to a distant galaxy. In some senses, maybe we were.

Eighteen hazy hours later, amid screams and body-wracking exertion, the dilation of Christine's cervix remained stubbornly stalled at eight centimeters. Eventually the midwife and obstetrician agreed: the huge baby inside Christine was not going to pass through her narrow hips.

"You need a Caesarean," the obstetrician explained. "Right now. OK?"

Christine gazed at me, her muscular body exhausted, hair matted. She was beyond deciding. We had discussed a "birth plan" beforehand, both agreeing that the only thing that mattered was a healthy baby. The manner in which our child entered the world was not important. Still, I hesitated. The doctor glanced at me over his eyeglasses and waited.

I nodded. Immediately the room was bustling with activity. An anesthesiologist, whose meaty hands looked more like a mechanic's than a surgeon's, deftly slipped an epidural into Christine's spine. Then she was wheeled to the operating room, where the shocking physical process unfolded out of her sight, beyond a hanging sheet.

"Have they started yet?" Christine asked weakly.

"Just getting going," I lied as a team of doctors used fists and forearms to press on her distended belly, as if popping a gigantic zit. For an eternity, nothing happened. Then a tiny head burst out, dark hair glistening, eyes staring directly at me. The room was silent, apart from the ticking of a wall clock. Then a scream shattered the universe.

Shoulders followed, and the entire glistening body slipped out like a foal.

"It's a boy!" someone yelled. "A healthy boy."

Behind the sheet, tears streamed from Christine's reddened eyes.

❦

That first year passed in a haze of cotton onesies, milky skin, curious blue eyes, wonderment and love. And exhaustion. And stretches of boredom.

Neighbors and friends had long encouraged us to procreate. *You'll be such wonderful parents. A child brings joy and love like you've never known.* Now they were suddenly singing from a different song sheet. *A full night's sleep? A quiet dinner? Sex? Bahahah!* At times, I wondered if those bastards had simply been seeking company for their misery.

Our lives had been seismically altered, and along the way, Christine and I discovered that parental life does not entirely resemble the broadly marketed myth of soft blankets, cooing babies and unicorns. Yet despite such challenges, those early years felt *normal* to both of us, and everything appeared to be progressing the way it was meant to—until the age of two and a half, when Bodi abruptly began displaying both unusual behaviors and extraordinary abilities.

While his peers watched cartoons, he perused Lego instructions online, scanning schematic diagrams for models he didn't even own. At other times, he sat alone and lined up toy trains, perfectly straight, over and over. Sensitive to sounds, he screamed whenever the freezer drawer squeaked open. Sensitive to touch, he refused to wear shorts or short-sleeved shirts, and insisted Christine tear every tag from his clothing. He wore a specific shirt for every day of the week ("my Monday shirt") and vehemently refused all others. Christine began cutting his sandwiches in half; he begged her to stop. When she asked why, he explained between sobs that he couldn't decide which half to eat first.

At the local supermarket, Bodi memorized the grams of sugar per serving for every cereal in stock, a habit he picked up from Christine, who checks such statistics fastidiously. When he spotted a woman dropping a box of Sugar-Crisp into her cart, young Bodi accosted her.

"That has seventeen grams of sugar!" he shouted. "It's no good for you!"

The confused woman shuffled off, leaving our son in hysterics.

"Why did she take it, Mom? Why?" he screamed. "I told her it was bad."

The tiniest transgression was capable of triggering a tantrum: arranging apple slices the wrong way, putting a book on a different shelf, pausing to chat with a friend on the street. Our days became a cacophony of tears. Bodi cried before breakfast, during breakfast, on the way to preschool and on the way home, while shopping, during dinner and as he drifted to sleep. He even sobbed in his sleep, haunting screams that brought us sprinting to find him bolt upright, drenched in sweat, clawing at the darkness.

Neither firmness nor compassion seemed capable of corralling his tears. Ignoring the outbursts only made the situation worse, and we felt increasingly powerless. At malls and supermarkets, Christine and I shrank from withering glances. *Control your child.*

I'd always blithely assumed I'd be a great dad, fun to hang out with, full of wit and wisdom, and able to cheer up my kids on even the greyest of days. But if those first years were any indication, it seemed I'd grossly overestimated my aptitude.

Worst of all, Christine and I were both plagued by a vague sense that Bodi was drifting away from us. Whenever we nestled beside him, on a sofa or bed, he would shuffle away, insistent on maintaining a space between our bodies. If I stooped to kiss him, he would look aside. When I held out my arms for a hug, he turned his back and then slowly inched toward me in reverse, as if my love were a spotlight too blinding to endure head-on.

Such signs and symptoms are so classic—so "textbook"—that if there is someone in your life facing similar challenges, you already know what is going on. Otherwise, the behavior probably appears to you just as disconcerting and mysterious as it did to Christine and me.

From the outside, I suspect we appeared happy. We had a healthy boy, lived within a supportive community, were blessed with a network of wonderful friends. We both remained physically active, jogging with Bodi in a stroller and cross-country skiing with him in a backpack. During the evenings, Christine continued to pursue her academic studies. I'd been recently cast to host an adventure television series for CBC and was writing for increasingly prestigious publications. Everything, it seemed, was on the upswing.

But behind closed doors, we were drowning. Taking Bodi to any type of social function was torturous. At backyard barbecues and neighborhood dinners, while the other little children ran in packs, our tearful son clung to our knees, demanding to return home.

"Never again," Christine sobbed after attending a neighbor's birthday party. "Why do I always fool myself into thinking it's going to be better the next time?"

Having lost the capacity to deal with any social interaction, we stayed home, where every bleary-eyed day felt like an eternity, stretching from morning coffee to ever-more-copious glasses of evening wine. Along the way, Christine and I bickered, fought, grew depressed, went to counselling and then fought some more.

Our parental instincts clashed. Christine's impulse was to smother our child with love, regardless of his behavior, while mine was to respond to Bodi's outbursts with firmness. Neither approach worked, and as our frustration grew, I lashed out in anger, at times leaving the entire family in tears. We took a parenting course together—not a very romantic way to spend our first evenings alone since Bodi's birth—but it didn't help.

Early parenthood is supposed to stand among the happiest times of life, yet as we slipped deeper into despair, an unsettling divide existed between how I thought I should feel, and what I actually felt. For that, I was beset with guilt, sorrow and, at times, resentment.

❧

One beacon remained in our lives. Christine and I always cherished our wilderness journeys together. So when Bodi arrived, we just kept going—and packed him along.

Looking back, I'll admit I was driven at least in part by a desire to prove the naysayers wrong, to show that our adventurous lifestyle was not doomed to evaporate with the arrival of children. Yes, safety was our foremost concern, and yes, we modified our ambitions, but without question we stretched the boundaries of what is considered "normal."

When Bodi was just three months old, we packed him up into the alpine spires of Canada's Bugaboos. Soon after, he spent a month camping on the windswept coast of Vancouver Island. At seven months, he was sea kayaking in Argentina. At eight months, we trekked through the Torres del Paine in southern Chile with our infant bouncing on our backs. By the time he was eighteen months old, Bodi had spent a quarter of his life in a tent.

To those who questioned our choices, I trotted out the standard arguments about the intrinsic value of fresh air, the wonder of sleeping under the stars, the improved immunity that comes with ingesting a bit of dirt, but in retrospect, the real reason we planned such long, challenging journeys—and took Bodi along—was selfish: the wilderness was the only salve we knew.

Whatever our initial motivations, it quickly became clear that such escapes provided immense benefits to our family. Unplugging from busy lives allowed Christine and me to connect with Bodi (and each other) in ways we could never replicate at home. On these journeys, I glimpsed again the woman I'd fallen in love with: confident, secure, happy. And I'd like to think she recognized the same in me. Most notably, such journeys calmed our anxious son, perhaps because of the simple daily routine; rise with the sun, break camp, move, set camp, sleep packed together in a tent, repeat.

So we continued, cycling in France, hiking in Wales, sea kayaking along Canada's West Coast, canoeing in Canyonlands National Park, even goat packing for one hundred miles across Utah's Uintas Mountains.

The arrival of Taj didn't slow us. When the tiny boy was just eight months old—and heroic Christine still breastfeeding—we flew to Georgia (the country, not the state), bought a pair of pack horses and spent sixty days trekking the length of the Caucasus Mountains, skirting a war zone while surviving on the yogurt, honey and bread offered by passing shepherds. Perhaps because of the length and challenge of that journey, it was particularly impactful; for an entire year after returning home, I enjoyed a previously unknown depth when gazing into my boys' eyes.

But such glories fade, and old habits return. I bought an iPhone. Opened a Facebook account. Joined Twitter. Bodi began sleeping less and tantruming more. We sunk deeper beneath the surface.

❦

At some point in that whirlwind I started referring to Bodi as the "stress beaver."

It was an epithet borrowed from my days of Northern river rafting, and Christine hated it. In the high Arctic, day after day of remorseless winds can gnaw on a guide's nerves. Gusts blow rafts helter-skelter across the river. In camp, tents are sent tumbling and hats are torn from heads. Fires become a struggle to light. Sand and grit infiltrate every meal. Plates and cutlery are tossed from serving tables. At night, tents flap incessantly and sleep proves elusive. After just a few days, the entire crew is shattered, gnawed to the bone by the "stress beaver."

Like these Arctic gales, Bodi seemed to unintentionally make even the simplest daily tasks more challenging. He struggled to settle at night, rose long before dawn and only seemed to sleep soundly if we needed him awake. He was never hungry at mealtimes, but famished to the point of tears whenever food was unavailable. He refused to wear hats in the winter or short sleeves in the summer. The list goes on and on, and viewed individually, such issues appear trivial—it feels embarrassing even to mention them—but in concert they had become overwhelming, and although we were loath to admit it, something didn't feel right.

When Christine shared such concerns with doctors, she unfailingly received the same response: "You are an over-anxious mother. Bodi is fine. Stop worrying."

For years we accepted this advice and plodded along. But suddenly Taj gave us a new yardstick. While the tiny boy brought many things to our life—a mischievous, stubborn spirit with an infectious laugh—he was also the unmistakable embodiment of *neurotypical*, though we didn't know the word yet. When we gazed into his eyes, he gazed back. Rather than avoiding physical contact, he sought it. He said hello and goodbye to strangers without prompting. He didn't writhe on the floor at the mention of leaving the house. Day in and day out, Taj required just a fraction of the parenting energy that Bodi demanded, and his presence made it irrevocably clearer that something was "different" with Bodi.

Absorbed with work, I remained blithely optimistic that somehow, someday, everything would work out. But Christine would not be swayed, and driven by the seismic forces of motherhood, she took matters into her own hands: scouring the internet, calling university colleagues, and poring through academic texts. Gradually, a theory began to form. To test her suspicions, Christine slipped from her chair one day at lunch and crawled beneath the kitchen table, even as Bodi talked to her. When he didn't pause or ask what she was doing, she knew.

A month later, we drove to the Child Development Centre in nearby Cranbrook, where Bodi was assessed by a team of child-assessment experts. Later, as he played with plastic dinosaurs, they gathered Christine and me, looked us in the eye, and gently confirmed that Bodi was on the autism spectrum.[*]

A deluge of other words followed, but I don't remember any.

Driving home, I felt numb. *Fuck.* Then confused. *What the hell is autism anyway?* Then hopeful. *I'm going to love Bodi so damn much that I'll love this right out of him.*

Beside me, Christine was sobbing so hard I doubted she could see the dashboard. Even before the grief began to ebb, she had entered protection mode. "No one can know about this," she wept. "Ever."

She'd grown up in a small town. She knew how rumours spread.

❧

---

[*]   His specific diagnosis was PDD-NOS, or pervasive developmental disorder, not otherwise specified, which sounds unsettling, but denotes a high-functioning umbrella encompassing what was formerly referred to as Asperger's syndrome.

Unless you have family or close friends on the autism spectrum, or are on the spectrum yourself, there is a chance you know as much about the condition as I did when Bodi was diagnosed: almost nothing.

In a nutshell, autism spectrum disorder (ASD) encompasses an extremely broad palette of neurodevelopmental challenges, ranging from non-obvious eccentricities (such as aversion to eye contact or tendencies toward repetitive behaviors) to the completely non-verbal (individuals who may suffer from impaired motor function, sensory processing deficits and self-harming behaviors, such as headbanging.)

Despite talk of a modern "epidemic," autism is not a *disease* (i.e. an illness caused by a known biological agent), but rather a *syndrome*, or a cluster of symptoms.

While sweeping generalizations are dangerous, one characteristic common to many on the spectrum is difficulty interpreting social cues. Tony Attwood, author of the definitive *Complete Guide to Asperger's Syndrome,* uses this analogy: Imagine a driver unable to comprehend traffic signs. While perfectly capable of driving in isolation, they would suffer disastrously on a shared road. Similarly, a child blind to common social cues—the *green light* of a smile; the *slow down* of crossed arms; the *stop* of a teacher's "ahem"—is prone to mishaps, misunderstandings and, ultimately, isolation.

Today, the US Center for Disease Control estimates one in fifty-nine children are on the spectrum, making ASD twice as common as it was just seven years ago. Despite raging conspiracy theories, this increase is completely unrelated to childhood vaccinations. Rather, it is driven by expanded diagnostic criteria (the funnel has grown wider) and improved diagnostic opportunities (more children are passing through the funnel).

What this all means is someone in your life is almost certainly affected by ASD, and there is an equally good chance you don't know it.

❧

Somewhere deep inside every parent live unspoken dreams for their children: happiness, freedom, a loving partner, an engaging and meaningful career.

In the days following Bodi's diagnosis, such aspirations were cast aside as Christine and I found ourselves considering, for the first time, if he might succeed in more modest goals: making a friend, getting a job, living independently. It felt, at times, as if our lives were balanced on the edge of oblivion.

But oddly the diagnosis was also a source of hope.

For one, it explained our struggles. More importantly, it gave Christine and I something to work on—together. In that respect, it might have saved our marriage; or in all fairness, I should say Bodi saved us. Suddenly we found ourselves facing the most difficult and confusing challenge of our lives.

Parenting a child on the autism spectrum is not intuitive, at least it wasn't for me, and our support counsellor began by explaining that Bodi was awash with anxiety caused by noise, people and changing routines. In such an emotionally elevated state, he was incapable of responding appropriately to even simple requests. Thus our first job became finding ways to methodically and repeatedly reduce Bodi's angst, calming nerves jangled by the clamor and uncertainty of a modern world, bringing some measure of certainty to his life. Then, and only then, could we start making headway with his behavior and relationships.

We also faced a race against the clock, for research suggests that early intervention, notably before the age of five, offers profound advantages to children on the spectrum. Bodi was diagnosed at age four and a half.

While I was determined to help our son as best I could, my efforts were dwarfed by the ferocity with which Christine addressed these challenges. She devoured books, subscribed to scholarly journals and attended conferences, quickly becoming an expert in social theory and behavioral modelling. She sought expert help and ferried our son to endless appointments. Her laminating machine worked overtime, preparing visual schedules for every part of Bodi's day—little Velcro-backed images organized his life into series of discrete and manageable events.* Together, we used a five-point scale to help him understand and manage both external noise and internal emotions. Week after week, we prompted Bodi to say "hello" when meeting a friend and "goodbye" when we left.

The fundamental goal, our support counsellor explained, was to stretch Bodi like a balloon, over and over—gently pushing his boundaries outward, then letting them relax in again, just not quite so far.

At the same time, we wanted to prepare Bodi for a society that would almost certainly be confused by his eccentricities, and at times perhaps judge them harshly. In today's increasingly busy and distracted world—I'll be the first to

---

* A Velcro strip in the bathroom held squares for 1) Toilet, 2) Wash Hands, 3) Wash Face and 4) Brush Teeth. Before bed, as Bodi completed each task, he flipped these squares in sequence to the "done" column.

admit I'm a prime example of this modern condition—anything "different" demands extra attention, and thus has the potential to become an imposition or irritant. The result, I suspect, is that we have developed a boundless taste for homogeneity; we like things predictable, in our coffee shops, in our hotel rooms and in the people surrounding us. Mustering the time and empathy required to bridge differences can often exceed society's collective capacity.

But amidst a constellation of therapists, support groups, interventions and counselling, it was impossible to say if our efforts were helping Bodi. All we could do was everything we could do.

The only thing we didn't do in those early years was share Bodi's diagnosis with him. Our support counsellor suggested he was too young to grasp the implications. Better to wait, perhaps until he was seven or eight.

But as our departure for the monastery loomed, the approaching presence of the film crew presented a dilemma. They would surely notice something was different about Bodi, and we wanted our son to be portrayed fairly. Yet disclosing his diagnosis to the crew meant sharing it with the world. It was a decision we agonized over.

Friends and relatives urged us to keep Bodi's autism a secret. We'd be labelling our son, they suggested, making him a target for judgment amongst peers. He should be the one to choose when and where to share his diagnosis, later in life—if he wanted to at all.

While Christine and I understood this rationale, in the years since Bodi's diagnosis we'd come to see the situation differently. At the core of our thinking lay one simple conviction: we tend to hide the things we are ashamed of. And Bodi had nothing to be ashamed of. So why keep it a secret?

Having learned the telltale signs of spectrum behavior, Christine and I could see indicators everywhere—at the cinema, on the skating rink, in school. All around us, children and adults were slipping through the cracks. If our television series could help reduce the stigma of ASD, or play a role in improving early diagnosis—even for one child—that would be worth it.

So we told Wes a month before departure, explaining that Bodi's symptoms were subtle and included such things as rigidity of thinking, preference for routine and avoidance of eye contact. I didn't share my suspicions that, for Bodi, a camera lens might resemble a gigantic eye.

❦

The day after the pink bracelet incident, we departed from Busan on a high-speed train bound for Seoul. Bodi sat beside me, carefully sketching the *Hanjin Ottawa* in his journal as the lush peninsula flashed by at three hundred kilometers per hour. While he worked, I gazed affectionately upon our blue-eyed son, who loved sushi, whose favorite color was "sparkly purple," and who would one day surely grow taller than me.

This pencil sketch, like all the others found in this book, comes from Bodi's journal.

With his keen insights, black-and-white beliefs and searing honesty, Bodi was changing the way I viewed the world—for the better. In the luminous words of Temple Grandin, one of autism's leading advocates, he was "different, but not less." My only desire was that Christine and I could help him come to see his autism spectrum diagnosis not as a curse, but rather as an essential part of what makes him special.

3

AN ARMY OF TROJAN HORSES

―――――――――――❖―――――――――――

Seoul appeared like a scene from *Blade Runner*: neon lights, sirens, drizzle and twenty-five million people.

We took shelter in an ancient *hanok* neighborhood, an oasis of tile-roofed dwellings intersected by cobble footpaths, nestled in the city's core. The barren rooms were divided by paper walls, and we slept on hardwood floors, atop thin mattresses lavished with silken pillows. The boys gathered these to create a foam pit which they leapt into, despite Christine's reservations. The ceilings had been built with fourteenth-century farmers in mind, so low that even my stooped shoulders touched them, and we were forced to eat outside in a bamboo-shaded courtyard, slurping noodle soup and devouring yellow melons the size of softballs.

For two frenetic days we criss-crossed the city, travelling by subway, ascending Seoul Tower, taking the boys to Lotte World (an exhausting indoor theme park) and visiting the demilitarized zone that borders North Korea.

On the third morning, a taxi carried us to a cavernous ferry terminal in the nearby port city of Incheon. We passed the hours before departure playing cards and reading. Gradually, throngs of Chinese tourists started to arrive, returning home with the spoils of shopping. Thrilled at the sight of our porcelain-skinned, fair-haired boys, they gathered around us, snapping selfies. Bodi irritably waved them off, but Taj obliged, happily posing with gaggles of strangers who all stood poker straight.

I was reading a Chinese travel guide when I heard him scream. Leaping up, I spotted the writhing boy being carted away in the arms of a short, middle-aged woman. Christine and I sprinted to intercept, but Taj had already escaped. The woman, wearing designer sunglasses and thick makeup, apologized profusely. She was clearly mortified and meant no ill, explaining she only wanted to photograph Taj with her family. Still, it marked a shocking cultural divide. It was hard to imagine a Canadian stranger plucking up a child and carrying them away without asking a parent first, or going to jail after. Even more staggering: the woman still wanted to take Taj's photograph. Once again, she tried to drag him toward her waiting family. Christine lost her patience and waved the woman off.

Since arriving in Asia, Taj had revelled in the attention his strawberry-blond hair drew, but now as strangers continued to seek photographs, he rebuffed all. Christine felt dreadful. "He's so sensitive. I should have realized it was becoming too much for him."

Then an extraordinary metamorphosis began to unfold. Bodi, of his own volition, started jumping up and offering himself as a photo subject when strangers approached, enduring the loathed act as a decoy to protect his brother.

When a whistle sounded, the throngs pressed toward escalators, boarding an aging ferry reminiscent of TV's *Love Boat*, where the carpeted hallways were scented with mildew and dolphin statues spouted rust-colored water. After dropping our duffels in a cramped berth, we were picking over a buffet of seaweed and congee (rice porridge) when the ship cast its lines, departing on an overnight journey across the Yellow Sea.

❧

Great overland journeys, once common among backpackers, are no longer in vogue. I suspect the limiting factor is time; no one has enough. Vacations of more than a week are widely viewed as an indulgence. And the concept of taking time off without pay, or god forbid, quitting work altogether for the sole purpose of travelling on a shoestring across continents, appears even more unsettling. *How will you survive? What about your mortgage? And the blank space on your resume?*

Months earlier, as we started planning our journey to the monastery, the idea of jetting across the globe in search of stillness felt wrong. So I'd suggested to

Christine that instead of flying to the Himalaya, we travel by surface, embarking on a long, slow journey in the style of yesteryear, with kids in tow.

She did not initially share my enthusiasm.

It wasn't the hazards of such a journey that worried her, but rather the sheer and unrelenting effort required. How could we shepherd our two young sons halfway across the globe when just the four-hour drive to Grandma's was often a marathon of squabbles and tears. But as we pored over maps and considered possible routes traversing a tapestry of environments and cultures, the idea of an overland journey grew more enticing.

Friends and family, on the other hand, thought we were insane. *What? Why? Seriously? What about school?* When we asked Bodi's teachers about home-schooling, they scoffed, assuring us he'd learn more on the road than in any classroom.

The first major hurdle we faced was finding passage across the Pacific. In a world connected by airlines, steamships no longer ply the oceans. A handful of cruise liners make the journey to Asia each autumn, but the timing didn't work. Buying a small sailboat and crossing the Pacific ourselves was more than Christine and I wanted to tackle, especially with young boys. The only solution was to seek berths aboard one of the massive container ships criss-crossing the globe.

"There is no way you'll get a three-year-old aboard," declared the first freighter agent we called, part of a relatively unknown cadre who specialize in booking passage aboard cargo ships. "Marine insurance covers passengers between the ages of six and seventy-nine. No one is going to risk millions of dollars of cargo to get you and your babies across the ocean."

After weeks of digging, we managed to uncover a German carrier whose insurance covered three-year-olds, and immediately reserved four bunks aboard the *Hanjin Ottawa*.

Neither of the boys' grandmothers (both grandfathers had predeceased them) raised questions about our overland journey plans—either they trusted our judgment or had learned by now we weren't going to change course. But as word of our impending departure spread, some ferociously negative responses erupted, usually from strangers who itemized the morbid ways our boys might perish: communicable disease, traffic accident, pollution, poisoning, diarrhea, snake bite and stampeding yaks. No one mentioned the perils of high altitude—which of all the dangers swirling through my mind was the one that kept me awake at night.

The train across Tibet would ascend to a dizzying 5,074 meters, and we would encounter even higher elevations on the trek into Zanskar. When I contacted a long-established American outfitter in the Himalaya, seeking assistance with permits and logistics, they refused to help.

"Tibet is no place for children," the manager scolded. "We won't take anyone under twelve years of age on our trips."

"Why not?"

"Because they can't acclimatize. Their lungs are not properly developed. Do you know who Peter Hackett is?"

Funnily enough, I did know Hackett. I'd met the Telluride-based doctor, who specializes in high-altitude illness, at Everest base camp during the '90s, and on my desk were two papers he'd co-authored, "High Altitude Disease: Unique Pediatric Considerations" and "Children at High Altitude: An International Consensus Statement by an Ad Hoc Committee of the International Society for Mountain Medicine." Neither said anything about undeveloped lungs or the inability of children to acclimatize.

The advice contained in those long reports can be boiled down to something like this: Go ahead, but be sure you know what you are doing, make conservative decisions and always give yourself an out.

To my mind, it's an adage that fairly reflects how all risks should be managed, kids or not.

❧

Bodi joined me on the ferry's upper deck when China appeared on the horizon, allowing me to nuzzle his warm body close. Then he borrowed my camera and took photographs of me standing before the approaching hillsides swathed in apartment buildings.

The muscular presence of this ascendant country was unmistakable. It could be felt in the great rafts of plastic floating offshore, in the glassy towers that loomed over the once-impoverished fishing village of Qingdao, in the red flags that fluttered on rooftops, in the lavish waterfront parks teeming with joggers and walkers.

Stumbling through a sweaty immigration hall riddled with soldiers and CCTV cameras, we spotted the glum-looking television crew surrounded by customs agents. A furtive glance from Wes telegraphed that they were in trouble.

So we marched straight past, pretending we didn't know them, and joined a snaking lineup. Eventually a stamp slammed down on our passports and we were in. Pushing through crowds outside the station, we leapt into a derelict taxi and melted into the city of ten million.

"Will we ever see the TV crew again?" Taj asked.

I didn't know. Christine shrugged. They'd surely reappear, at some point.

Our cab raced down narrow streets, past steaming noodle vendors, mobs of mopeds and markets overflowing with curious vegetables. The humid air carried pungent scents of fish, flowers and decaying compost. Asia never fails to awaken in me a boundless sense of possibility, akin to young love. Christine and I, who had visited China together a decade earlier, stole a knowing glance; it was good to be back.

For nine US dollars, we crammed into a family room at a Qingdao youth hostel, a former observatory perched on a lush hilltop near the city center. Outside, a vendor sold fresh-pressed sugar cane juice, and after downing several cups, we wandered the leafy grounds. Taj and Bodi watched elderly beekeepers as they plucked larvae from hives. Later, the pair joined a herd of local children who were making bubbles from dish soap, chasing the glimmering orbs as they tumbled away on a warm wind.

❧

A pink slip of paper waited on the front desk of the youth hostel. The message advised that the television crew had been granted Chinese visas and were staying on the far side of the city, in the sparkling new Radisson Hotel. We were requested to drop by the lobby that evening at five for a round of interviews.

The Radisson lay two hours away, the manager estimated, because of rush-hour traffic. So I called Wes, suggesting we film the interviews the next morning. But he insisted.

"Are you kidding me?" Christine moaned as we climbed into another taxi. "Clearly those guys don't have kids."

We didn't get back to the hostel until long after dark.

The following morning, we waited for the crew outside the central train station. Taj cowered away from curious strangers while Bodi again offered himself as photographic fodder. As our scheduled departure neared, I searched the crowds frantically for the crew, but to no avail. Time ran out, and not knowing what else to do, we let our tickets pass unused.

Were we at the wrong station? Did we have the wrong time? Without a mobile phone, there was no way to contact the crew. So we waited, sitting atop our duffels beneath the relentless sun.

Eventually a line of taxis pulled up and the crew tumbled out, haggard, red-eyed and devastatingly hung over. They had fallen prey to the cheap lures of Qingdao's nightlife: beer, karaoke and who knows what else. Nerves were frayed. Arguments erupted. A few were still drunk. One senior producer, unable to stand, was dispatched to the airport by Wes, her job terminated. Christine sarcastically suggested we film an episode about the crew, but it might have been too early for that joke. A tray of strawberry milkshakes from McDonald's helped calm tensions.

Soon new tickets were booked, and within an hour, we were rocketing toward Beijing, some eight hundred kilometers north, inside the hushed carriage of a high-speed train. Our boys sat beside two exhausted camera operators, their noisy iPad game of *Plants vs. Zombies* keeping the pair awake.

Outside the windows, rice paddies gave way to transmission lines, factories and nuclear cooling towers. Like South Korea, but on an entirely different scale, it was apparent that China was being dizzyingly reshaped.

Upon reaching Beijing's central train station, our family bid farewell to the television crew for the night. Christine had made reservations in an ancient *hutong* guest house, while they were headed to a glassy downtown hotel. It seemed a shame for the young crew not to experience more authentic accommodation—a Los Angeles–based production company arranged their lodging—but it did offer our family a welcome respite each evening.

We crammed our duffels into the trunk of a yellow cab and jumped inside. But it was some time before the car was able to move an inch, the road ahead completely gridlocked. Nowhere is China's rapid growth more visible than on the streets of Beijing, where unrelenting congestion and smog have led to space rationing, and new licence plates are awarded on a lottery basis.

As our taxi crawled on, the driver—a jolly old man, unable to speak a word of English—reached over and began stroking my forearms with a concerned look on his face.

"I don't think he can believe how hairy you are!" Christine giggled. Perfectly hairless himself, the driver appeared aghast that I should suffer such a cruel fate.

Gazing out the window across snarled traffic, toward skyscrapers obscured by pollution, I felt similarly for him. The midday sun was orange and cast no shadow. Pedestrians and cyclists alike wore white surgical-style masks, like extras in a low-budget horror film. How could over twenty million live amidst such apocalyptic conditions?

I was reminded of a television interview in which a Beijing university student was asked what she liked best about Microsoft Windows.

"The screensaver," she declared.

Why?

Because the twenty-year-old had never seen a blue sky before.

❧

After four days in Beijing, we pressed westward, toward the grasslands of Qinghai province, where our family spent a week acclimatizing—methodically exposing ourselves to progressively higher altitudes. Then we boarded the Qinghai Express, bound for Tibet.

Crawling into a cramped cabin, our boys discovered nasal cannula on each bunk, meant to deliver oxygen to any passengers suffering the effects of altitude. Immediately, the pair donned the plastic tubes.

"Look! I'm drinking oxygen up my nose," Bodi beamed, looking like an ER patient. "And it tastes so, so good."

"Me too," Taj hollered. "I'm drinking oxygen too."

"This all makes me feel nervous," Christine whispered as she squeezed in beside me.

A few days earlier, Taj had collapsed in the back seat of our rental car while crossing a mountain pass, though it wasn't clear if this was due to the flu or altitude. After descending to thicker air, his rambunctious ways quickly returned. In the days that followed, I had carefully monitored his blood oxygen saturation, using a pulse oximeter—a tiny device I'd brought from home that clips to a fingertip, commonly seen in hospitals—and his readings, like Bodi's, remained in the high nineties, a sure sign the pair was adapting well. We would pass even greater elevations on the train journey, but with pressurized carriages and personal oxygen supplies, I felt confident that Taj would be fine.

"Rationally I know that," Christine agreed. "But once this train leaves the station, there is no turning back."

At that very moment, the carriage lurched forward.

❧

Constructed at the staggering cost of 4.2 billion dollars, and inaugurated in 2006, the new Qinghai–Tibet railway is a marvel of modern engineering, with elevated bridges traversing swaths of permafrost and long tunnels piercing the tall ranges.

It is also another nail in the coffin of free Tibet, for the railway has allowed China to consolidate control over the far-flung province, accelerating the pace of resource extraction. But its most insidious objective appears to be drowning Tibet's ancient Buddhist culture with relentless waves of Han Chinese immigration.

I have always felt outraged by China's treatment of the Tibetan people, but now as we peered from UV-shielded windows, watching the forlorn Tibetan Plateau slip by, I recognized the uncomfortable similarities with what had occurred in North America, where Indigenous peoples were subsumed by a flood of immigrants eager to exploit the resources of the New World. *Why did the Tibetan situation tweak my fury while issues in Canada felt easier to overlook? Perhaps because my culture had done the flooding at home? And was our presence on the train making us complicit in atrocities here?* There were no easy answers.

Hour after hour passed. Occasionally we spotted shaggy yak wandering the barrens, and small herds of slender gazelle, but far more common were uniformed soldiers, standing poker straight outside grubby tents, saluting the passing locomotive.

Later that night, as the train lumbered over the 5,231-metre Tanggula Pass, Bodi and Taj delighted in racing between carriages, oblivious to the stumbling Chinese tourists who clogged the aisles. Many, having been dragged straight from sea level in Beijing, were collapsing in pools of vomit.

❧

We reached the Forbidden City of Lhasa at high noon, having completed in twenty-four hours a journey that had thwarted even the boldest explorers for centuries.

Battalions of Chinese soldiers marched in formation through the cavernous new train station. Outside, our government-assigned guide waited beyond barricades, a short Tibetan woman who gently slipped *khata* scarves around our necks, welcoming us with a whispered Tibetan greeting, *"Tashi delek, tashi delek."**

The midday sun was blinding, and around us, gleaming office towers rose in every direction. The newly paved streets were a mess of billboards, fast-food outlets and malls. The city had swollen to twenty times its size since I'd last been there a decade earlier, and stationed amid the squalor, our guidebook advised, were 224 karaoke bars, 685 brothels and three hundred thousand Chinese troops.

But still the Potala Palace floated above the fray on a distant prow, and my heart soared. The magnificent fortress of the Dalai Lamas is home to some thousand rooms, ten thousand shrines and two hundred thousand statues. Eagerly, I recalled to Christine and the boys the wonders I'd witnessed there. The snaking lines of sheepskin-clad nomads carrying buckets of yak butter, which they spooned into flickering candles. The pilgrims crawling on hands and knees beneath shelves of scripture, in the belief the knowledge contained within would shower down and bathe them in merit. The impoverished herders tossing bills at golden statues of Buddha until the money fell like snow, only to be swept up by Chinese caretakers, stuffed in bulging garbage bags and carried away.

While the television crew checked in to a marble hotel on the city outskirts, we headed to the old town and to a colonial guest house appointed with teak and mahogany. In a courtyard shaded by chrysanthemum and hollyhocks, Christine and I sipped tea while the boys lay on their bellies beside shallow ponds, watching lazy schools of koi. A pamphlet on the table advertised Blind Tibetan Massage, and Christine quickly arranged for a treatment.† Within twenty minutes, a sightless man stood at our door.

Leaving Christine in peace, I took the boys to wander cobblestone alleys, joining streams of pilgrims. Toothless men in cowboy hats shuffled past on bowed legs. Elderly women wearing pigtails and colorful aprons bowed

---

*   *Tashi delek* conveys blessings, along with wishes for good health and good luck. It is often translated directly as, "May all auspicious signs come to this environment."

†   Dust, soot and intense UV radiation have led to elevated cataract levels on the Tibetan Plateau, and these massage programs help support the region's visually impaired.

wordlessly to our boys. Families of nomads with electric eyes and tangled hair
had travelled from the distant reaches of the Chang Tang plateau, some five
hundred kilometers away.

Some pilgrims prostrated themselves with every three steps, throwing themselves across the cobblestones, then rising and taking three more steps before
repeating the process. Wearing crude wooden boards affixed to hands and
knees, these devout souls were using their physical body to draw an unbroken
line across the surface of the earth, connecting distant homesteads with Lhasa's
sacred sites. One man bore a callus as thick as a heel on his forehead, where it
repeatedly grazed the ground.

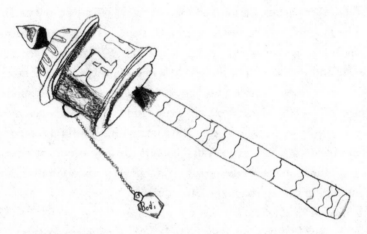

A hand-held prayer wheel. The brass drum has been embossed with
Om mani padme hum, *and Buddhists believe that spinning the wheel*
creates the same meritorious effects as chanting the mantra.

Bodi and Taj delighted in spinning the long rows of brass prayer wheels
adorning the walls of temples and shrines. Soon a group of elders had gathered
around them, stroking their cheeks, giving me the universal thumbs-up sign.
A few yanked mobile phones from their robes and photographed the pair, who
now danced gaily in their midst.

Meanwhile on rooftops overhead, silhouetted against a darkening sky, soldiers
stood stock-still, gripping combat staffs and rifles. A Chinese flag fluttered
above the Jokhang, Lhasa's holiest Buddhist temple, like a raised middle finger.

❦

How could we describe to our boys the tensions at play here?

Amid a complex history, perhaps the place to start was the eighth century, more than a thousand years after Buddha's life on the plains of India, when his teachings first began drifting northward across the Himalaya. Carried by wandering mendicants and scholars, Buddha's message spilled across the high plateau, absorbing local customs and faiths as it went.

Eventually the colorful tradition of Tibetan Buddhism emerged—known as Vajrayana, or the "thunderbolt path"—which bore fleeting resemblance to the more established and staid schools of Southeast Asia. Depicting a fantastical world where tigresses soared among the clouds, gurus left footsteps in stone and horses rode on the wind, perhaps the most defining characteristics of this new doctrine were the radical meditation techniques, which promised the possibility of swift enlightenment, possibly even in a single lifetime.

Grand monasteries rose, a quarter of Tibet's male population became monks and with time, the reclusive country closed its borders. Gradually, a society emerged different from anything the world had previously known: a nation where the ideals of non-attachment, non-desire, material renunciation, compassion and transcendental wisdom were institutionalized. Shrouded in secrecy, Tibet became synonymous with a lost paradise or Shangri-La—a sequestered land of simplicity and peace.

All that changed in 1949. Following the formation of the People's Republic of China, Mao Zedong wasted little time exerting territorial claims over Tibet, which lay nestled on China's western frontier. Forty thousand troops were dispatched to the cloistered kingdom, which at the time possessed not a single airstrip and just fifty artillery pieces. When Tibet's spiritual and political leader, the fifteen-year-old Dalai Lama, appealed to the United Nations for support, his calls went unanswered, and the small nation had no choice but to submit. For several years, an uneasy truce endured.

A decade later, when rumours of a Chinese plot to abduct the Dalai Lama began to swirl, disgruntled Tibetan peasants took to the streets in protest. China's crackdown was swift and severe. Amid the ensuing upheaval, the young Dalai Lama slipped away, disguised as a soldier, travelling by foot across the Himalaya toward sanctuary in India, launching a diaspora that continues to this day.

Far greater horrors were to follow.

As China's Cultural Revolution swept across the plateau, in a period stretching from 1966 to 1976, Tibet's great monasteries were systematically laid to waste by artillery fire until just thirteen of an original six thousand stood intact. Religious artifacts were stolen. Scripture was incinerated, or used by soldiers as toilet paper. Nuns were forced to publicly copulate with monks. Others suffered forced sterilization, electroshock and rape. Parents were made to applaud as children were executed. Crops failed and starvation ensued. In the space of a generation, one out of every five Tibetans perished—more than a million in total.

Today the cultural genocide continues, but now rifles have been replaced by state-sponsored immigration programs that flood Tibet's cities and villages with Han workers. Travellers are warned of recording devices in hotels and soldiers disguised as monks who infiltrate monasteries, rooting out subversion. At schools, Tibetan youth are taught in Mandarin under the steely gaze of Mao's portrait.

As I watched my own children dance among the beaming pilgrims—with closed eyes and outstretched arms—I wondered: *Should my boys know this sad history? Might it later inform their own behaviors at home? Or was it better, at this age when they still believed in magic, that they simply saw with their own eyes and felt with their own hearts?*

In the days ahead, Christine and I would relate some of Tibet's dark history to the pair, but we chose to largely focus on the wonders of this still-enchanted kingdom.

❧

The next afternoon, our family visited Drepung Monastery on the outskirts of Lhasa. Once one of Tibet's great learning institutions and home to ten thousand monks, there were just five hundred in residence now (by Chinese decree) and the massive complex felt more like an abandoned movie set.

We were wandering slopes above the temples when Bodi spotted a cave. Inside was an altar littered with scarves, water bowls and flickering candles. A grubby cushion sat on the dirt floor.

"What is this for?" he asked.

"Cave very special place," our guide explained. "From ancient days, senior monks here coming to meditate." The monastery's founder had spent seven years sitting here in silence, she told us. Did Bodi want to try?

To my surprise, our fidgety boy agreed and settled on the cushion. Our guide crouched beside him, showing him how to clasp his hands in prayer, mindful to leave a small space for Buddha between his arched fingers. I glanced around for Christine, but she'd sprinted off with Taj in search of an outhouse.

"Just rest now," the guide urged, "and your mind will become very clean. Very pure."

Bodi closed his eyes, and his breathing settled to a gentle rhythm. He remained motionless for what seemed like an eternity. At first I thought he was pulling our leg, or putting on a show for the television cameras, but as minutes ticked by, and Bodi didn't budge, I began to suspect something unexpected— maybe even profound—was transpiring.

Perhaps I shouldn't have been surprised. From an early age, Bodi had always displayed an uncanny ease with all things spiritual, particularly Buddhism. When I brought home a pewter statue of Buddha from a photojournalism assignment in Cambodia, he placed it at his bedside and buried the figurine beneath a pile of offerings: glass beads, feathers, pebbles, necklaces. On family canoe trips, he gently shooed mosquitos from our tent, sobbing if he ever caught Christine or me surreptitiously swatting an intruder. His resistance to harming any living being reminded me of Tibetan monks I'd seen in archival documentaries, on their hands and knees outside the Potala Palace, painstakingly plucking earthworms from irrigation ditches as local farmers dug.

Even Bodi's name was a nod to a mythic Buddhist figure, the bodhisattva, one who upon achieving enlightenment chooses to forsake Nirvana and instead returns to earth to assist others on their own journeys toward enlightenment. (In fairness, I had originally suggested the name as a reference to Patrick Swayze's freedom-loving surfer character in *Point Break*, a Hollywood bank heist film; however, Christine was drawn to the bodhisattva slant, and thus the name pleased us both.)

Half an hour later Bodi blinked. Slowly opening his eyes, he sat silently for some time.

"I forgot where I was," he finally whispered. "It was like I was nowhere."

Then he jumped up and ran to join Taj, who had just returned from peeing in bushes, while I tried to explain to Christine what I'd witnessed.

❧

Packed into a Toyota Hilux, our family set out the next morning for Nepal, some eight hundred kilometers and five days distant. We followed the Friendship

Highway, a lonely ribbon of asphalt weaving across the southern edge of the Tibetan Plateau.

Upon reaching the dusty outpost of Tingri, we took a detour and emerged from a constricted valley below the towering north face of Mount Everest, its crystalline summit piercing an unblemished blue sky.

I'd previously visited the mountain several times from the south, but this iconic view left me unexpectedly overwhelmed—the site of so much mountaineering history. Until becoming a father, I'd never been much of a crier. But now I seemed to well up at the slightest provocation: acts of kindness, sad songs on the radio, even cheesy television advertisments. Tears leaked from my eyes.

"What do you think, Bodi?" I asked with wavering voice.

"It's OK."

OK was his standard response for every question I asked, and had become a joke between us.

"OK? Seriously? It's Mount Everest! What would it take to make it a *good* day?"

"Winning the lottery, I suppose. Getting elected president. Or maybe getting married. If I'd been looking for a long time."

"And what about a *great* day?"

"Dad! You already know that," he yelled, voice tinged with frustration. "Going to Mars would be a *great* day."

"Well, that takes a long time," Taj interjected. "It would be more like a great day and a great night."

Bodi rolled his eyes.

❧

The next morning, the Friendship Highway plunged off the edge of the Tibetan Plateau, dropping into the Sun Kosi gorge. Ahead of us lay the jungles of Nepal, and beyond, the scorching plains of India. In just a few kilometers, barren plains were replaced by thick forests. Waterfalls floated down from above, hammering on the Toyota's roof as we passed beneath.

Caught in congested traffic near the border, we bid our driver farewell and tipped him generously. Then we leapt out, racing onward by foot, duffel bags bouncing between us and boys tumbling alongside. The TV crew struggled to keep pace, burdened with a mountain of their own gear. We reached the border bridge just as steel barriers were lowered for the night. Slipping underneath, we stepped into Nepal, drenched in sweat.

A beaming customs agent stamped visas in our passports, then draped garlands of marigolds around our necks. Moments later, a goat darted out from beneath a tour bus, grabbed a hold of the flowers around Taj's neck and almost dragged our poor boy away.

We spent three days in steamy Kathmandu, wandering markets, eating cake from German bakeries, visiting the iconic Boudhanath stupa (a massive Buddhist shrine adorned with all-seeing eyes) and later a local orphanage, where our boys joined a game of barefoot soccer and both picked up a stubborn case of warts.

Then we pressed on, toward India.

❦

Fifty-two days and sixteen thousand kilometers after leaving home, we crossed our final border, entering India near Lumbini, the birthplace of Buddha.

Despite frantic efforts, the television crew members were unable to obtain working visas, and found themselves turned back toward Kathmandu. Only Wes and a clandestine camera operator managed to sneak across. An interim crew of Indian camera operators was arranged, and the jolly men waited for us on the far side of the border, beneath a mango tree.

Travelling by rental car—Wes and his camera operator packed alongside our family, the crew of Indian videographers in a separate vehicle behind—we followed dirt roads through unruffled villages, past mud-brick homes and shady banyans, where the dusty air was scented by charcoal, paraffin and dung.

In Prayagraj, we boarded a rickety wooden riverboat and set off down the Ganges River towards Varanasi—a journey of 150 kilometers and two days. The boys jousted with pillows on a cushioned deck above the wheelhouse as we slipped past gaunt cattle and white egrets, past glistening fishermen who poled slender boats, past wispy cooking fires on sandy banks. A riotous symphony of frogs and crickets bid the flaming sun farewell.

Sadly, our makeshift berths in the cramped bilge reeked of diesel and were plagued by mosquitos. A bedside thermometer read thirty-eight degrees Celsius, and that sweltering night marked the most uncomfortable of our journey—perhaps of my entire life.

The boys rose sodden and cherry-cheeked before dawn, having slept little. Wes appeared haggard too, but the Indian camera crew, who had spread out on the wooden deck without even sheets protecting them from insects, were no worse for wear.

Temperatures were crippling by the time we reached the ancient city of Varanasi. Tossing our duffels into a tuk-tuk, a three-wheeled auto rickshaw, we negotiated a fee then raced off toward an air-conditioned guest house, which Christine had carefully booked in advance.

But instead of taking us to the guest house, the tuk-tuk driver entered a maze of narrow streets, spluttered to a stop and demanded more money. Exhausted, soaked in sweat and desperate to get the boys into a cool room, I blew a gasket—which is inevitably going to happen sooner or later on a long trip, but never a proud moment in front of one's kids. Ripping the duffels from the back of the tuk-tuk, I set off by foot, ploughing down crowded streets, scattering strangers as I went.

Christine raced after me, tearful boys in hand. "Kirkby! I know this sucks, but you've got to pull yourself together. Please, this isn't the example we want to set."

She was right, and her patience disarmed me. We both wanted to teach our boys that travel, just like life, delivers an unending series of challenges—and how we respond is what makes us who we are.

But when she discovered the air conditioning in our guest house was kaput, Christine herself nearly collapsed. Desperate to cool off, all four of us piled into the small shower at once, shoulders and buttocks pressing against mildew-stained tiles. A group of monkeys watched curiously from outside a window, perched in a strangler fig. Later, generous bowls of mango ice cream, served on a breezy rooftop patio, restored our disposition. Then we set out to explore.

Varanasi stands among the most auspicious locations on the planet for a Hindu cremation, and in those crowded streets, sobbing men bore corpses atop homemade litters. A taxi inched past, a cadaver lashed to its roof. The tang of charred flesh was inescapable.

At a cremation pyre, we paused to watch as a linen-shrouded corpse was consumed by flames. Eventually the skull fractured, spilling steaming pink brains on the ground, and I instinctively pushed the boys onward. But they would not be rushed.

"What's the matter?" Bodi asked. "Everyone dies. Afterward you go to heaven. Then you come back."

I glanced at Christine and she grinned. Clearly she'd been exposing the pair to ideas different from mine.

"I'm coming back as a honey badger," Taj declared.

"Oh Taj, you can't know that for sure," Bodi retorted with annoyance. "It's not your choice."

"Yes, it is my choice," Taj insisted.

Surrounded by scorching heat and pungent smoke, jostled by loincloth-clad men who unloaded firewood barges, the boys argued about reincarnation until they grew red in the face and tears streaked their cheeks.

Eventually Bodi relented, just a bit.

"Well, if I can choose, which I don't think I can, I'd like to come back as a human. Or a hummingbird."

❧

Two and a half thousand years earlier—just nine kilometers from the riverbank where our boys stood engaged in esoteric discourse—a gaunt man gathered five disciples and gave a sermon that would change the world.

Siddhartha Gautama was born the son of a chieftain around the fifth century BCE, a time when iron was spreading across the subcontinent and elephants were still employed for transport. After spending his youth in the opulence of his father's court, Siddhartha renounced his privileged existence, and at the age of twenty-nine, set out to wander the plains as a mendicant, seeking spiritual guidance from mystics and yogis.

Six years of rigorous asceticism failed to deliver the decisive understanding he sought, and eventually Siddhartha abandoned his austere path, his body in collapse.* After bathing in a river, he drank a bowl of milk offered by a villager and then settled beneath a Bodhi Tree with an ascendant moon in the east, vowing to remain motionless—even if it meant death—until he attained Supreme Enlightenment.

---

* These struggles proved to be the foundation for what would later become a key Buddhist precept, that of the Middle Way, the concept that neither extreme self-denial nor self-indulgence lead to realization.

How long Siddhartha sat in a meditative state is the stuff of legend. Some accounts suggest hours. Others claim forty-nine days. But after a long and probing search, he glimpsed what he described as "the true nature of reality."

Immediately seeking former ascetic companions near Varanasi, he shared his vision: if we can change the habits of our mind, we can change how life is experienced. Siddhartha proposed a doctrine of compassion, non-attachment and impermanence, which was meant to end human suffering in this lifetime.* He placed no faith in an unseen god, instead suggesting all that mattered was the here and now. Finally, he urged his disciples not to blindly accept his teachings, but rather test everything themselves.

For the next forty-five years, the man who would come to be known as Shakyamuni (Sage of the Sakya), or more simply Buddha (the Awakened One), wandered the plains of India, teaching all who came to him, no matter their status, rich or poor, noble or thief.

Upon reaching the age of eighty, Buddha gathered his followers and implored them to recognize their own impermanence while continuing to strive for liberation. Then he lay down on his side and entered a meditative state, never to rise again.

In the centuries that followed, his teachings would sweep across India and Southeast Asia, flowing north over the Himalaya (where they blossomed into Tibetan Buddhism) and continue onward into China and Mongolia, then across the sea to Japan.

Today, more than half a billion people worldwide follow the simple principles set forth in those shady groves outside Varanasi, just a few kilometers downstream from where our boys stood arguing about reincarnation.

❧

Thundering trains carried us onward. The hot season had settled on the plains, and in crowded carriages we crammed onto hard benches, reading tattered

---

* More specifically, Buddha preached the Four Noble Truths: life is suffering; suffering arises from desire; suffering stops when desire stops; and cessation of suffering comes from adhering to the Eightfold Path (right view; right intention; right action; right speech; right livelihood; right effort; right mindfulness; right concentration).

storybooks to the boys over and over, perspiration dripping from our noses while curious throngs peered over our shoulders.

For their part, our boys dealt with the jostling, heat and pungent odors heroically. And they derived great amusement from the local form of air conditioning: men's T-shirts hiked up, exposing globular bellies.

"Dad! It's really good," Taj gushed, when he and Bodi pushed their bare bellies against the barred window. "My stomach feels icy." So I joined my two beet-faced boys, shirts jacked up and bellies stuck out, as the entire carriage watched in disbelief.

Every few hours, passing stations brought a small measure of relief. Slender hands passed paper cups of chai through open doors in exchange for a wad of rupees, and our boys devoured this sweet, creamy drink. But finding food they could tolerate proved more difficult. Men in singlets raced through the aisles, selling greasy curry on paper, but Bodi gasped in horror after just one bite. "Way too spicy!" The local version of potato chips—cellophane-wrapped packs of fiery lentils and split peas—left their eyes watering. So we resorted to tiny bananas, which Christine caked with peanut butter from a precious jar in her backpack.

We paused to visit Taj's namesake, the Taj Mahal, in Agra.* Of course we'd seen pictures of the marble mausoleum beforehand, but Christine and I were unprepared for its magnificent presence. Regretfully, our boys were unimpressed, and their indifference, coupled with crippling heat, made our stay fleeting. That evening an argument erupted between Christine and me, and after slamming the door to a room she shared with Taj, I spent a restless, lonely and regret-filled night lying beside Bodi in an adjacent chamber, listening to the tap drip.

The next morning, at the breakfast buffet, we hugged and all was forgiven. Soon we were laughing, for neither of us could remember what we'd actually been arguing about in the first place. India is famous for wearing travellers thin, but the pre-monsoon heat coupled with two months of unceasing television production had left us both in tatters.

---

* The Sanskrit name Taj loosely translates to "the jewel in the crown," and once again weds Christine's affinity for Indian culture with my love for surfing; Taj Burrow was an ascendant surf champion at the time of our second son's birth.

We were granted an unanticipated reprieve that evening, when Wes's permits for filming along India's strategic northern frontier were denied. A week in a posh Delhi hotel followed, while he frantically chased bureaucratic approval. While we waited, producers—the whole crew had joined us again—arranged for an unending stream of activities: Christine took cooking lessons in a private home, the boys joined a Bollywood dance class and at a busy spice market, we all received temporary henna tattoos. Despite the challenges of being constantly filmed, I was also aware the crew afforded our family experiences we would have never contemplated (or afforded) alone.

Then it was on toward the perfectly straight streets and leafy boulevards of Chandigarh, a planned city built following Indian Partition in 1947. From there, a narrow-gauge railway carried us into misty Himalayan foothills. Two days in a bumpy bus brought us to Manali, just as the monsoon skies opened.

A knock on the door of our stone cottage interrupted our duffel packing. A short man with coppery skin and chapped cheeks stood in the downpour, T-shirt sodden, baseball cap backward. It was Sonam Dawa.

This Zanskari native had guided many groups of friends on treks in the region, and months earlier, I'd arranged for Sonam to lead us over the Great Himalaya Range, on a 150-kilometer hike into Zanskar. Gentle and quiet, like most of Tibetan lineage, the reserved man gave me an immediate feeling of kinship.

We'd postponed the start of our trek by almost two weeks, due to delays in Delhi. And during this time, Sonam's team of porters and horse wranglers had been waiting at the remote trailhead. Anxiously, in broken English, he asked if we would pay for these extra days. Instead of agreeing, Wes's production team bartered over the porter's already meager daily wages while Christine and I listened in embarrassment. Later, we privately counselled Sonam to stand his ground.

Whether such frictions wore on Sonam, or he was preoccupied by other worries, the forty-two-year-old appeared beset by some distant heaviness.

❧

A computer in the lobby of our "hillside resort cottages" allowed me to check email for the first time in months. What a mistake. Amidst the piles of spam

I learned a Calgary-based developer had recently purchased the forest behind our Kimberley home and was already levelling it for a subdivision. Nameless, faceless lawyers for the Travel Channel delivered a contract so devoid of humanity that it read more like an eighty-page straitjacket.

Christine and the boys shopped for monastery school supplies on Manali's historical Mall Road, and I joined them. On a visit twenty years earlier, I'd found the walking bazaar crammed with donkeys, street hawkers and boisterous merchants. While the carnival atmosphere still existed, the street was now lined with fast-food franchises, luxury hotels, nightclubs and high-end fashion shops. We had witnessed the same thing in every city and town we visited on the journey, across continents and oceans. *Was it ridiculous to worry about such change? Was it really progress?*

Traditional neighborhoods were being bulldozed, leisurely laneways paved over and ancient trees felled to make way for glassy towers. Self-sufficient villages rapidly gave way to cities of concrete, crammed with busy workers. And an unmistakable sense of loss swirled in the wake. A tidal wave was sweeping the land—we'd seen it everywhere—bringing the very things we had left home to escape. It made me wonder if our journey was in vain?

"In appearance everything is fine these days," writes Tiziano Terzani, a long-time correspondent for *Der Spiegel*, who himself spent a year travelling overland across Asia and Europe. "Everywhere people speak of nothing but economic growth. And yet this great, ancient world of diversity is about to succumb. The Trojan horse is *modernization*."

❦

The following morning, we crammed our lightened duffels into the trunk of a dented minivan. The driver, a stern man with a red *tilaka* ("third eye") daubed on his forehead, slammed the doors, revved the engine and raced north, following the Leh–Manali military highway toward the Rohtang La—which, translated from Tibetan, means "Field of Corpses Pass."

The road ascended steep switchbacks, weaving through monsoon-drenched forests of pine, oak, chestnut and rhododendron. Roadside tea stalls displayed racks of sun-faded ski suits. These were rentals, awaiting the hordes of lowland Indians who ascend this pass each summer, seeking a first giddy glimpse of snow.

Mists parted as the minivan struggled higher, revealing sheer rock faces and jade-green alpine grasslands. At the windswept summit, two enterprising young men were using a blowtorch to heat a vat of sweet coffee, which they sold to exhausted long-distance truck drivers. Christine and I joined the lineup.

Beyond the Rohtang the land grew drier. Shrubby junipers dotted the rocky mountainsides and, far below, groves of green poplar traced the banks of the churning Chenab River. Icy summits floated to the north. The driver shut off the engine to save gas, and we coasted downward in silence. The boys drifted to sleep. Christine and I stared out the windows, grappling with the enormity of what lay ahead.

In the village of Keylong, at a colonial guest house, we took what might be our final showers for six months, later drinking Kingfisher beers on a patio trimmed with strings of colored lights.

The next day, our minivan entered a parched landscape devoid of trees. It was late afternoon when the military checkpoint of Darcha appeared amid the wastes, a cluster of stone huts, olive tents and sandbags. A balaclava-clad soldier thumbed through our passports, then waved us on.

Following a rudimentary track, we ascended a barren valley bounded by dark, snow-streaked peaks. Eventually the minivan bounced to a halt beside a lone splash of green—a small spring. Two wall tents stood in the surrounding meadows, and at the sound of our motor, a dozen or more men burst out, wearing threadbare sweaters and khaki pants. Despite waiting for two weeks, these porters, with calloused hands and twinkling eyes, greeted us as warmly as long-lost relatives.

Christine and I set up our tent, while Bodi and Taj floated an armada of sticks in the shallow spring waters. A midstream boulder bore an odd hand-painted message: BATH 5 RUPEES PLESE. But who collected such a fee, amid this desolation, remained unclear.

As shadows engulfed the valley, Christine dozed off. With the boys playing merrily together, I wandered up the valley alone. Nothing moved amid those desiccated plains, not even a bird, and a sense of vast isolation descended.

A deep chasm appeared, blocking my way. Whitewater thundered from hidden depths. A small Hindu shrine stood beside me; on the altar a bronze statue of Ganesh, the elephant-headed remover of obstacles, was buried beneath nubs of incense and melted candle.

A chorten *(or stupa in India) is the universal dome-like monument of Tibet, symbolizing the universe held in Buddha's enlightened mind.*

A rudimentary bridge of rusting girders led to the opposite bank, where a whitewashed *chorten* rose: the dome-like monument of the Himalaya, symbolizing the entire universe held in Buddha's enlightened mind. Quartz pebbles and ibex horns littered its base, and sun-bleached prayer flags fluttered overhead.

After eighty-seven days, we stood at last on the doorstep of Zanskar's Himalayan Buddhists.

ॐ

AMONG THE ANCIENTS

Centuries ago, texts were discovered in Tibet describing *beyul*, hidden-lands where the essence of the Buddhist Tantras is said to be preserved for future generations. They describe valleys reminiscent of paradise that can only be reached with enormous hardship . . . Pilgrims who travel to these wild and distant places often recount extraordinary experiences similar to those encountered by spiritual practitioners on the Buddhist path to Liberation.

—His Holiness Tenzin Gyatso,
the Fourteenth Dalai Lama

4

ACROSS THE DIVIDE

***

Breath billowed in frigid air when we awoke. Wooden fingers crammed sleeping bags into stuff sacks. Bodi poked his head out of the tent door and discovered boots and duffels coated with thick frost.

"Who spilled baby powder over everything?" he asked with sincere concern.

The television crew emerged from their tents looking exhausted. Their numbers had been pared to seven for the trek, but they still required a dizzying amount of gear, including twenty-three waterproof briefcases, six tripods and two diesel generators.

Pulling on puffy jackets and woollen hats, we sat together atop cold boulders, wolfing down curried eggs and chapatti delivered by smiling cook boys, while nearby, the Pony Men separated a mountain of gear into carefully balanced loads, whistling as they worked.

"Pony Men" is the historical name given to wranglers of the western Himalaya, but it is inaccurate, for the animals they drive are actually lithe horses. Sonam had hired six men from Manali and a pack train of twenty-two animals. Rake-thin Tsewang Yetok was the oldest wrangler at sixty-four, bearing a lone golden tooth, which he exposed with every smile. The youngest, eighteen-year-old Ramesh Singh, wore mismatched tennis shoes and a soiled rag around his head. His nose was daubed with zinc.

When the sun hit camp, temperatures soared. Woollen toques were quickly replaced with wide-brimmed sun hats. After smearing sunscreen across the boys' cheeks, we gave them each a pedometer to measure footsteps in the days ahead. The pair were thrilled, dashing back and forth across the meadow, watching their step count grow. Christine and I didn't expect them to trek the entirety of the 150-kilometer trail ahead, but we hoped the pedometers might encourage them to walk just a bit more often.

Despite being blessed with quasi-Olympian strength, Christine had raised the white flag for this journey and asked Sonam to hire an extra porter—to carry Taj. Additya (Adi) Lama was a bashful twenty-one-year-old with spiked hair and a sparse moustache. Hailing from the Sherpa enclave of Darjeeling, he wore the discards of previous expedition clients: skateboard shoes, reflective sunglasses, a down jacket. Taj shook his hand warily, then hid behind Christine's legs.

But I couldn't possibly ask one of the porters to carry Bodi—he was almost the same height as the sinewy men. So after cramming his thirty-kilo frame into a far-too-small child carrier, I hoisted him myself.

The porters immediately protested. "No sir! Not possible."

Sonam appeared skeptical too, and dragged a mangy white mare toward us. "Riding more comfortable," he suggested. "And more easy."

But Bodi recoiled from the horse, as I suspected he might. From the earliest age he had been uncertain around animals, turning his back on dogs, cats, even gerbils. Now he began to whimper.

"Let's not force him, Bruce," Christine whispered, so I moved off. Perched in the child carrier on my back, Bodi was soon humming happily again.

❧

There was no celebratory moment or rousing cheer to mark our departure. Instead, after filling water bottles and glancing at maps, we simply started walking.

Ahead loomed the Himalaya, or "Abode of Snow" in Sanskrit, an enormous mountain range stretching 2,400 kilometers, from Pakistan in the west to Bangladesh in the east. Separating the humid plains of India from the sere Central Asian plateau, this natural barrier has thwarted the passage of weather, trade, armies and caravans for centuries. It now stood between us and Zanskar.

A jeep track led up the narrowing valley, a scar bleeding mud and boulders across loose slopes. The track was a remnant of the ambitious Zanskar Highway

Project, a plan to carve a strategic road across the Himalaya, from Manali to Leh, allowing the Indian Army rapid access to contested northern frontiers. Construction started following the '99 Kargil War with Pakistan, but funding dried up when political winds changed, and the foreign workers had long since departed. The fate of the project remained unclear.

I had been unaware of this incursion, and felt mildly disappointed, for despite its flat nature, a road makes for unpleasant walking. It doesn't blend into the landscape the way a footpath can, giving way to rises and dips, gracefully following contours. Instead it ploughs straight ahead, an incongruous line in a world of curves. For all its ease, walking on a road is comparable to riding a stationary bike; you get some exercise, but the experience remains a ghost of the real thing.

"Track ending soon," Sonam promised.

Beyond, we would follow ancient footpaths of traders and shepherds.

❧

The high-altitude sun was relentless and my shirt was soon sodden. Walking beside me, young Adi wore his puffy jacket.

"Keeps me cool," he explained when I asked.

The television crew dashed ahead to set up shots, soon red-faced from exhaustion. A string of porters trailed behind, carrying heavy cameras and tripods. Occasionally Wes would ask our family to pause while his team prepared. Then, with a whistle, he would signal our advance.

On one such occasion, we rounded a corner to find the cameras set up around a flooding rivulet. They were clearly hoping to infuse our journey with drama, but it pissed me off, because the water wasn't a serious obstacle; it was barely ankle deep. So I strode across nonchalantly, without pause, carrying Bodi on my back. Christine, Sonam, Adi and Taj rushed to follow.

"For Chrissakes, Kirkby," Wes grumbled when he caught up. "It would make better television if you stopped and talked to your wife in a situation like that. Try to help our viewers understand what's going on. And what's at stake."

I nodded. He was right.

Christine was less annoyed, and taking my hand, she dragged me out of earshot. We unclipped tiny microphones from our shirts—which recorded every word we said—and popped them into pockets.

"You don't seem to be yourself today," she said. "There have been plenty of times when I didn't think I could take another minute of filming. But let's try to finish this on a strong note."

I marvelled again at Christine's ability to gently rise and counterbalance the frustrations of travel, no matter how trivial.

❧

We camped amid rocky flood plains, at the end of the jeep track. Nearby, a derelict yellow sign declared—or warned—BORDER ROADS ORGANISATION BRINGS PEOPLE OF REMOTE TO THE MAINSTREAM.* The next morning we would leave the valley, climbing upward, following a small creek toward the soaring Shingo La pass, still three days' walk away and hidden from view.†

As the sun dropped, the stout cook, Ani Rai, settled cross-legged on a foam mat inside the cook tent. He chopped onions and carrots while two kerosene stoves bathed his face in blue light, and a pair of cook boys hovered nearby, ready to retrieve anything called for: spices, knives, pans.

Adi soon delivered scalding tomato soup and popcorn to a shaky table. A dinner of fried yak, steamed okra and rice followed, and as we ate, a scattering of clouds flushed pink. The valley sagged toward darkness. A pair of alpine choughs whistled past, their caws echoing across the barrens, and in the silence that followed, I caught myself counting crows.

❧

Carrying a seventy-pound child is, in my estimation, far more physically challenging than carrying seventy pounds of gear. Gear doesn't swing wildly from side to side, or peer down at passing wildflowers. It doesn't press elbows into your spine, or request that you kneel to retrieve shiny pebbles, or deafen you by shouting in your ears. And the rarefied air of the Himalaya only amplified such challenges.

---

* Border Roads Organisation is a goliath Indian military contractor, tasked with blasting a route through these peaks.

† *La* means "high mountain pass" in Tibetan, so to say "Shingo La pass" is redundant, but I have included it here, and elsewhere in the text, for clarity.

But for me, the costs of schlepping Bodi paled before the rewards, for a back-pack full of gear will never run its fingers through your hair, or absently stroke your neck while counting clouds, or engage in an endlessly spiralling game of I-love-you, I-love-you-more.

"Kirkby, don't kill yourself." Christine broke my reverie as we ascended steep switchbacks the next morning. "We've got a long way to go."

I was huffing and puffing, but I enjoyed the exertion and pressed on. Adi followed close behind, carrying Taj. Thirty minutes later, the incline eased and we joined the television crew on a high ridge, where they'd been filming our struggles. While the audio technician replaced a sweat-soaked microphone on my chest, Sonam once again dragged the white mare over and encouraged Bodi to give riding a try. He again refused, which confused Sonam, for Zanskari children all ride from an early age. Trying to be helpful, he plucked Bodi from his feet and tossed him over the mare's back. But Bodi writhed frantically and refused to let go of Sonam's shirt. Embarrassed, Sonam returned him to the ground.

So Bodi and I climbed hand in hand up the rocky trail, entering an alpine valley where ribs of dark granite soared above and remnants of last winter's avalanches spread across the floor in sloppy fans. Meltwater freshets, swollen with the summer heat, burbled across these slopes and we leapt over the smallest. Others we crossed hopping from rock to rock. The deepest forced us to remove boots and socks, tiptoeing through water so frigid that sharp rocks passed unnoticed underfoot.

Taj soon fell asleep on Adi's back, mouth agape, head bouncing at a ghastly angle. Christine tried to stuff a jacket beneath his chin, but it was a hopeless effort.

Bodi raced ahead on the trail and then slowed down, causing me to bump awkwardly into him, over and over. It was a frustrating habit, and for years I'd complained—until finally realizing it was his instinctive way of calming nerves. For many on the spectrum, physical pressure can tame sensory overload. As a teenager, Temple Grandin famously built her own "squeeze machine," a wood-framed, foam-lined device that she crawled into, and which was capable of inducing a relaxed state that persisted for hours.

Rather than building Bodi a squeeze machine, I chose instead to become one, and for years had tried to coax the reluctant boy into my arms at every oppor-tunity, holding him tight. It was challenging, for like many on the spectrum, as much as Bodi enjoyed pressure, he also recoiled from personal contact.

"Stop, Dada!" he would scream whenever I bear hugged him. But as soon as I let go, he would quietly ask, "Can you do that again?"

With time he learned to seek out such physicality, which led to this frustrating walk-bump-stumble routine. But we developed our own solution to that. Wrapping an arm around Bodi's neck as we walked, I tightened my hold until I grasped him in a headlock. Bent in half at the waist, he stumbled along beside me, and anyone witnessing the act would surely judge me an abusive father. But Bodi loved it.

Eventually Bodi paused to collect a handful of colorful pebbles—white quartz, red chert, green serpentine, black andesite lava, mocha limestone—and I asked Sonam how many times he had crossed the Shingo La.

"Too many times. Thirty? Maybe forty."

As a youth, he'd crossed the Shingo La twice a year—once after harvest in the fall, when he departed Zanskar to attend school in Delhi, and again in spring when he returned to help his family plant crops. Travelling with a pack of schoolboys, he crossed the snowy slopes by night, when the snow was frozen and less prone to avalanche. Wearing thin nylon jackets, their pockets stuffed with barley flour, the boys would rest in a cave near the summit before reaching the first Zanskari village of Kargiak in twenty-four hours—a distance it would take our cumbersome group a week to travel.

❧

On our third day of trekking, Sonam set out lunch beside a burbling stream—curried potatoes, fried rice, fresh chapattis and tuna salad. Wes ate with us, but the rest of the television crew had not yet appeared, and I kept glancing down the trail, wondering where they could be. Eventually Wes and I decided to jog back and take a look, and Sonam joined us.

From a high prow, we scanned the valley. Nothing appeared to move in that world of rock and ice, where only lavender pools of dwarf fireweed broke the monotony. A sea of icy peaks spread before us, and the high-altitude air was so uncannily clear that I could discern details on their flanks as if peering through binoculars: snow flutings, sapphire glaciers. Far to the south, monsoon clouds boiled. Overhead, a ceramic blue sky spread to the horizons.

Eventually a figure appeared in the distance, striding up the dusty switch-backs. It was a herder in indigo robes. A grimy rag obscured his face, and four black mules scampered ahead, dented jerry cans lashed across their backs.

"Oi!" shouted Sonam, as the man neared, asking in Hindi if he had seen our missing companions. The herder plowed past without breaking stride, only muttering (which Sonam again translated) that a foreigner was lying on the trail far below, being tended by friends.

Before disappearing, the herder turned and shouted back, "If that man comes higher, he will die."

For a moment, the immense valley was filled with a crystalline silence, broken only by the sound of pebbles shifting underfoot. "That man" was almost certainly Jonathon, the audio technician, who had been struggling with headaches for days.

"I'll run back and sort Johnny out," Wes declared and sprinted away. Sonam followed. I watched the pair fade to distant specks with sadness, for I doubted I'd see Jonathon again.

Our party had now reached an elevation exceeding any summit in the American lower forty-eight or the Alps. And much climbing still remained ahead. For Jonathon to ascend farther, while displaying symptoms of altitude sickness, would be irresponsible. The only solution was to dispatch him down the valley in the care of a porter, toward the warm, oxygen-laden air below.

❧

The afternoon dragged on. With Bodi on my back, I stared at my boots, breath heaving, counting footsteps.

Not until dusk did the tents appear ahead, tucked amid rocky slopes. At the sound of our voices, a cook boy came bounding, swinging a thermos. We sat together on a boulder, gulping cup after cup of sweet, milky tea, dipping orange cream biscuits. When the sun ducked behind a cloud, cold air came roaring down the mountainside like an avalanche, engulfing us.

Our camp stood at 4,500 meters, and once inside the family tent, I checked everyone's acclimatization using the pulse oximeter—as I did each evening—relieved to find healthy readings. Afterward, Christine and I dozed while the boys crawled back and forth, waging an imaginary battle with Lego mini-figures. Before leaving home, we'd given each a toiletry bag, allowing them to bring whatever fit in. While Taj haphazardly crammed in handfuls of Lego, Bodi painstakingly built a solid cube that filled the bag.

It was almost dark when a clattering of hooves roused us. I unzipped the tent flap horrified to discover Sonam leading the white mare into camp with Jonathon perched atop, pale and unstable.

"What else could we do?" Sonam shrugged.

After coaxing a glass of warm juice into Jonathon, we stuffed him into a tent and he fell into a catatonic sleep. Sonam's medical kit thankfully included two bottles of compressed oxygen, which could save Jonathon's life if his condition deteriorated. Otherwise I would have insisted they turn around and descend in darkness.

But Jonathon was not the only crew member suffering. An Indian camera operator, summoned at the last minute from Delhi, succumbed to a debilitating headache, and two exhausted producers retreated to their tents without dinner.

With budgets weighing on his mind, Wes was loath to slow our pace, but the only option was a rest day. No one would be going higher tomorrow.

❧

Two days later, the snowy summits above camp burned like candles at sunrise. In the kitchen tent, singing cooks prepared omelets. After a day of hibernation, the television crew appeared rejuvenated. Even Jonathon was smiling, and his oxygen saturation had returned to normal.

We set out early, hoping to move fast and cross the Shingo La by lunch, then quickly descend on the far side, eliminating the risk of sleeping at even higher elevations. The trail beyond camp was steep and frequently blocked by massive snow drifts, which had become a sloppy mess in the summer sun. Wildflowers bloomed along the fringes of such oases: Himalayan mini sunflower, yellow larkspur and pools of blue iris that appeared to reflect the sky above.

After several hours, a strange noise brought our party to a halt. Thunder? A distant jet?

Sonam pointed to slopes high above. A yellow excavator was carving a path across the mountainside. Dark smoke belched from its exhaust, and the bucket swung to and fro, sending boulders crashing downward with muffled booms. Sonam shouted and waved his arms, and eventually the machine shut down. The operator clambered to the roof. For some minutes the pair shouted back and forth. Sonam reported that a Zanskari monk-turned-businessman, frustrated with the Indian government's inaction on road construction, was personally financing this excavator.

"One of the brave men of Zanskar," a porter whispered.

Only a single dirt track penetrated the Zanskar valley currently, running over mountains to the north, near the Pakistan border. Built in 1976, it was notoriously difficult to access, and closed for six months of every year by snow.

"Zanskar need more roads," Sonam said. "For more education. More doctors. More business. More money."

Young Zanskari parents, he explained, still tried to time childbirth for summer, when it was possible to reach a hospital in Ladakh's distant capital of Leh. The porters nodded solemnly, and after more yelling, the digger lurched back into action.

"He is making one hundred feet a day," Sonam reported. "By August he will cross the Shingo La."

It was already early July.

❧

We crested the Shingo La just before noon, finding a mess of prayer flags marking the summit—so many it appeared that an entire village had hung its laundry to dry. Offerings were scattered around the base of countless cairns: quartz, pages of scripture, bronze talismans, empty rum bottles and horns of ibex and bharal—the massive wild goat and sheep of the Himalaya.

Christine grasped my cheeks and pulled me close for a kiss, staring into my eyes. The boys joined, jumping up and down with arms wrapped around our legs till we almost tumbled. In a biting wind, we yanked on hats while Sonam excavated almonds and carrots from his pack.

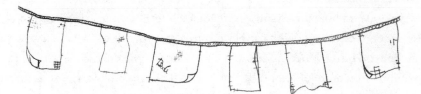

Prayer flags, or Lung-Ta *in Tibetan, are strings of rectangular cloths bearing the five elemental colors of Buddhism (blue, white, red, green and yellow). They can be found across the Himalaya, strung outside homes, on flag poles, and adorning every high pass and summit. Most bear an image of the wind horse, surrounded by Buddhist prayers in Tibetan script. Tradition holds that the winds scatter these prayers, bringing benefit to all.*

When the television crew set up tripods and prepared to interview Christine, I took the boys and scrambled higher up the ridge. We'd only gone a short distance when the view opened before us, revealing row upon row of crumbling peaks ahead, their steep slopes a swirl with lollipop shapes of red, green, purple and mocha rock.

This was our first glimpse of Zanskar: a scene torn from the pages of Dr. Seuss.

❧

Tucked between the Himalaya Range to the south, and the Tibetan plateau to the north, the Kingdom of Zanskar remains among the highest permanently inhabited places on the planet.

The valley is formed by the union of the Stod and Tsarap Rivers, whose combined waters meander across broad gravel plains before crashing into a nearly impassable gorge,* giving Zanskar what may be its most defining feature: inaccessibility. There is no easy way in or out.

For more than a thousand years, a close-knit society has endured here in isolation, eking out a scant living from the glacial till, growing crops of barley during the short summer with the aid of glacial meltwater irrigation.

When Tibetan Buddhism entered the valley during the seventh century, it quickly became entrenched as cultural bedrock. Stately monasteries sprang up—built inside caves, atop spires or perched on sheer cliffs as a means of balancing meditative seclusion with proximity to an alms-producing village—and soon a quarter of the male population had entered monastic life.

With time, Tibetan culture came to permeate all aspects of Zanskari society—art, architecture, astrology, medicine, clothing, cuisine and music—and the hidden valley, along with the entire surrounding state of Ladakh, came to be regarded as "Little Tibet," a de facto appendage of the great Tibetan kingdom.

Only an inconsequential quirk of fate tilted Zanskar's fortunes away from Tibet and toward the subcontinent. In 1834, as part of an effort to increase pashmina wool production, the maharaja of Jammu and Kashmir dispatched a raiding party that laid claim to the remote kingdom. As a result, more than a century later, Zanskar was spared China's crushing annexation of Tibet, and the ensuing atrocities of the Cultural Revolution.

---

*   For centuries, butter traders, monks and lay people wishing to access the amenities of Leh tiptoed over the frozen rapids of the Chadar during the depths of winter, but it was a perilous journey.

Today, the hidden valley stands among the last places on the planet where Tibetan Buddhism remains intact, undiluted and still freely practiced in its original setting.

❧

Beyond the Shingo La, hours of knee-knocking descent brought us to a flooding creek blocking our way. Muffled thuds emanated from the rapids, the sound of boulders tumbling downstream like bowling balls.

Sonam suggested we wait for the Pony Men, and then ride the horses across, but I recoiled at the suggestion. The thought of our boys perched atop mares, amid such whitewater, was too perilous to consider. So we ranged up and down the banks, searching for a way across, eventually discovering a bridge of avalanche debris. I went first, carrying Bodi on my back, carefully kicking steps into the narrow catwalk of snow while trying not to look at the rapids roaring beneath. Sonam followed, carrying Taj in a piggyback, as sure-footed as a Sherpa. Then Christine, the porters and finally the television crew.

I was relaxing on solid ground when a thud caused me to jump. One of the camera operators had slipped, but instead of falling off the bridge he had landed in a crevasse. Shaken but uninjured, the man crawled to safety.

We followed the creek downward, and with every step, the air grew thicker and the slopes greened. Sedges and wildflowers appeared. Bodi gathered fistfuls of "Dirty-Sock Flowers" (pink bistort) while Taj collected a bouquet of "Forget-Me-Nuts."

"Look!" Christine shouted, pointing to a herd of prehistoric-looking beasts grazing on the opposite bank. "Yaks!" For their immense size, the shaggy animals moved with astonishing grace.

"How can they see?" Bodi asked. "Their eyes are covered by hair."

"Please come back Mr. Yak," Taj shouted as they disappeared over a rise.

A gathering of stone huts stood nearby. This was a *doksa*,* Sonam explained, grazing lands for the village of Kargiak, still a two-day walk away.

Counterintuitively, Zanskar's high alpine meadows are far more biologically productive than the valley bottoms, and every summer, women accompany herds of cow, yak, horse, sheep and goat to these exposed slopes, where they produce butter, cheese and yogurt to see the village through the winter ahead.

---

* *Doksa* translates literally to "nomad land" from the Tibetan *drokpa* (nomad) and *sa* (land).

Sonam hollered and clapped, but no one appeared. Perhaps they were out gathering yak dung, he suggested. Easy to gather and stack, yak dung provides an invaluable fuel in this treeless land, used for heating homes and cooking meals. These Frisbee-shaped patties dry rapidly in the parched Himalayan air, devoid of mold or fermentation, and every Zanksari household retains claims to well-defined collection zones. Dung, Sonam explained with a laugh, was the only commodity in the remote valley that money could not buy.

Wearily we trudged on, reaching the muddy flats known as Lakong ("Gateway") as silver light drained from the western sky. A chill wind blew, and the Pony Men hastily unloaded their animals. Kerosene stoves soon screamed. In perfect darkness, we put up our tent.

The boys were brushing their teeth by flashlight when a group of ragged men stumbled into camp, leading a team of horses. These wranglers were headed home to Manali after a summer spent leading tourist treks. A small girl travelled with them. Dark-eyed and barefoot, she wore a fraying pink sweater and blue skirt. Bodi and Taj approached curiously, but she ducked beneath a low plastic tarp, where the men were huddled around a brass stove. By the time we rose at dawn, she and the wranglers had already vanished into the dark peaks.

❧

We descended a wide, U-shaped valley. The flooding Kargiak River ricocheted back and forth across the shale flood plains, and we crossed the torrent regularly, atop wobbly bridges of log and flagstone. Dotted along the trail were purple vetch, pink rose and in places, the extremely rare blue Himalayan poppy. Prayer flags rippled from passing headlands, the only sign of habitation in this otherwise barren land.

A magnificent fin of white granite appeared in the distance. This was Gumbarajan, Sonam explained, and he was unsure if anyone had ever reached its summit. I marvelled at the possibility, for elsewhere in the world such a spire would be covered by a web of climbing routes. By noon we were scuttling beneath its sheer face, ears alert for the clatter of rockfall. Soon the tall, triangular cliff floated behind us, like a sail on the blue sea of the sky.

After a lunch of curried potatoes and peas, Sonam dragged the white mare toward Bodi again. This time, Bodi glanced uncertainly at Christine and me.

"It's up to you, sweetie," Christine said. "If you want to ride, we'll stay close. You'll be safe. I promise."

Without waiting for an answer, Sonam plucked Bodi from the ground and plopped him atop a blanket of boiled yak wool on the mare's back. I braced for a tantrum, but Bodi said nothing, his face expressionless. Tiny stirrups hung on frayed nylon rope from a rudimentary pack frame, but Bodi's hiking boots wouldn't fit in, which was fine by me, for if he ever tumbled, foot entrapment could pose a grave danger. With no reins for purchase, I stripped the bandana from my head and knotted it to the pack frame, creating a loop for Bodi to hold.

"You OK?" I asked quietly. Bodi nodded without looking. I glanced at Christine. She gave a thumbs-up. Sonam tugged the halter, and the horse clattered forward.

I struggled to stay close behind, arms held aloft in case Bodi lost his balance. But our son appeared to be a natural rider, sitting tall with relaxed hips. When the mare crossed a stream, and water swirled to her belly, Bodi nonchalantly raised his feet. On the far side, he leaned forward and grabbed her mane as the mare clattered up a steep bank. Before long he had let go of my bandana entirely and was staring upward, pinching fingers before his eyes as if plucking clouds from the sky.

❧

On the sixth morning of our trek, *mani* walls began to appear, rising in the center of the trail and running for hundreds of meters. Constructed from intricately carved stones, most bore the famous Buddhist exhortation, *Om mani padme hum*. Every rock represented a long, cold winter spent chiselling, and viewed cumulatively, they were a humbling testament to local devotion.

Om mani padme hum, *the ancient mantra of Avalokiteshvara, is commonly translated as "Hail to the jewel in the lotus," and is meant as a reminder that just as the lotus grows in muddy water, so too can wisdom take seed in an impure mind.*

Like all sacred Buddhist objects, *mani* walls were meant to be passed on the left—keeping a traveller's right hand, representative of right thoughts and right action, closest to the divine, while creating a clockwise circumambulation, which in Buddhist doctrine is the direction that both the earth and universe revolve. If any of our party accidentally passed a *mani* wall to the right, as the television crew was prone to do, a porter or Pony Man would invariably notice, even from a great distance, and send them back to correct their miss.

Chortens came next, the iconic Buddhist monuments rising like giant chess pawns along the trailside, two storeys tall or more. Some were freshly white-washed, others ghosts of their former selves, eroded by wind, rain and time.[*]

Whitewashed chortens grace the entrance to most Himalayan villages,
often holding relics or the remains of esteemed lamas.

The boys took particular interest in the offerings left at the feet of these monuments. When Bodi asked if he could keep a particularly nice coin he'd found, Sonam wagged a finger. Taj popped an aging lump of dough into his

---

[*]   Used to protect buildings across the Himalaya, whitewash is created by baking limestone that villagers mine from surrounding peaks. When mixed with water, the resulting slurry cures to calcite and forms a thick, weather-resistant coating.

mouth, which Christine frantically dug out with a finger. I suspected illness, not impiety, was her concern.

Bodi had paused to sketch a trio of *chortens* when a horse came thundering down the trail toward us. Two young boys were perched on top, riding bareback, and they charged straight past without slowing.

Eventually a cluster of whitewashed homesteads appeared ahead. We had reached Kargiak, the first Zanskari village.

The mud-brick structures were set deeply in the earth, which Sonam explained served as protection from intense winter cold. Prayer flags flapped upon flat roofs, and dung dried beside piles of russet fodder.

Fields of barley surrounded the village. The crop was already waist high, with fuzzy green heads that rippled in the wind. Barley is a staple of Himalayan culture, a hardy grain blessed with a short growing season and remarkable drought tolerance. But here—at the very limit of habitable altitude—the grain would never fully mature. Instead, these fields would be cut as the first snows of autumn fell, left to ripen on the ground.

"*Jullay, jullay, jullay, jullay!*"

A pair of elderly women materialized beside us. Wearing homespun robes and chunky turquoise necklaces, they'd been stooped amid the crop, weeding by hand. Scrambling over a stone wall, the pair showered our party with greetings.

"*Jullay, jullay, jullay, jullay!*"

Jullay is the luminous greeting of the Zanskari people, meaning by turn hello, goodbye, good morning, good night, please, thank you or whatever else is needed. Similar to the manner in which Nepalis employ *namaste*, it is a salutation that defies being said without a grin.

"*Jullay, jullay,*" we echoed back.

The women were enthralled by our boys and reached out to brush soft cheeks with crooked fingers while peppering Sonam with questions. At the mention of Karsha Gompa, the women beamed and touched their hands in prayer. "Good, good, good, good."

Next they turned their attention to Christine.

"I'm so embarrassed," Christine moaned as they yanked on her braids. "My hair is a mess."

Indeed, wild strands escaping from her braids left her looking like a static electricity experiment, but the elders were far more interested in the elastic bands holding her pigtails. By chance, Christine had a spare pair in her pocket, which she handed to the women. Then we all stood together, beaming at one another, unable to share a word.

We could have lingered for hours, but Sonam wanted to establish camp, so we departed, chased down the trail by a cascade of "*Jullay, jullay, jullay, jullay!*"

Flocks of dark-eyed children tailed us, their cheeks darkened and cracked by sun. Tiny laminated photographs of the Dalai Lama hung from red strings around their necks. The youngsters crowded around as we pitched our tents in a nearby meadow, but when our boys held aloft biscuits and a thermos of milky tea in offering, they melted away into the barley.

❧

With every passing day, more and more quiet hamlets appeared, where tendrils of smoke spiralled from scattered homesteads, and irrigation canals, crafted by hand and running arrow-straight across slopes above, delivered precious melt-water from distant glaciers. Only the occasional shouts of children, or groans of livestock, broke the tranquility.

Late on the eighth day the valley began to narrow, and we arrived at the mouth of a deep gorge, where the path had been carved into precipitous cliffs. Sonam pressed on without a pause, dragging Bodi behind him atop the white mare, but I didn't like the look of what was to come.

"Stop!" I shouted. Rushing to catch up, I asked Bodi to dismount, but he was hysterical at the intrusion.

"Why? Why do I have to get down, Dad? Tell me why!"

The chance of a hoof slipping might have been slim, but the result would have been catastrophic. So instead we all inched along the trail together, Bodi grasping my hand, Taj in Christine's.

In places, cantilevered logs and hand-fitted stones formed airy catwalks. Elsewhere, rock slides had obliterated the path, and we followed Sonam carefully across these loose slopes, placing our boots softly in his prints. Pebbles whistled by from above, disappearing into the chasm with a yawning silence, possibly landing in the silty Kargiak River somewhere far below.

When a train of pack horses appeared on the ledge ahead, we pressed our backs against the rock wall and sucked in our breath.

"Don't worry," Sonam yelled back. "You will be safe."

And indeed, the sure-footed animals marched straight past, swaying loads never grazing us, their hooves balanced on the very edge of oblivion.

That night we camped at the outwash of a gulch. A dusting of icy stars beckoned from above, and the silence reminded me of a desert, or the high Arctic when the winds abate. It seemed even the birds and locusts had abandoned this land.

❧

Two days later, Christine and I were reading bedtime stories to the boys when Sonam appeared at the tent door with unexpected news: tomorrow would be our last day on the trail.

Karsha Gompa still lay four days of walking away, but a footbridge had recently been constructed downstream, leading to a new jeep track on the far side. While Christine and I would have happily trekked the entire way to the monastery, to Sonam, the idea of walking when a road was available seemed ridiculous.

So the next morning he set off before sunrise to seek drivers. After a lazy breakfast, we followed, taking our time, savouring the final moments of our trek, lingering on riverside beaches while our boys wrote their names in the sand.

We crossed the swaying footbridge shortly after lunch, and on the far side, scrambled up loose slopes to find Sonam waiting alongside a convoy of jeeps. After unloading their animals, the Pony Men prepared to leave. They would follow the same path back to their homes in Manali. When I handed the men a modest tip, eighteen-year-old Ramesh Singh held the bills to his heart and Tsewang Yetok flashed his golden tooth.

Then our family crammed into a dented jeep and bounced away.

❧

After an hour, the canyon walls parted like curtains, and the central plains of Zanskar spread before us, an extraordinary expanse hidden amongst the world's highest peaks. These rocky flats—surrounding the confluence of the Tsarap and Stod Rivers—were dotted with villages, fields of barley and swaying poplar, but my eyes sought Karsha Gompa.

And there it was, in the distance! A tangle of whitewashed temples and dormitories clinging to cliffs the color of rusting iron. After months of gazing at Internet photographs, I recognized the monastery instantly.

"Look, look," I shouted, pointing through the windshield.

Sitting in the front seat, Christine shook her head in silence. When she turned, tears streaked her dusty cheeks. Beside me, Bodi and Taj were busily dividing the crumbs of a biscuit package, and didn't even glance up.

❧

We stayed that night in a half-finished concrete guest house on the outskirts of Padum, Zanskar's administrative center. I slept fitfully, as excited as a child on Christmas Eve.

Wes and the crew departed at dawn to scout the monastery. I desperately wanted to accompany them, for I was nervous about first impressions. During the trek, the crew occasionally ran roughshod over locals, directing them to "stand here" and "say this." But Wes bristled at the suggestion his team might be disrespectful. So I acquiesced. What else could I do? As I watched jeeps carrying the camera team bounce away, I wondered what reception they might receive.

Sonam repeatedly assured me Lama Wangyal was anticipating our family's arrival, but something in the way he averted his eyes felt unsettling, and recently I'd begun to wonder if Lama Wangyal actually knew we were coming at all.

Bruce, Taj,
Christine, and
Bodi (clockwise
from bottom).

Departing from their home in Kimberley, British Columbia (OPPOSITE TOP), the Kirkby family canoe down the Columbia River (OPPOSITE BOTTOM) to the town of Golden, where they catch a train bound for the coast (BELOW).

The *Hanjin Ottawa* container ship passes beneath the Lions Gate Bridge while departing Vancouver, bound for Asia (OPPOSITE TOP). Bodi at the helm with Captain Klugscheisser (OPPOSITE CENTER). After a seventeen-day sea voyage, the ship makes landfall in Busan, South Korea (OPPOSITE BOTTOM). The family explores a fish market in Busan (ABOVE TOP). Awaiting an overnight ferry to China, alongside the two heavy duffel bags, in Incheon, South Korea (ABOVE BOTTOM).

Pilgrims surround the energetic boys in the Tibetan capital of Lhasa (ABOVE). Christine and Taj below the north face of Mount Everest (BELOW). Bodi enjoys an elephant ride in Nepal's Chitwan National Park, while the television crew shoots from an adjacent elephant (OPPOSITE TOP). A fleeting visit to the Taj Mahal during India's hot season (OPPOSITE CENTER). Henna tattoos at a Delhi market (OPPOSITE BOTTOM).

A narrow-gauge railway carries the family up into the Himalayan foothills, toward Shimla.

A ten-day trek over the Great Himalaya Range. Bodi riding a pack horse (OPPOSITE TOP). An oasis of wildflowers (OPPOSITE CENTER). The route followed ancient footpaths, carved into precipitous canyon walls (OPPOSITE BOTTOM). Karsha Gompa, a thousand-year-old Buddhist monastery in the Zanskar valley, where the family's hundred-day journey ended (ABOVE).

Lama Wangyal, the former Head Lama of Karsha Gompa, took the family in (ABOVE).
Bodi on the day of arrival at the monastery, gazing out across Zanskar's central plains
(OPPOSITE).

Taj in Lama Wangyal's rudimentary kitchen (ABOVE). Bodi, Nawang and Taj at play (BELOW).

Lama Wangyal in ceremonial attire during a *jin-sek,* or fire ceremony, (LEFT). Strong winds buffet the courtyard, scattering novice monks, as the jin-sek reaches its crescendo (BELOW).

Lama Wangyal and Taj.

5

ONCE IN A FULL MOON

Our jeep bounced along mud lanes lined with mud-brick homes and shaded by poplar, finally pulling to a stop in Karsha's village square, beside a gin-clear creek. Through gaps in foliage, I peered up toward the wondrous, otherworldly tangle of whitewashed buildings plastered to steep cliffs above. Our boys gazed up too, uncharacteristically silent.

It was only ten o'clock, but already the high-altitude sun burnt like an ember on my neck as I dragged duffels from the jeep. Nearby, a plump, ruddy-cheeked man sold tomatoes and dried apricots from the trunk of a dented Fiat. Two elderly women in robes sat motionless in the shade of a prayer wheel. Beyond, a dirt path led upward.

I was vaguely aware of camera operators and producers scrambling in our periphery, but my attention was fixed on a tall figure standing a short distance up the trail, beside a crumbling *chorten*. He wore maroon robes and a pointed orange hat with upturned earflaps, and while I'd never seen a picture of Lama Wangyal, I knew it was him.

Christine started up the steep path with the boys in hand, and I followed, struggling with our duffels. As we neared, Lama Wangyal opened his arms and whispered hoarsely, *"Jullay, jullay, jullay, jullay."*

A traditional Zanskari monk's hat, made of felted orange wool
and bearing the distinctive upturned dog-ear flaps.

Resting a large hand atop each of Bodi and Taj's heads, he drew the boys close. I pulled a crumpled *khata* scarf from my pocket and clumsily placed it around the old monk's neck. Then Lama Wangyal reached out and wrapped Christine and me in a hug. We stood in silence for some time, simply gazing at each other.

He was a tall man and powerfully built, probably in his sixties, with smooth forearms and a square chin. Every ounce of hair-growing energy appeared to have been channelled into his eyebrows, which curled upward and reminded me of a ram's horns.[*]

Eventually Lama Wangyal took Bodi and Taj's hands in his thick paws and without a word, started up toward the monastery. Christine and I followed, marvelling at the sight of our boys flanking this tall robed monk. It was unusual for them to accept a stranger so readily, especially Taj, who had remained withdrawn since the quasi-kidnapping incident at the Korean ferry terminal.

"This all gives me goosebumps," Christine whispered.

Slowly we ascended slopes as steep as a ski run, plodding around switchbacks, gasping for breath in the thin air. After twenty minutes we reached a colossal *chorten* guarding the monastery entrance. A darkened tunnel led through its

---

[*]   Lama Wangyal had retired from his Head Lama position two years before our arrival, but remained a respected senior member of the monastic community.

base, and inside, Lama Wangyal paused to spin a soot-stained prayer wheel. We followed suit. Then he led us on, toward the light.

The monastery's courtyard was ringed by whitewashed temples whose thick mud-brick walls sloped gently inward as they rose. Silken drapery of red, yellow and blue fluttered from open windows. We paused, trying to take it all in, but Lama Wangyal was impatient and dragged us on, up pathways burnished by centuries of shuffling feet, past dormitories with hunched wooden doors and shuttered windows, past abandoned homes and *chortens* thick with generations of whitewash, past ornate frescoes and magnificently carved boulders, past shady willow groves where wrens hopped underfoot.

Twenty more minutes of breathless climbing brought us to a simple mud-brick home, standing alone on steep rocky slopes, near the top of the monastery complex. The front door was made from rough-hewn timber. Only a meter tall, it appeared fit for a hobbit. Using a lanyard of keys around his neck, Lama Wangyal opened a rusty padlock and ducked inside. Then his large hand reached out and pulled our boys in after him.

Stooping, Christine and I followed. Plunging into darkness, our fingers traced earthen walls down a long, narrow passageway. We passed tidy stacks of dung, a rickety ladder of twisted branches and the entrance to a small stable (actually the kitchen), before finally emerging into a sunlit chamber the size of a child's bedroom.

Mud-plastered walls were painted lime green and adorned with faded photographs—snaps of the lama proudly posing with foreign trekkers. A squat table held a homemade prayer wheel (built inside a jam jar) and a geranium (sprouting from a rusty paint can). Wooden transportation pallets covered in red carpets ringed the walls. A bank of cracked windows offered a sweeping view across Zanskar's central plains.

"Sitting, sitting," Lama Wangyal waved us in. As I entered, I bonked my skull loudly on the log ceiling, and the old monk laughed. "First day, bang! Second day, bang! Third day, bang! Fourth day, no problem."

Then he disappeared.

The boys raced in circles, bare feet raising clouds of dust. I collapsed on a pallet beside Christine, feeling a tremendous weight lift from my body.

"Wow," Christine grinned. "Just wow."

Wes scrambled in through the low door, bent in half at the waist and pouring sweat. "Is this where you're gonna stay, mate?" he whispered, eyes wide.

I shrugged, uncertain.

Lama Wangyal returned with a biscuit tin, which Bodi and Taj rushed to investigate. After pouring cups of sweet black tea for family and TV crew alike, the old monk plopped down between Christine and me, and with a broad smile, stuck out his tongue—a greeting once common throughout Tibet, meant to demonstrate one was not a black-tongued demon.

❧

A guest house had recently been constructed at the base of the cliffs, below the monastery. Funded by a French benefactor and operated by the monks, it offered passing tourists a place to stay while providing a new source of income for the monastery. After tea, Sonam suggested we stroll down to take a peek.

"Maybe guest house better for family?" he whispered with Lama Wangyal out of earshot. "Maybe nicer."

Built from concrete blocks, the square structure held six bedrooms, a porcelain-tiled kitchen and a spacious common room. While clean and modern, it was also devoid of spirit. The sterile environment held no interest for me.

"What do you think?" I asked, pulling Christine aside, conscious of her need for space and privacy. We were careful not to let Bodi hear our discussion, for if he knew there was a choice in lodging, he would undoubtedly voice a strong opinion, and invariably it would be different than ours.

"I'm not sure. I feel a bit rushed," she admitted. "This place is nice enough. And the lama's house feels cramped. But I think it would be crazy not to live up in the monastery. I mean we've come so far."

Just then I was summoned outside, where Sonam and Lama Wangyal sat cross-legged, engaged in a heated discussion. For some time the men yelled back and forth in Zanskari, ignoring my presence, and as I waited, I felt sheepish for understanding nothing of the local tongue.

Eventually, Sonam turned to me and declared, "Better you staying at guest house. Now special celebration time for harvest. No one allowed staying at *gompa*. Besides, guest house more better. More clean."

My face must have betrayed a whisper of disappointment, because Lama Wangyal and Sonam immediately dove back into their animated debate. Eventually Sonam stood and brushed his hands. "Okay. We going Lama Wangyal's now."

Assuming he meant to retrieve our duffel bags, I suggested dashing uphill myself to save our boys the climb.

"No, no. Everyone," Sonam said impatiently. "Family living upside. With lama."

I was taken off guard, feeling simultaneously pleased and concerned. Was Lama Wangyal breaking monastery protocol because he felt pressured? Or had Sonam been trying to steer us toward the guest house in his belief the modern facility would suit a Canadian family better? I tried to ask, but both men walked away.

I never learned what transpired between Sonam and Lama Wangyal that day, and as with so much we experienced in Zanskar, I suspect the truth lay masked beneath layers of language, culture and tradition.

❧

Later that afternoon, the television crew organized a final round of interviews. I offered a few summary thoughts about the journey behind us and the experience ahead. Both boys said a few cute things about being happy with their new home. Then we sat on boulders and watched as Christine lined up before the cameras, a reflective panel lighting her face.

Wes began by asking why she wanted to take this trip.

"I feel kids can only benefit from an experience like this," she started. "The opportunity, to live with people who are so different, and less fortunate, it just feels so precious . . ." Emotions welled that went beyond words, and Christine's voice wavered. As Wes asked question after question, tears spilled down her cheeks.

"The lesson I want to impart to my kids is that it's not about the stuff. It's more about being solid within yourself."

After what seemed like an eternity, Wes called, "Cut."

"Damn it, Wes," Christine sniffed, rubbing her reddened eyes. "I promised myself I wasn't going to cry. But you made me!"

Then she wrapped her arms around the beaming Aussie, who we'd both grown so fond of.

Despite the inevitable tensions and frustrations of any journey—particularly given the nature of our relationship of documentarian and subjects—special bonds had formed between the crew and our family. Wes had even floated the idea of staying at the monastery for a few weeks and crafting a final episode about our time at Zanskar. But the presence of cameras would undermine any chance of our family quietly fitting in, so without malice I refused.

Now, as the crew prepared to bid a final farewell, we pressed gifts of turquoise into their palms. More bittersweet tears flowed. Then the audio technicians, camera operators and producers who had travelled alongside us since departing from our home in Canada three months earlier disappeared down the trail, dust rising from their vanishing feet.

They left in their wake an oceanic stillness, a sense of quiet and profound relief broken only by the occasional bawling of a calf and cries of village children far below.

❧

Bodi wanted to visit an enormous brass prayer wheel he'd spotted near the monastery entrance, so I took him and watched as he ran in dizzying circles, spinning the drum faster and faster. With every rotation, a nail driven into the upper rim crashed against a bell, announcing to all within earshot that merit was being accrued.

We returned to find Christine in the dim kitchen, working under the supervision of Lama Wangyal. He was teaching her to cook dal, or curried lentils, in a pressure cooker atop a single-burner propane stove.* My job in the months ahead, he explained, would be to supply the household with tea, and he demonstrated precisely how much water, loose tea, masala spice and sugar he wanted in each pot.

Afterward, we ate together in our room, sitting on pallets. Lama Wangyal was curious about everything in our duffels: toothbrushes, Lego, camera, journal, deodorant. Christine was pulling cotton pyjamas onto Taj, when she addressed him by the familial nickname, "Taji."

The old monk froze, looking perplexed. He pointed at Taj in disbelief. "Tashi?"

"No." Christine explained that Taji was a nickname, but Lama Wangyal waved her off.

"Tsering Tashi," he repeated, pointing at Taj. Eventually it dawned on me he was bestowing Taj with a Tibetan name.

---

* Pressure cookers are ubiquitous across the Himalaya, where water boils at markedly lower temperatures because of thinner air.

Next, Lama Wangyal turned his attention to Bodi, closing his eyes and placing a hand atop Bodi's knee. Was he searching his memory for someone Bodi reminded him of? Or waiting for an appropriate name to enter the stillness of his mind? Assigning Tibetan names wasn't new for Lama Wangyal, for senior monks routinely rename the novices in their care.

"Norbu," Lama Wangyal finally declared, opening his eyes. "Tsering Norbu."

"Tsering?" I asked.

"Very sorry. Tsering no good name." Lama Wangyal grimaced, raising his shoulders in mock helplessness. "Old person name."

His full name was Tsering Wangyal, and by sharing it, in the same manner a guru names a student, he was placing our boys under his umbrella of care.

Lama Wangyal then pointed at Christine, declaring she would hereafter be known as Angmo. Months earlier, at a public teaching in Leh, the Dalai Lama had suggested that the traditional Zanskari name Angmo could benefit from more use. Lama Wangyal was now doing his part.

Christine tried saying the unfamiliar name a few times, and Lama Wangyal beamed. "Good, Angmo, good."

Finally, the lama turned to me, and declared after a pause, "Mortub!"

What? I'd never heard the name Mortub (pronounced More-Toob) before, and felt a momentary flush of disappointment. With so many fond and familiar Tibetan names to choose from—Kami, Nima, Purbu, Tenzing—why had I been given a title that sounded like a dark wizard from *Harry Potter*?

Pragmatically, I knew it would be easier for locals to remember Tibetan names instead of our unfamiliar Western ones, but the deeper truth was that I felt honoured. Something rare and enchanting occurs when one is bestowed with a local name in a foreign land.

I'd experienced the phenomenon decades earlier, when Bedu companions in Arabia named me Saleh. Until that moment, I had assumed I would never be anyone but Bruce. Initially Saleh sounded strange, its usage forced, but within days I found myself responding to even a whisper of the name. In conversations between Canadian teammates, we soon referred to each other by Arabic names. The Bedu knew us by no other. Ultimately, Saleh came to represent who I was during those seventy days in the desert.

So here amongst the monks of Karsha Gompa, we became Tashi, Norbu, Angmo and Mortub.

❧

Later that evening, as I rinsed dinner bowls in a dented pewter basin outside the hobbit door, a full moon appeared in the east. Climbing free of tangled peaks, it drifted skyward like an enormous yellow balloon.

We had arrived, I realized, on an auspicious day, for Buddhists hold the full moon in highest regard. According to legend, every important event in Siddhartha Gautama's life transpired on a full moon: his birth, his renunciation of earthly desires, his enlightenment, his first sermon and his eventual passing into nirvana.

Back inside, I found the boys sleeping soundly. Christine had arranged our sleeping bags atop the pallets—head to toe, head to toe—so the family slept in a continuous loop, ringing the room. My bag was pressed up against the bank of windows.

I crawled in and was about to start reading when Lama Wangyal appeared, carrying a candle. After gazing at the sleeping children, he sat beside me, placing a hand on my sleeping bag while quietly muttering, *"Om mani padme hum,"* over and over.

I watched as the old monk kneaded a rosary of *mala* beads through his fingers. Noting my curiosity, he plucked another set from a nail on the wall and held them toward me as a gift. I tried to refuse, but he insisted. He showed me how to advance a bead at a time, rolling each between thumb and forefinger, prompting me to chant as I went. Feeling like an imposter, I began. *Om mani padme hum. Om mani padme hum.*

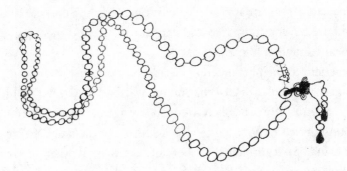

A set of mala *or prayer beads. The Tibetan rosary comprises 108 beads, and is used to count mantra recitations during meditation. Beads on two smaller strings are used to record rotations of the primary rosary.*

"No, Mortub." Lama Wangyal gently corrected my pronunciation of the final syllable. "*Om mani padme* HEUNG! In Zanskar, all people saying HEUNG."

I continued while Lama Wangyal drifted to an adjoining puja (prayer) room, no larger than a walk-in closet, where a small altar held seven small silver bowls filled with water. One by one, Lama Wangyal emptied these into a bucket. Then he lit a multitude of yak-butter candles, illuminating three brass statues: Buddha, flanked by his famous Tibetan disciples, Guru Rinpoche* and Je Tsongkhapa.†

Christine glanced up from the book she was reading by headlamp. "He gave me a set of *mala* beads earlier. I love them."

Eventually Lama Wangyal emerged from the altar room carrying a single candle, still chanting. I listened as his footsteps faded up the twisted ladder in the passageway outside. We were left alone in darkness.

Christine was soon breathing rhythmically. I could feel Taj's warmth on my feet, and somewhere above my head, Bodi rustled. Cool air cascaded down the windows, and I pulled my sleeping bag tight, gazing out at the broad valley silhouetted in milky moonlight. I was drifting toward sleep when a faint scratching caught my attention. It sounded like hundreds of tiny claws and came from the ceiling overhead.

Mice? A rat? Did I hear purring? A cat?

On and on these peculiar sounds went, building to a crescendo then falling away, again and again. Eventually I surmised a colony of bats were roosting in the ceiling. As they clawed their way through the thatch, struggling to emerge into the moonlight, their wings whirred like a moth held in cupped hands.

---

* Guru Rinpoche, also known as Padmasambhava, "the Lotus Born," was an eighth-century master widely credited with bringing Buddhism to Tibet.

† Je Tsongkhapa (1357–1419) was a prominent teacher of Tibetan Buddhism who founded the "Yellow Hat" or Gelugpa lineage, to which Karsha Gompa belongs.

6

TOUCHING DOWN

The sharp note of a chime woke me. My cheek was pressed against a chill window. Outside, glaciated peaks smouldered in the sun's crimson rays. From upstairs came the sound of shuffling feet. Then chanting.

I sat up slowly, careful not to rustle my sleeping bag, for Christine and the boys still slept. A dog-eared copy of Peter Matthiessen's *The Snow Leopard* lay beside my pallet, where I'd dropped it the night before, but I wasn't in the mood for reading. Instead, I reached for the *mala* beads, gently passing the polished spheres between my thumb and forefinger. At home I would have recoiled at the thought of passing time in such a way, but here, surrender came more easily.

I had completed three rotations of the rosary when footsteps padded into the nearby kitchen. The click of the gas stove was followed by a jangle of pots. Lama Wangyal soon appeared, chanting as he placed a thermos of sweet black tea on the table before me, indicating I should pour myself a cup. Then he disappeared down the passageway and out the hobbit door.

Not long after, horns echoed across the mountainside.

Christine moaned; she was too exhausted to rise. Taj remained motionless. But Bodi sat bolt upright. I told him I was going to investigate, and to my surprise, he asked if he could tag along.

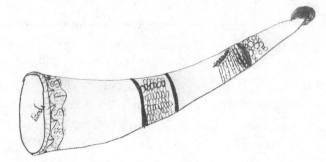

Every morning, a pair of rag-dung, *short Tibetan brass horns, called the monks of Karsha Gompa to puja, or ritual prayers.*

Hand in hand we climbed rocky trails, winding between whitewashed buildings, seeking the source of the racket. Maroon-robed monks floated up the paths around us, some swinging bare arms to stay warm, others hunched and muttering, hands clasped behind backs. Most ignored our presence, but a gaggle of curious novices dropped in behind us, whispering excitedly.

A dark tunnel led to the monastery's upper courtyard. A wooden pole rose in the center, festooned with prayer flags and topped with a yak tail. Beneath, two teenage monks were zealously blowing into brass horns. Beyond rose an ancient fortress.

This was the *lhakhang* ("hall of the gods"), also commonly referred to as the assembly hall. Constructed from mud, stone and rough-hewn timbers, it was four hundred years old and now gently slumped, walls and roof askew. Like autumn leaves, a scattering of plastic sandals lay before the entry. We added our hiking boots to the pile, then pulled aside a heavy yak-hair blanket and slipped in.

We found ourselves inside a darkened room about the size of a school gymnasium, where a scattering of twisted wooden pillars supported the low roof. Frescoes lined the walls. A sea of flickering yak-butter candles on the altar warmed a giant golden statue of Buddha.

Row after row of monks sat silent and cross-legged. A young man wandered the aisles, swinging a censer that billowed with the blue smoke of burning juniper. A single sword of sunlight cut down from above.

Unsure of what to do, we lingered beside the door. Eventually an older monk spotted us and scurried to a dark corner where he unfurled a carpet and then motioned for us to sit. Awkwardly, I lowered myself cross-legged. Bodi did the same, driving a sharp elbow into the flesh of my leg as he leaned against me.

"What happens next?" he whispered. I shrugged.

We sat in silence as monks and novice boys continued to stream in, each prostrating three times in the central aisle before finding their place.* Eventually a single, sonorous voice filled the room. The others quickly joined in, their rhythmic chants gently rising and falling like ocean swells.

Distracted by aching knees, I adjusted my position, but only made matters worse by grinding an ankle against the hard floor. Soon one foot had fallen asleep. I straightened my leg and then glanced at my watch. We'd only been sitting for seven minutes?

Apart from crouching on haunches, sitting cross-legged may be the most ageless form of repose. As a young boy, I could spend hours on the floor, but decades of chair-bound living had tightened me in ways I had never realized. None of the lamas showed any discomfort as they swayed, and I made a commitment that if I achieved nothing else during my time at Karsha Gompa, at the very least I would teach my body—or more accurately re-teach it—how to sit cross-legged.

Bodi was experiencing no such problems. He sat serenely with eyes closed, upturned hands resting on his knees, thumb and forefinger touching, mirroring the Buddha statue at the front. Whether this was a continuation of what he'd learned in the Tibetan cave, or simply another expression of his comfort with all things spiritual, he had drifted into a realm I knew nothing of.

I have long viewed meditation with skepticism. Sitting around and thinking of nothing did not seem like a productive use of my precious time. So decades earlier, when my mother gently suggested that meditation might help calm my busy mind, I ignored her. Christine had meditated daily when we started dating, and I'd often discover her sitting in lotus position with eyes closed and a distant expression on her face. Usually I'd sneak up and gently tug on an ear, which infuriated her. She too had implored me to give meditation a shot, which I did, for a short time. But I found it impossible to concentrate on my breath and gave up.

So it came as a surprise, just weeks before our departure, when I happened upon a review of contemporary research that showed meditation was having unexpected and far-reaching effects: decreasing blood pressure, decreasing stress hormones, even decreasing dangerous cholesterol in the blood, while

---

* Three bows or prostrations are meant to show reverence for Buddhism's Three Jewels: Buddha, the dharma (his teachings) and the sangha (spiritual community).

simultaneously increasing immune response and positively influencing such seemingly unrelated conditions as binge eating, irritable bowel syndrome, psoriasis, ADHD, depression and addiction.

But the most astounding results of these studies were the brain scans, which revealed even short bouts of meditation were literally rewiring the brain, adding measurable grey matter while altering attributes previously thought to be set from birth: happiness, resilience, kindness.

Whether these studies had softened my resistance, or whether it was just the thin Himalayan air, I can't say, but I decided to give meditation another shot. Gently shutting my eyes, I took a deep breath and tried to clear my mind, focusing only on my breath.

What does that mean, "focus on your breath"?

What exactly should I be thinking about?

The tickle of air at my nostrils?

My chest moving up and down?

Wasn't I supposed to breathe with my belly?

A pair of stockinged feet tiptoed past. A cymbal clanged. Then a scratching sound, and I opened my eyes to find a young monk sweeping the aisles. Another boy was lighting candles.

Damn it, what happened to my breathing? Clearing my mind, I again closed my eyes and focused on the air moving in and out of my nostrils.

How long would my camera batteries last? Would I be able to recharge them in Zanskar? What about the upcoming TV show? Would it be a success? Would it change our lives? Would there be a second season? My thoughts drifted to home. Had I collected enough firewood to see us through the coming winter? Had I waxed my skis before putting them away for the summer?

For something that appeared so simple, meditating was damn hard work.

Sunlight flooded the room, and my eyes popped open again. The heavy drapes covering the door had been flung aside, and two barefoot boys rushed in, carrying fire-blackened kettles so heavy they were forced to balance the urns against a hip and walk askew. Starting with the Head Lama (who sat on a raised dais near the altar) the pair poured steaming tea into outstretched bowls as they scampered up and down the aisles.*

---

* Known as *phor-pa*, these shallow wooden bowls are carried inside the robes of monks and the coats of villagers, always on hand for drinking tea or mixing barley porridge.

A lama with severe eyebrows—he could have passed for Soviet politician Leonid Brezhnev—shuffled from the room. Moments later the man returned, carrying two china tea cups, which he handed to Bodi and me. The novices raced over, one filling Bodi's cup, the other mine. Unfortunately, my server was so distracted that he poured right over the rim, spilling scalding liquid across my pants. A loud tut from Brezhnev sent the pair scurrying toward the door.

I expected to taste *po cha*, or butter tea, a gamey concoction common across Tibet. But instead I found myself drinking sweet, milky chai, spiced with cardamom. In a few gulps I had drained my cup. After fastidiously blowing on his own tea, Bodi took a sip and gave a thumbs-up.

More chanting followed. With knees and back aching, maintaining focus on my breath felt impossible. I fidgeted endlessly. Eventually Bodi whispered, "I'm done praying. I want to leave." I asked if he could find his own way home, and he nodded. He stood and tiptoed out, with every eye in the room following him.

Soon the tea urns appeared again, and this time a layer of molten butter floated atop the tea in my cup.

Made by churning yak butter with boiling water, salt and tea leaves, *po cha* is celebrated across the Tibetan Plateau for its capacity to hydrate, replace salts, provide energy and even prevent chapped lips from cracking. Common estimates suggest villagers drink anywhere between forty and sixty cups daily. I wasn't so keen on the stuff, and on previous journeys had gagged on the briny flavor and congealed fat.

"The trick is not to think of it as tea," a French traveller told me years earlier, in a Sikkim guest house. "Imagine you are drinking bouillon. Or chicken noodle soup."

His advice proved useless, and for years I had surreptitiously tossed the fetid liquid beneath tables and out tent doors—never a successful strategy, for Tibetans relentlessly refill every guest's cup.

But when I tried this batch, I found it creamy and surprisingly palatable. I finished my cup and held it out again when a second round was served.

Chanting resumed, and I had closed my eyes, pondering why the butter tea of Karsha Gompa seemed so agreeable—Non-rancid butter? Less salt?—when the lamas leapt up in unison and began streaming out. Struggling to my feet, one leg asleep, I was carried by the tide of crimson robes toward blinding sunlight beyond.

❧

After a breakfast of garlic and tomato omeletes, Bodi and Taj were both desperate to visit the village below. I suspected they wanted to ascertain what candy was available in Karsha's only store. I was curious to poke around as well, so the three of us set off, leaving Christine at Lama Wangyal's to read in peace.

Bodi skipped gaily down the trail, and I followed with Taj on my shoulders. Soon three white goats came bounding toward us, intent on licking Bodi's face. He shooed them away furiously while Taj giggled. Later, a pair of women overtook us, scarves drawn across faces and wicker baskets piled high with dung slung across shoulders.

At the village entrance, the women paused to give the prayer wheel a mighty spin. We followed suit, Bodi and Taj taking turns getting the enormous brass drum revolving at a frantic rate.

Karsha's "store" was actually the ground floor of a mud-brick homestead. Two garage-style doors had been thrown up, and a silent man in a maroon sweater and cream fedora sat behind a wooden counter. The shelves were laden with biscuit packages, soda crackers, noodle soup, powdered milk, black tea, spicy Indian snacks, cellophane tape, flashlights, sticks of incense, prayer flags, and *khata* scarves. On the dirt floor, plastic crates held eggs, butter, a few wrinkled potatoes and one head of cauliflower.

To my delight, there was no soda pop or bottled water—making Karsha one of the rare places on the planet where you can't buy a Coke. I wasn't so happy to discover a corresponding lack of coffee and beer, which meant we'd be drinking nothing but creek water or tea during the months ahead. It was probably for the best. A full detox.

A collection of clear plastic jars held bulk candy: sours, lollipops, mints, chocolates and a mango-flavored chewing gum called Center Fruit. Digging into his pocket, Bodi extracted a wad of Indian cash, earned for good behavior, and purchased ten Center Fruit at one rupee (two cents) apiece. Taj started to cry, for he had no money, and having come without my own wallet, I begged ten rupees from my little banker.

Afterward we lingered by the village stream, balancing pebbles and later trying to corral black beetles that skittered across the glittering pools. Riverside cottonwoods were releasing seeds, and the fuzz drifted ceaselessly across the blue sky above, as if carried on a conveyor belt. It was August. Back in Canada, the same seeds would have flown in May, but Zanskar's stunted growing season demanded reproduction remain in full swing, even as autumn approached.

Clambering back up to the monastery, we found the hobbit door padlocked. We didn't have a key, so all we could do was wait in the shade of nearby rose bushes. I mused this was a chance to practise the Buddhist virtue of acceptance and focused on my breathing. The boys discussed which superhero could open the hobbit door.

"Hulk would smash it down," Bodi declared.

"Not Spidey," Taj said, lip starting to quiver as if he might cry. "His webs are too weak."

Taj brightened when Bodi declared Superman capable of burning the lock off with his X-ray vision. And Thor could smash it with his hammer. There was no consensus whether Captain America's shield could shatter the wood.

"I miss home," Bodi said unexpectedly. "How long until we go back?"

"Not long!" Taj beamed. "Just three months."

Bodi rolled his eyes. "Taj, that is a very long time."

We sat in silence again, then Bodi said, "I wish Nain was here."

Nain is the Welsh word for grandmother, and referred to my seventy-five-year-old mother.

"Nain can't come to Zanskar," I explained. "It would be too difficult for her here. There are too many stairs. And Lama Wangyal's passageway is too low."

Bodi thought about this for a moment, then suggested, "Why not wait until she shrinks some more. Then she won't have to bend over."

I laughed, but he wasn't joking.

"Dad! You shrink as you get older. You know that."

I admitted he was correct.

"And it will be easier for you to go into Lama Wangyal's house this afternoon."

I looked at him quizzically.

"When you sleep, your body stretches out. Even an old geezer like you. But all day you shrink again. You'll be shorter this afternoon. We can measure."

"Will you and Mom die before me?" Taj interjected.

"I certainly hope so," I replied, taken by surprise.

"Why do you hope so?" asked Bodi.

I launched into a clumsy explanation of how no parent wants to outlive their child, but Taj interrupted with more pressing concerns.

"When will you die anyway? When I am ten?"

And so it went, back and forth, for forty-five minutes, until a novice monk came rambling down the path, with shaven head and sleeveless robes.

He stopped before us and stared at my two boys, open-mouthed with disbelief. Then he pulled a key from his robes, opened the hobbit door and disappeared up the wooden ladder at the end of the dark passageway.

❧

That afternoon I was stretched across my pallet, enjoying the warm sunlight while watching a little wren collect nesting material from the sill, when Lama Wangyal burst in.

"Teaching," he shouted, pointing to his wristwatch.

I knew Lama Wangyal was eager for us to teach English to Karsha's novice monks, but I hadn't realized the role would commence so soon.

Christine and I had planned that she would teach at the monastery while I spent the afternoons with Bodi and Taj—a change of routine for both of us. But with Christine and the boys down in the village, buying eggs for supper, today would fall to me. Cramming supplies into a backpack, I raced to catch Lama Wangyal, who was already climbing up the steep trails.

The classroom sat near the top of the monastery. Screams and laughter echoed from an open door. Inside, a horde of boys were tossing cups of water over shrieking compatriots. Others whipped their classmates with damp robes.

"Big Teacher coming soon," Lama Wangyal assured me before striding off.

Tattered cushions rested against the classroom's mud-brick walls. Two sheets of plywood—painted black and perched on easels—acted as rudimentary blackboards. A hot plate and teapot sat in the back corner, while a bank of windows at the front provided gorgeous views of the wide valley.

The monk boys remained oblivious to my presence, and after waiting ten minutes for backup, I decided to break up the pandemonium myself.

"Hello!" I shouted.

A few of the novices glanced my way, but no one stopped running.

"HELLO!" I hollered, this time at the top of my lungs.

Everyone froze.

Hurriedly the boys gathered satchels and arranged themselves in what appeared to be order of youngest to oldest. There were twenty-one in total. All wore maroon robes, except for one little cherubic youngster, who sported a brown satin coat and orange monk's hat with upturned earflaps. Placing their hands together, the class bowed toward me.

"Good afternoon!" I said, enunciating the words slowly.

"Good afternoon," the class replied in unison.

"My name is . . . Mr. Bruce."

Until that moment, I hadn't thought about what the monk boys should call me. But instinct told me Mr. Bruce was better than Mortub, for half the battle of learning a foreign language is growing accustomed to its unusual sounds.

"My name is Mr. Bruce!" the class repeated, beaming.

Well, that didn't work. I tried pointing to the oldest boy, asking, "Your name is . . . ?"

"Your name is . . . ?" he repeated.

Not wanting to be excluded, the entire class joyously joined in, "Your name is . . . ?"

"Mr. Bruce!" I replied, and I moved along the row of boys, banging on my chest then pointing quizzically to each in turn. "My name is Mr. Bruce. And your name is . . . ?"

Eventually, someone understood.

"Stenzin," he said proudly, pointing to himself.

Finally we were getting somewhere. Except the boy beside him was named Stenzin also. And the boy next to him as well. In fact, every boy in the classroom told me his name was Stenzin.

That was the starting point: twenty-one identical boys, all wearing maroon robes, all with shaved heads, all called Stenzin.

Unsure what to do next, I retrieved a world map from my backpack. As I unfurled the chart, the boys crowded close, some sitting on my lap, others standing behind and poking through my hair the way a gorilla might search for fleas. I pointed to Canada. So did all twenty-one boys. Then we all pointed to India together. Then to the valley of Zanksar.

A knock at the door interrupted us. Seven French tourists were being shown around the monastery by a young Indian man wearing a leather motorcycle jacket and Ray-Ban sunglasses. After bowing deeply to the novice boys, he asked if his group could watch my lesson. I invited them in.

"How long have you been teaching?" one woman asked.

"Five minutes," I replied, leaving her unsure if I meant today or in my entire life. The answer was the same either way.

I continued, asking each boy his age and home village, while the tourists wandered amongst us, distributing ballpoint pens, unsharpened pencils and pink erasers. Apparently, the boys received plenty of such discards, for their satchels brimmed with broken and leaking tokens of such generosity. After snapping several photos, the group departed without a word.

Left in peace, I discovered the novices came from villages across Zanskar, the majority drawn from a cluster of neighboring hamlets. As we chatted I overheard the name Purbu, so I stopped and asked, "Who is Purbu?"

An impish looking boy raised his hand.

"Not Stenzin?" I asked.

"Stenzin Purbu!"

The boys had all been renamed upon entering the monastery, I would later learn, and every single one received the name Stenzin in honor of the current, and widely popular, Dalai Lama, Tenzin Gyatso. But they also received secondary names, by which they addressed each other, and those names now came in an avalanche.

There was sunny RamJam, solemn Joray, tall Tsephal, earnest Skarma, square-jawed Nawang, runny-nosed Thurchin, blue-eyed Nima and quiet Sonam. Impish Norgay, who wore the unusual brown robes, was the youngest, at seven years old. The eldest, Changchup, was seventeen. A stocky fourteen-year-old named Norphal spoke the best English, and in the months ahead would become an essential translator.

I glanced at my watch. It was two thirty. I'd been in the classroom for thirty minutes, but it felt like an eternity. What next? I wrote the colors of the rainbow on a blackboard, and tested the boys' comprehension by pointing to various things: the sky, the carpet, the walls, my backpack.

"What color?" I asked, and the boys leapt over each other in their eagerness to answer.

Two lamas eventually appeared in the doorway. One was Brezhnev, who now introduced himself as Lama Tsering Wang Chuk. The other was a short, smiley lama: Kachen Tenzin Chosang.

Wang Chuk raced around the classroom, snatching pink erasers from students' hands, whacking a few who refused to let go.

"Eating!" he said angrily, shaking his head in disgust. "No good."

He held out his palm to show me, and indeed a few of the confiscated erasers had been nibbled down like apple cores.

Then the pair of lamas leaned against the back wall, muttering as they watched me teach. I worried they might not approve of my improvised lesson.

When three o'clock finally arrived, I dismissed the boys, who leapt up at once, dangling satchels across their foreheads and sprinting out the door. I was packing my own backpack when the lamas approached.

"You teaching daily days, one hour?" Chosang asked. "Or two?"

"As you wish," I replied.

"No, as you wish," he smiled.

Then the two monks whispered between themselves for some time. "One hour OK," Chosang finally nodded. I was relieved, for today's lesson had felt interminable. But Wang Chuk held up a hand, and the pair launched into further discussion. Eventually Chosang reversed his decision. "Two hours better. First English. Then mathematics. OK?"

I agreed, but when I asked if they would be helping, or if they had a curriculum for me to follow, the pair looked confused and shook their heads.

❦

A green patchwork of fields spread across the plains below the monastery, in the shape of two butterfly wings centered on the small village stream. And that stream emerged from a deep canyon, which cut right through the cliffs upon which Karsha Gompa was perched.

While visiting the village store, I'd spotted an unusual line zigzagging up the sheer walls of the canyon toward the monastery, but it seemed impossible that a trail traversed such steep terrain, so I'd assumed it was just a cleft in the rock—until I spotted a maroon robe floating up the rock face.

"Winter trail," Lama Wangyal explained when I asked after class.

The path had existed for a thousand years, he told me: since the monastery was established. As a young boy, Lama Wangyal had struggled up and down the steep trail each morning, carrying sloshing buckets of water to and from the kitchen. But just three years ago, PVC piping had been strung to a natural spring, high in the peaks behind the monastery, which filled a cement cistern beside the assembly hall. Ever since, the winter trail had fallen into disuse.

Intrigued, Bodi and I set off to investigate.

Behind the monastery's ancient granary, we found a faint footpath, which led toward a precipitous drop. We approached the brink cautiously, tiptoeing over loose shale. Below, a catwalk of cantilevered logs and flagstones descended the cliffs in a series of airy switchbacks.

Bodi skipped on, unperturbed. Cognizant of the void beside us, I gripped his hand tightly. Eventually we emerged in the depths of the canyon, beside a jade pool. The air was chilly, and a sliver of silver sky ran overhead, mirroring the creek at our feet.

Downstream, a collection of squat stone buildings lined the banks, each roughly the size of a hot tub. Known as *rantok*, these tiny mills were used to grind roasted barley into flour. A hollowed log diverted stream water into each, where it turned a gigantic stone.

While Bodi tossed pebbles into the creek, I lay back across a flood-smoothed boulder. A blue butterfly tumbled past on the breeze, and I spotted a dipper flitting upstream, heading deeper into the peaks.

"Dad! Look at this quartz. Can I keep it?"

Bodi held out a dirty rock the size of a baseball, and reluctantly I crammed it into my pocket. His rock collection was growing at a frantic rate, and I suspected the future might hold a surreptitious culling.

Later we tossed pebbles at a flotilla of sticks Bodi had launched. As we dug for ammunition along the banks, I paused to marvel at the patterns adorning each stone.

What a rare feeling, with nothing calling.

At home, the pace of life was growing faster with each passing year, my days crammed with phone calls, appointments, emails, business travel, house chores, writing assignments and fitness. The boys too had piano lessons, soccer practices and even homework (already?). And for Bodi, there were hours and hours of additional therapy. If we didn't make time for trips like this, I wondered how many simple wonders we'd forget: the scent of damp earth, a tadpole in the palm, the iridescence of a dragonfly's wings.

An hour later, we scrambled back up the winter trail, and voices floated down from above. Two lamas were silhouetted against the sky. The men reached for Bodi's hand as we crested the final rise, pulling him close and stroking his hair.

"Norbu?" they asked, old and toothless. "Tashi?"

Word of our arrival was spreading.

7

EVERYTHING OLD IS NEW AGAIN

❈

The next morning, a novice stumbled from the hobbit door at sunrise. I was sitting nearby on a boulder, sipping tea, and watched as the boy—who I recognized from class—went to the rusty barrel, peeled off his robes and began scrubbing face, arms and gaunt torso with frigid water. Three other boys had soon joined him.

It seemed inconceivable that four novice monks shared Lama Wangyal's squat house with us. How had we not noticed them before?

"Yes," Lama Wangyal insisted when I asked after puja, leading me up the rickety ladder to the low attic. A single candle stood on a metal trunk, overlooking a scattering of paper and books that appeared to be homework. A nest of blankets on the rough plank floor revealed where the boys slept, huddled close.

Next, Lama Wangyal showed me where he slept, in a tiny room (secured with a padlock) no larger than a double closet. Beside a foam mattress sat brass chimes, a pile of books and a pink highlighter.

That evening Lama Wangyal marched the novices into our room. I recognized them all from the classroom. First came seven-year-old Tashi Topden, the age of Bodi and the size of Taj. Dark skinned, with generous eyebrows and a bewildered look, he reminded me of a young Mr. Bean.

"Mother dead," Lama Wangyal said. "Father too poor. So giving boy to me."

Next came Paljor, a slender fourteen-year-old who gazed at his feet as he mumbled, *"Jullay."* Then Jigmet. Thirteen years old with almond eyes, unblemished skin and full lips, he could have been a magazine model. Finally, a seventeen-year-old poked his head through the door. Rinchen wore a red hoodie over his robes. Having recently graduated from the monastery school, he now belonged to a shadowy crew of monastic teenagers that we would come to call the Lost Boys.

❦

After I described the boisterous schoolroom to Christine, we decided rather than her facing the class alone, it would be better to teach side by side and split the novices in half.

This meant Bodi and Taj would have to tag along, but it wouldn't hurt for them to join in the lessons, and more importantly, it would provide them with an opportunity to interact with the novice monks, who thus far had proven elusive.

"I'm so glad we are doing this," Christine said, as all four of us traipsed uphill. "You love an audience, Bruce, but I've been stressing about this for months. Standing in front of a classroom was going to be way out of my comfort zone."

We arrived to find bedlam. Red-cheeked novices threw rocks, books and pens at each other. One small boy arrived carrying the still-twitching tail of a skink.

"Frog," he announced proudly, handing it to me.

Taj watched with fascination as the tail wiggled in my palm.

Bodi burst into tears. "He killed it! Dad, he killed it!"

I promised Bodi the skink was still alive, probably darting among the monastery's stone walls, its detachable tail an evolutionary adaption allowing it to escape predators. Then I ducked inside.

"HELLO, HELLO!"

The ruckus faded and the boys settled on cushions, staring at the strangers by the door.

"Hello, class."

"Hello, Mr. Bruce," the monk boys replied in unison.

"This is Angmo," I said, motioning for Christine to come forward.

"Angmo! Angmo! *Jullay*, Angmo!" The boys shouted a tidal wave of welcome, apparently elated that a foreign woman held a Zanskari name.

Next, I introduced Norbu (Bodi) and Tashi (Taj).

"*Jullay*, Norbu! *Jullay*, Tashi!" the novices screamed. To my amazement, Bodi and Taj walked up and down the line of seated novices without prompting, bowing low and shaking every boy's hand.

I recognized awkward Tashi Topden, shy Paljor and striking Jigmet from Lama Wangyal's home, but the other names would take time.

Neither Christine nor I had any background in education, so over the coming days, we would blindly fumble forward, focusing first on learning names and then gauging abilities. In time the monk boys' individual personalities began to shine through. Some were gregarious. Others were timid, reminding me of injured birds. Some studious. Some social. Some earnest. Some impetuous. Many were rambunctious.

What struck me was that there appeared to be no outcasts in their midst, no cool group within the group. Removed from parental affection at a young age, and living amongst gruff lamas, the boys seemed to have closed ranks. They huddled together at puja, roamed the monastery in packs—holding hands, or arms wrapped around shoulders—and nestled close during the frigid nights. While occasionally appearing callous toward the suffering of peers—I suspected these boys gauged physical and emotional discomfort on a scale different than the one I was accustomed to—their genuine affection for one another rarely faltered in the months ahead.

But the spread in their scholastic abilities was shocking.

At fourteen, wispy Tsephal had attended the monastery longer than anyone else (six years), but he still couldn't add single digits. On the other hand, ten-year-old Lakdan—a studious boy who had recently arrived at the monastery—could solve three-digit multiplication problems.

The most accomplished mathematician was tall, butter-cheeked Sonam. But at the age of fourteen, he was only enrolled in Second Standard (the equivalent of North American grade two). When I asked why, he explained he had already completed Fifth Standard, but Karsha Gompa didn't have textbooks for higher levels, so Wang Chuk had started him over at the beginning.

❧

Bodi and Taj were reading quietly when Jigmet appeared at the door of our room. The teenage boy leapt onto the pallet beside Taj and began tickling the youngster. Meanwhile, Bodi watched furtively from the other side of the room, occasionally making silly sounds.

"It is so clear that he wants to join in," Christine whispered, leaning against me. "But he doesn't know how. It's heartbreaking."

Despite not speaking the same language, Jigmet and Taj shared some intangible connection. Perhaps it was the way Taj turned toward Jigmet when he spoke, or how he smiled in response to certain words.

Most of us take the skills of human engagement for granted, effortlessly interpreting complex social cues while navigating hundreds of daily interactions: high-fiving a passing friend, nodding at a stranger who holds the door, waiting at a discreet distance while others argue. For neurotypicals, such moments pass unnoticed, allowing us to harvest the magic of companionship instinctively and easily. But for those on the spectrum, such apparently simple interactions can pose severe challenges. I once attended a support group for spectrum kids alongside Bodi, staggered by the roadmap the children were given for even the most basic playground interactions.

"As you approach a group, listen to the tone of voices. And scan faces for expressions. Are they excited? Happy? Sad? Maybe you can guess. How are they standing? With arms crossed? If so, they might be angry. Slouched could mean they are bored. Before talking, listen to what the others are already talking about . . ."

How could any child remember all that, and apply it in every single daily interaction? It seemed impossible. Most days, I can't even remember where I've left the car keys.

I often imagined Bodi's social challenges as akin to sitting in a noisy pub, able to see people's lips moving, but struggling to catch a word of the conversation. Frustratingly, no one else at the bar appears to have a problem hearing. And some tend to grow annoyed when you can't understand them.

That's a lonely place to be, alone in a crowded bar.

❧

The temples and dormitories of Karsha Gompa had been built from the only raw materials available in Zanskar: stone, mud and logs. Crafted by hand rather than machine, nothing was perfectly square or plumb. Walls and pillars leaned. Ceilings slumped. Shelves, windows and doorways stood slightly askew. The overall effect was a sense of looseness that echoed the natural world and appealed to me immensely.

But the Achilles heel of these buildings was their flat rooftops. Created by spreading mud across a twig thatch—which dried hard as kiln-baked pottery in the parched air—these roofs were not waterproof. And sitting in the rain shadow of the Himalaya, that hadn't mattered for millennia.

But things were now changing.

In recent years, storms had begun descending on Zanskar with disastrous results. Even a light drizzle often seeped into temples and dormitories, destroying ancient frescoes and books of scripture. Downpours brought the threat of collapse, and buildings that had stood for centuries were being washed away with grim regularity.

Every day, on the way to and from school, we were reminded of the monastery's fragility. On the slopes below the assembly hall, a centuries-old dormitory had caved in with spring rains, and a new residence was being constructed atop the ruins.

I knew at a glance that the crew of dark-skinned workers—packing mud and straw into brick molds—came from Nepal.

"Namaste daju bhais!" I shouted the first time our family approached, bastardizing a colloquial Nepali greeting that roughly translates to "I salute you, older brothers, younger brothers."

Leaping to their feet, the men replied in unison, *"Namaste daju bhai! Namaste didi!"* ("We salute you older brother! We salute you older sister!")

Pulling aside soiled face masks, they gathered around us. The men hailed from the Kathmandu Valley and would stay at Karsha Gompa until snow fell. Their scant wages were paid not by the monks, but rather by the Indian government as part of a program to refurbish deteriorating monasteries in the northern provinces. They spoke staggeringly good English—once again a reminder of my own linguistic shortcomings.

In 1997—just months after one of my many visits to Nepal—a Maoist insurrection boiled over, ravaging the economy and leaving the already impoverished nation among the world's very poorest. Today, as a result of unchecked population growth, an estimated 2.2 million Nepalis (or 10 percent of the domestic workforce) must seek work abroad, and the money these migrant workers send home accounts for a staggering one-third of Nepal's GDP. From Darjeeling in the east to Kashmir in the west, Nepalis have become the hard laborers of the Himalaya, paid miserable wages to perform menial jobs—breaking rocks by hand, melting tarmac in barrels, carrying heavy loads on bent backs. Yet despite such hardships, I am always struck by the defining lightness of Nepalese culture.

As we talked, the men laughed and smiled and reached out to tousle our boys' hair. When we pulled ourselves away, their happy calls followed us down the trail.

In the months ahead, I would watch this bony crew splitting hardwood logs with hammers, staggering beneath immense loads of stone and excavating foundations by hand. Through it all, they appeared to find pleasure in each other's company, and to perform the most menial work with pride. I felt a deep admiration for them and whenever our paths crossed, we always exchanged a hearty round of "*Namaste daju bhai!*"

I noticed with sadness that the lamas seemed to pass these laborers without so much as a second glance.

❧

Another empty building—the abandoned shell of a half-constructed dormitory—was perched on steep cliffs below Lama Wangyal's residence. Its flat roof was easy to step onto from above, and offered a commanding view of the valley's broad central plains. The novice monks often played here in the golden hours before sunset, when the day's unforgiving heat had broken. Senior lamas lingered too, standing with hands clasped behind backs, gazing toward distant peaks.

Our family began joining these impromptu, late-afternoon gatherings. Occasionally our boys sketched in journals or shared Lego mini-figures with curious monk boys. But most days we stood together, balanced together against the parapet, delighting in watching the monastery's squadron of resident choughs as they patrolled the cliffs below.

Similar in appearance to the North American crow, with coal-black feathers and brilliant yellow eyes, the choughs were magnificent acrobats, rivalling terns and frigate birds for aerial agility. Rocketing past in small groups, they engaged in endless games of what appeared to be follow-the-leader, wheeling around temples, zooming down narrow alleyways. At other times they soared impossibly high, fading to specks in the endless blue before retracting wings and plummeting earthward like fighter jets, skimming past us with wind whistling through feathers.

I was admiring the choughs' antics one warm afternoon when seven-year-old Nawang appeared beside me. Missing both front baby teeth, the boy possessed a fierce ruggedness, and I'd seen him strike bigger boys fearlessly. I ran a hand across his shorn skull, and he leaned against my leg, gazing at Bodi and Taj.

Taj winked at Nawang. Nawang winked back. Soon the pair were chasing each other through a maze of collapsing brick walls, playing a wordless variation of King of the Castle. Bodi stood beside me, weaving a hand through the air, imitating a flying chough. Was he listening to the sounds of the other boys' laughter? He appeared unperturbed. But was he? Was I wrong to worry?

From the outside, it often appears that people on the autism spectrum prefer to be left alone. But John Elder Robison, whose book *Look Me in the Eye* documents his life with undiagnosed Asperger's, suggests isolation is usually due to limitations, not desire. Many on the spectrum, Bodi included, experience powerful emotions—just like neurotypicals. They just don't always possess the tools to share their inner life.

I often think of this when a stranger is unexpectedly rude or abrupt—turning their back while I talk, avoiding eye contact, barging into line. Now, instead of judging their behavior as harshly as I might have a few years ago, I find myself wondering what unseen challenges they may endure. It is one of the small but many wondrous ways Bodi has made me a better person.

Even as I fretted, Bodi began inching his way toward Taj and Nawang. Then, with one awkward lunge, he joined them, running alongside the giggling boys, making strange sounds and exaggerated movements. For a moment he remained outside their partnership, but soon was absorbed, laughing with Nawang, smiling at Taj, even eventually suggesting a new game. For an hour, the three boys clambered together up a pile of rubble, then leapt down in unison, again and again.

When Christine came striding down the trail, carrying a thermos of tea and fresh chapattis, she pulled up open-mouthed. Playing with a group of children represented a simple milestone for Bodi—one that parents of neurotypical children probably gloss past—but for Christine and me, it felt like a glimpse of the divine.

❧

Long after the boys were asleep, Christine slipped out the hobbit door, toiletry bag tucked under one arm. Moments later, she stormed tearfully back in. Apparently a pair of lamas had materialized from the darkness as she brushed her teeth, watching her intently without saying a word.

"For three days, I've been trying to scrub my pits," she moaned. "But every single time I go out that bloody door, someone is watching."

Our family had been at the monastery for a week, and it seemed no matter what we did at Karsha Gompa, someone was always watching us do it.

At any time of the day, a glance across the skyline revealed silhouetted monks, standing on rooftops, watching. The Nepali workers had begun constructing a trail on the slopes above Lama Wangyal's house, and the moment one of us emerged from the hobbit door, they would stop what they were doing and crouch down on haunches, watching us as if we were a television set. If I visited the village store in the morning, that afternoon during class the novices would ask what I'd bought. When Christine missed puja, Wang Chuk dropped by to see if she was sick. Word just got around.

So when Sunday arrived—our only day clear of teaching responsibilities—we borrowed the guest house keys from Lama Wangyal, crammed laundry into a backpack and set off to wash in private. It had been three weeks since our last shower in Keylong, and a proper scrub was overdue.

We found the guest house empty and stale. After boiling metal buckets on the propane stove, Christine began scrubbing our filthy clothes (the water soon the color of espresso) while I gave our boys sponge baths in a plastic tub. Afterward, the pair ran outside wearing nothing but hiking boots, kicking a soccer ball they'd found in a closet, blissfully unselfconscious of their nudity.

I had stripped off my own clothes and was preparing to rinse myself, when I spotted a young girl peering in the window. Skittering about the wet tiles like a moose on ice, I grabbed a dish towel and covered up. Then I waved. And she waved back. Pulling on a pair of shorts, I opened the front door and invited her in.

Tsomo was eleven years old, with brown eyes and an impossibly wide smile. Her long black hair was held in pigtails, fastened by sparkly baubles. She had been filling her family's water jugs at an outdoor spigot when she'd noticed the guest house gate ajar.

We introduced ourselves as Mortub, Angmo, Norbu and Tashi, and she repeated the names in a husky voice. The boys began sketching in their journals while Tsomo watched over their shoulders. I offered her my journal, and she drew a stick figure with pigtails, standing in front of snow-capped mountains, beneath a rainbow.

Then she disappeared.

Soon she was back, holding a bowl of *cher-pay*, dried cheese curd. The tooth-breaking snack tasted exactly as you'd expect dried, unsweetened, unpasteurized milk to taste—like a barnyard.

Taj and Bodi took a nibble, then spat out the tart curd. Christine turned up her nose. So I ate the entire bowl myself, for it reminded me of *arrulth*—a similar Mongolian delicacy, containing copious amounts of sheep hair, that once sustained Christine and me on a sixty-day horse journey across the steppe.

Tsomo disappeared once again.

Next she returned with an infant in her arms, holding her six-month-old brother, Tuksten Chimba, toward me. I happily accepted the chubby-cheeked boy. How wonderful it felt to hold a baby again! It had been three years since Taj was so delicate, and already I'd forgotten that incomparable scent of a baby's skin, the heavy head that bobbed unpredictably.

When Chimba began to fuss, Tsomo jammed a piece of *cher-pay* in his mouth. Milky drool spilled down the infant's chin, and I worried he might choke, but when I looked for Tsomo, she was gone. I was standing all alone, holding a stranger's baby.

I found Christine outside, hanging laundry. Immediately she yanked the *cher-pay* from Chimba's mouth. "You can't let him eat this, Bruce! He'll choke."

I took Chimba back inside, clutching the sleepy child to my shoulder and bouncing him gently.

An hour later, Tsomo returned for a final time, having finished filling her family's water jugs. Now she was off to collect yak dung, with a wicker basket strapped across her shoulders. Gathering Chimba from my arms, she flashed a broad smile and then skipped away down the path.

Before disappearing, she turning and waved, "Bye-bye, *Ama*. Bye-bye, *Aba*," calling us Mother and Father.

❧

The boys were sleeping when Lama Wangyal tiptoed into our darkened room. Flopping down beside me, he rested his head atop my raised knee.

Lama Wangyal often took my hand as we strolled the pathways, or draped an arm around my shoulder as we ate. Non-sexual physicality is common between men in Asia (particularly hand holding), and refreshing because of its near-complete absence in North America. I enjoyed Lama Wangyal's physical companionship, but I knew it could be wildly misconstrued back home—which seemed sad.

Reaching up, Lama Wangyal yanked off the headlamp I was wearing and began inspecting it, turning it off and on, sweeping the beam around the room like a lightsaber, catching dust in the air. Zanskaris tend to scrutinize every new object they encounter and assess it for utility, a habit surely born of need and seclusion.

Popping the headlamp open, he smiled. "Canadian battery very good! Indian battery no power."

We had four headlamps with us, one for each family member, which felt embarrassingly abundant, so I offered him mine to keep. The old monk refused, of course, but after much encouragement, acquiesced and appeared sincerely pleased.

Next, he turned his attention to Christine's toiletry kit, holding up the dental floss questioningly. Christine demonstrated how to use it, tearing off a strand and cleaning between her teeth. Then she held the roll toward Lama Wangyal. The old monk looked skeptical. Raised in a land where every commodity was precious, he tore off a tiny piece, no longer than a hand span. Struggling to wrap it around his fingers—it kept slipping free—he eventually scoffed and gave up. But instead of tossing the floss aside, Lama Wangyal folded it and slipped it inside his robes for some future use.

Christine, who was busy studying basic Zanskari words, asked Lama Wangyal for help with pronunciation.* On past journeys, we'd made concerted efforts to pick up at least a rudimentary understanding of the local languages. But so far in Zanskar, we'd made disappointingly little progress.

"Zanskari, no!" Lama Wangyal declared. "English teaching me, yes!"

Jumping up, he retrieved a faded English textbook buried amid Buddhist tomes. Produced in India, the content was dated—and often unintentionally hilarious.

Samar's football became soft after passing wind.
Vikram and I were on rocks when he popped off the question.
With all politeness I request you shutter your windows.

---

* Zanskari is a dialect of Ladakhi, which itself is a language of Tibetan origins. More details can be found in the Notes section at the back of book.

Such vocabulary felt painfully dated, so I tossed the text aside and instead scribbled out a list of basic vocabulary on a piece of scrap paper: *pen, pencil, book, pants, shoes, shirt.* Lama Wangyal carefully read each word aloud, while I clarified meaning and pronunciation.

"Shirt," I said, pointing to my T-shirt.

"Sure," he said, struggling with the new sound.

On and on we went, filling page after page. Lama Wangyal's energy appeared boundless. Christine's eyes fluttered. Soon she drifted off.

Every time I thought we were about to wrap up, Lama Wangyal flipped to a blank page and ordered me to continue. I wrote out lists of farm animals, office supplies, family members, geographical landmarks, common foods and, finally, kitchen implements: *cup, plate, knife, fork . . .*

"Fork," I read aloud.

"Fuck," he tried to copy.

"Fork," I said again, gently trying to steer him away from the profane.

"Fuck!" the tall monk said decisively, finally closing his notebook. He repeated the word as he shuffled toward the altar room and began lighting yak-butter candles.

"Fuck, fuck, fuck."

8

SAME AS IT EVER WAS

The eerie cry of the *kang-ling* (Tibetan brass trumpet) echoed across the mountainside every morning at dawn, calling the monks to puja.

And day after day, I was drawn back to that dim assembly hall. The quiet ritual began to feel so consequential that often, as I drifted to sleep at night, I found myself anticipating next morning's prayers. Such devotion was wildly out of character. In my youth, I'd complained bitterly whenever my parents dragged me to Anglican Sunday school, and I'd rebelled against all forms of organized spirituality since. But this felt different.

My behavior certainly astonished Christine. "I'm not saying I thought you were shallow, but it's not what I expected."

Perhaps it was only the overachiever in me, trying to tame the unfamiliar practice of meditation, but whatever the case, it marked a reversal of roles, because with increasing frequency, Christine moaned and pulled her sleeping bag around her ears at the sound of the horns, choosing warmth over the cool temple floor.

"I'm feeling a lot of resistance," she admitted. "I find the nonchalance of the lamas a bit off-putting. They are always talking, joking, coming and going. Anything but focusing on the ceremony. I know I shouldn't judge, but I expected the atmosphere in the temple to be, hmm, more austere or reverent maybe."

Conversely, it was the unpretentious nature of Buddhist worship that drew me.

And our boys seemed to enjoy it too. While we never forced them to attend puja, the pair frequently tagged along with me, amazingly content to sit through an hour or more of chanting, cross-legged and shoulder to shoulder. Occasionally one or both closed their eyes and meditated. At other times the pair waged silent wars with Lego mini-figures, while novices seated nearby craned their necks to watch.

Each day, a new pair of barefoot students was responsible for serving the tea. And after traversing the rows of lamas, they raced together toward the back of the assembly hall, eyes flashing in recognition as they filled our bowls, quietly whispering, "*Jullay,* Tashi! *Jullay,* Norbu! *Jullay,* Mr. Bruce!"

The same boys later returned carrying dented copper urns of *tsampa,* flour of roasted barley. When this fine-grained flour is mixed with tea, it forms a stiff dough that is the staple of the Tibetan diet.

As the young servers floated down the aisles, each lama in turn extended a bare arm into the urn, retrieving a handful of *tsampa,* which he dumped into a wooden bowl, over the dregs of tea. After stirring with a single finger, the dough was kneaded until silky. Finally, the lama broke off lumps roughly the size of a walnut, which he deftly popped into his waiting mouth with a flick of his thumb.

Our family was not offered *tsampa* during our first week at the monastery, but as time passed, the servers began glancing our way, as if silently asking: "Want some?" We always demurred, not wanting to overstep our welcome.

But one chilly morning, as I sat in puja alone, I thought, why not?

Butter-cheeked Sonam, the fourteen-year-old math whiz, sprinted toward me with a grin. I reached deep into the dark urn, the flour at the bottom cool to the touch. As my fist emerged, a dusting spilt across my lap, and I heard a chortle. Glancing up, I realized everyone in the hall was watching intently.

I gently dumped the handful into my bowl, where it formed a volcanic shape. Tiny avalanches sloughed over the edge, leading to more laughter. When I tried stirring as I'd seen the lamas do, my index finger became coated with sticky dough—puffy and white like the Michelin Man. I tried licking it clean, but smeared dough across my cheeks, and a dour lama sitting nearby burst into giggles.

In time I would learn that few things amused the monks more than watching a Westerner struggle to eat *tsampa.*

A second round offered a chance at redemption.

Surmising that the first sticky mess had been the result of leaving too much tea in my bowl, I overcompensated and left too little the second time. The result was a dry, unpalatable dough. As I struggled to choke the mess down, spilling crumbs everywhere, tears streamed down the cheeks of senior lamas. As chanting resumed, a middle-aged monk appeared before me and began vigorously sweeping both the floor and my lap with a whisk of sharp twigs, never once making eye contact.

❧

Differentiating between the sea of monks at Karsha Gompa was a challenge, for there were sixty or more men, all with shorn heads, maroon robes and unfamiliar Tibetan names. So for clarity in our own private conversations, Christine and I began assigning nicknames. It was a habit born of affection and our own linguistic shortcomings.

The Head Lama was obvious, sitting on a raised dais at the far end of the puja hall, beneath the great gilded Buddha. With unblemished skin, dark eyebrows and a gravelly voice, Meme Khampo Purbu appeared ageless. (His actual age was sixty, according to Lama Wangyal.) The genial man always nodded to our family on monastery trails, but never once said a word to us.

The next three monks in line—sitting directly beside the Head Lama in the central aisle—were *lopon,* senior lamas being groomed to one day assume leadership. In Tibetan culture, seating order is of profound importance and a direct reflection of prestige.

The first *lopon,* Lama Tsering Norbu, was a seventy-seven-year-old with ragged stubble and red eyes, who perpetually appeared to be recovering from a night of hard boozing. He wasn't, of course, but his unkempt, manic air reminded me of Heath Ledger's character in *The Dark Knight,* and we named him the Joker. A playful man, he enjoyed teasing our boys, often chasing the pair down monastery trails with an exaggerated grimace, pelting them with handfuls of rice. But I noticed the novice monks shrank as he passed, making it hard to tell where fun ended and fury began.

Tsering Wang Chuk, the school administrator—who had reminded me of Brezhnev on our first meeting—was the second *lopon.*

The third was Lama Tham Chouy, a hawkish man with tanned skin, fine features and a short shock of grey hair, who we called the CEO.

Next came Lama Yarsal Thakpa, the *ohm-zet*, or chant master, a plump-faced man with a groomed moustache who we dubbed NYC Cop. It was his clear voice that rang out at the start of each chant, for just a beat, before the others joined in.

Finally, at the end of the central aisle, sat Lama Lobsang Mortub, the *yar-vak*, or monastery accountant. With loose skin, pouty lips and a dour countenance, he was reminiscent of the Mr. Burns character in *The Simpsons*, and became known to us as Moneybags. Every day, as puja drew to a close, Lama Mortub stood and held aloft any donations received in the previous twenty-four hours—from either passing tourists or local villagers—for all to see.

Sitting opposite the leadership group, on the other side of the central aisle, was a group of wizened elders. These *lazur*, or retired Head Lamas, came and went from the assembly hall as they pleased, often arriving late and departing early, their formal obligations to the monastery complete.

Lama Wangyal was the youngest *lazur*, at sixty-one. And eighty-two-year-old Lama Ishay Sundup was the eldest.

A gruff and solitary man with sun-faded robes that dragged on the ground behind him, Lama Ishay wore a pair of cracked red sunglasses, affixed to his bald head by a loop of fraying yarn. His traditional yak-felt boots had cartoonishly upturned toes. The elderly man circumambulated the monastery seven times each day, despite fading sight and balance, with a small prayer wheel clutched in one hand and *mala* beads hanging from the other.

I often found myself pondering the seismic changes Lama Ishay had witnessed in his lifetime.

He was born in 1932, before currency, electricity or vehicles entered Zanskar. As a child, he had been visiting the distant city of Leh—a foot journey of some two hundred kilometers—when a Douglas Dakota C-47 landed on the nearby flood plains of the Indus River, the first aircraft to ever arrive in Ladakh. As news of this peculiar god spread, women began arriving with loads of hay on bent backs, offering it as food.

In the ensuing years, he had witnessed the horrors of Partition, endured the appearance of noisy trucks, transistor radios and mobile phones, and now likely sensed the looming collapse of Buddhism's role within Zanskari society. Little wonder the senior *lazur* had chosen to pass his days in silence.

Beyond the central aisle, row after row of lamas fanned out toward the edges of the assembly hall. Some were permanent backbenchers, fated by either politics or aptitude never to scale Karsha's hierarchy. Others were young and only beginning their ascendance.

Stenzin Jamyoung, known to us as the Young Scholar, was one such up-and-comer: a fresh-faced young monk always carrying an armful of books. Lobsang Strab was another, a homesick teacher dispatched from Leh to teach meditative techniques to the novices.

Sitting alone at the back of the assembly hall was Lama Jimba Sonam, an intimidating bull of a man with domed skull, broad shoulders and a scattering of crooked teeth, who we called the Hockey Player. As the *ghe-gheu*, or monastery disciplinarian, he stalked the aisles during puja, huffing like a bull and occasionally cuffing noisy novices upside the head.

Rarely spotted were the Lost Boys. This elusive group of teenagers had graduated from the monastery school, but were not yet fully ordained monks. As part of their apprenticeship, they were assigned a slew of menial tasks: sweeping floors, filling water bowls, whitewashing *chortens*, producing offertory *tsampa* statues. Slouchy young men, they often loitered outside the monastery kitchen, like teenagers in a mall. I always said *"Jullay!"* as I passed, but they rarely looked up.

Their leader, Stanzin Ta'han, was a striking young man with chiselled cheekbones, dark eyes and a stone pendant necklace. A brown fleece beneath his robes—a Chinese counterfeit of the famous North Face brand—bore a misspelled logo that inspired his nickname: the Noble Face.

❧

At noon, our family always climbed with bowls and spoons in hand to the upper courtyard, where we sat amongst the lamas, quietly waiting in rows for communal lunch.*

The monastery kitchen was tucked in a shady corner of the courtyard. Built from stone and timber, the windowless room was reminiscent of a stable, its floor strewn with barley. Cleavers and copper kettles were scattered across wooden benches, and all manner of pots hung from the walls—one remarkable vessel apparently large enough to boil a pony. From sunrise to sunset, cauldrons simmered over clay hearths, and smoke billowed from the door.

---

* The monks also ate a communal dinner in the courtyard, but to give Bodi a break from the crowds, we usually cooked our own supper at Lama Wangyal's house.

The cooks were both surly men who hailed from the village below, their skin and clothes darkened from decades of soot. Bowlegged Tashi Tsering wore a beanie and wool sweater, even on the hottest days, and spoke only in grunts. His assistant, Chagar, was a thin-faced man with a wispy beard. Neither stood taller than my shoulder.

A hush fell over the courtyard the moment Tashi emerged from the kitchen with a wash basin of rice balanced against one hip. Chagar followed, swinging a bucket bearing some sloppy combination of boiled beans, onions and lentils. The lamas were served in order of seniority. Then the Lost Boys. And finally the novices, with whom we sat.

As the cooks neared, I followed the example of boys around me, casting eyes downward and holding my bowl out. Tashi served the rice generously: two immense spoonfuls, sometimes three. But the stew was proffered more sparingly. Chagar appeared to eye each recipient, then fill his ladle according to some indecipherable system of merit. The schoolboys generally received a quarter cup or less. Being an outsider, I was offered a tad more, but always tried to refuse because I didn't want preferential treatment. On the rare days the gruel held meat, I noticed that grim-faced Chagar ensured all the boys—Bodi and Taj included—received a precious morsel.

The novices wolfed down their lunch at a frantic rate, using fingers or chopsticks of carved willow twigs. Christine and I ate with our fingers as well, and how delightful it was to actually *feel* the food, a sensual pleasure mostly lost in the West. Our boys preferred metal spoons.

The novices finished their food in minutes. Leaping up, they ran to rinse their bowls in a water barrel and then dispersed. Our boys, on the other hand, were painfully sluggish eaters, and we often found ourselves sitting in the empty courtyard long after the others had departed, melting under a relentless sun, waiting for them to finish. Passing lamas would look at the four of us in confusion. *What is taking so long?*

Even more disturbing to the aging men was the fact that Bodi ate with his left hand. Ambidextrous since birth, he wrote with his right hand but ate with his left. For the lamas, who never missed anything, this was appalling. Across many African and Asian countries, the left hand is regarded as the "dirty hand," used to clean backsides in the absence of toilet paper. Touching food with the left hand is unthinkable, and almost every day, one lama or another would approach Bodi as he ate, firmly explaining that he must eat with his right hand.

"Tell them to stop," he would scream, looking at us and not the startled men.

"Shhhh!" Christine and I both hissed.

"I wipe my bum with my right hand," Bodi would bellow. "Which means I can eat with my left."

He had a point, but it held no currency in Zanskar.

Lama Wangyal reprimanded him continually at home. "Oh, Norbu! Right hand good. All lama eating with right hand." Lama Wangyal then explained that just one lama ate with his left hand, and he was "very stupid."

"Who?" Christine and I asked in unison.

Jimba Sonam! Lama Wangyal shook his head with disgust, as if eating with his left hand had subordinated the *gompa* disciplinarian to the realm of village idiot.

This ongoing left-handed versus right-handed debate presented a parental challenge. Should Christine and I respect local customs and force Bodi to eat with his right hand? He certainly was capable of doing so, and his refusal was born at least in part of stubbornness. Or should we turn a blind eye?

We worried about screwing up Bodi's natural dexterity by imposing such restrictions. Stories of left-handed students being forced to write with their right hand are common. Christine suffered that fate, and still wonders what her handwriting and art might have looked like had her natural inclinations been allowed.

What was best for Bodi?

Ultimately, like so many things in life—particularly when raising a child on the spectrum—we chose the path of least resistance. And Bodi, with his iron will, easily prevailed over the obdurate monastery.

❧

Before departing on our trek into Zanskar, we explained to our boys there would be no way to recharge their new iPad at the monastery. It may have been a little white lie, but Christine and I would be cutting ourselves off from such distractions and believed the boys would benefit from similar sequestration.

So we charged the tablet for a final time in Manali, and for the first three days of the trek, the boys eagerly played their allotted half-hour at bedtime. Then the screen went black. Amazingly, the pair hardly fussed, and soon it seemed they'd forgotten the device entirely. As quickly as their addiction came, it eased. At the monastery, in place of the tablet, they filled their days with simpler things: sticks, rubber bands, discarded water bottles and dried leaves.

I noticed similar changes in myself.

Within days of leaving my phone behind in Kimberley, I'd stopped reaching for my pockets to check if it was there. The phantom buzzes of imagined calls faded. As did the desire to fill every lull in action by mindlessly browsing the web. The demands of email and texting, which comprised an embarrassingly large portion of my days at home, dropped entirely from my awareness, and for the first time in memory, my mind began to feel relaxed.

⩔

The novice monks attended monastery school six days a week: Monday to Saturday.

Their mornings were crammed with memorization of scripture, meditation, Tibetan language and Buddhist debate—a strikingly physical exploration of philosophical teachings, punctuated by flamboyant gesticulations, loud claps and, occasionally, by both contestants leaping into the air toward each other.

Our afternoon classes in English and mathematics appeared to be an afterthought. There was no curriculum, and when pressed, Wang Chuk suggested we assign exercises from the textbooks the boys carried in their satchels. Decades old and published by the Indian government in Delhi, these tattered books had answers scribbled beside every question.

When I asked Norphal where the answers had come from, he told me, "Last teacher writing them."

The situation was heartbreaking.

For a thousand years, Karsha Gompa had stood as the most prestigious learning institution in Zanskar, grooming students for post-secondary studies in Tibet's great monasteries. But now, as Buddhism's central role in this remote valley began to crack, it appeared the senior lamas had given up. Or didn't care. The result: the young monk boys, once destined for academic greatness, were reduced to copying answers from outdated exercise books.

The novices' plight was even more deplorable when viewed in the context of India's current obsession with education, an environment where standardized testing plays an enormous role in determining a student's future. Across the southern Indian states, photographs of top students grace newspapers, and billboards advertise "all-star" high school teachers in the same way a North American sports team might promote its franchise player.

What hope did these young novices have in the modern world that was about to engulf them?

Knowing our time at the monastery was limited, Christine and I felt the most valuable skill we could pass on to the boys was conversational English. So we cast the exercise books aside and began talking with the novices, not just in class, but on pathways, in the puja hall, at lunch.

"Hello!" we would call out whenever we spotted the boys. "How are you?"

Gradually, they learned to respond.

"Hello, Angmo. Hello, Mr. Bruce. I am fine. See you tomorrow."

Within our classroom, a routine began to emerge, and like all youngsters, the novices gelled around such certainty.

First, we sang. And how the boys loved to sing! Inveterate chanters, they bellowed the words in unison. We began with a simple alphabet song, adding a new letter every day.

A *says ahhh*. A *says ahhh*.
Alligator, Alligator. Ahhh! Ahhh! Ahhh!
(Performed with arms chomping wildly, like an alligator's mouth.)

B *says buh*. B *says buh*.
Bouncy ball, bouncy ball. Buh! Buh! Buh!
(Performed with the motion of dribbling a basketball.)

Then we settled into English, Christine gathering the senior students in a circle and practicing conversations, while I introduced the youngsters to basic vocabulary.

After an hour we took a "body break," spreading out across the classroom and completing twenty push-ups, twenty sit-ups and ten burpees to release pent-up energy. The monk boys, unfamiliar with such exercises, grew giddy with excitement. Everyone counted loudly in unison. The older boys raced each other to finish first, while the younger ones, yearning for physical contact, crawled all over Christine and me as if we were a jungle gym.

Then it was on to mathematics. Again we split the class in half, but this time I took the senior boys, who were practicing increasingly complex multiplication and division, while Christine worked with the youngest boys on addition and subtraction.

By four o'clock, when Wang Chuk arrived to brew a vat of milky tea, it felt like we'd been teaching all day.

❧

Despite ongoing efforts to meditate, it seemed like I was making no progress. I couldn't concentrate on my breathing for more than a few seconds without my mind wandering.

When I asked Lama Wangyal for tutelage, he brushed aside my request, as if it were a triviality. So I asked the smiley teacher, Lama Chosang, who suggested a trade: he would tutor me in meditation if I taught him English. I eagerly agreed, but the very next day, Lama Chosang received a letter from a friend at the Tashi Lhunpho monastery in southern India.

"Him mother very sick," Lama Chosang told me. "Friend wanting help. So I must go."

An hour later Lama Chosang left the monastery. An overnight bus would carry him to Jammu, and from there, it was a five-day train ride, wending southward. We never saw the jolly man again.

Lama Strab, the homesick teacher, told me not to worry. It took a long time to establish true calmness of the mind, he explained. Most students required five years, or more, to grasp *tong-ee*, true emptiness.

"If you mediate for five hours, but can only achieve a calm mind for one, this is natural."

I didn't ask him if trying for an hour and achieving only seconds was natural too.

A few days later, Strab appeared at the hobbit door holding a portable DVD player and a USB drive—it held a meditation instruction video he thought I might find of benefit. After our boys had drifted to sleep, Christine and I cuddled close and started the video with anticipation. To our disappointment, the lecture was in Tibetan, and at the abysmally slow rate we were learning the language, it remained cryptic.

We were about to turn off the DVD player when Christine noticed pirated copies of *Saving Private Ryan* and *Return to the Blue Lagoon* on the USB drive. In darkness, we watched the former, and for a brief moment, I forgot entirely that I was in Zanskar.

Unable to find meditative mentorship, I stumbled blindly along on my own, practicing every day in puja—not entirely sure what I was trying to achieve.

No matter how hard I focused on my breath, my mind wandered, and within seconds of closing my eyes, I found myself writing sentences for a book, or riding my mountain bike through groves of autumn larch.

Let the thoughts go, I told myself. *Don't judge your efforts. Be gentle. Return to the breath.*

Then I was gathering firewood. Getting a haircut. Skiing in powder. Eating nachos. Sleeping in. Cliff diving and feeling the sting of a bellyflop.

It seemed bitterly ironic that before leaving home, I often caught myself day-dreaming about living at the monastery. And now that I was here, I daydreamed about being home.

Even the very effort to silence my thoughts created more thoughts. What would meditating feel like when I got it right? Free falling? Bliss? Silence?

The continual background chatter was staggering. "Monkey mind," Buddhists call this: thoughts leaping randomly from place to place. The goal of meditation is simply to tame the monkey and regain control of our thoughts.

On the rare occasions that I started slipping toward stillness, I recognized the situation—*Oh my god, holy shit, I'm almost there, it's about to happen!*—and then, of course, the entire house of cards collapsed.

Try again.

I concentrated only on the movement of air through my nostrils, visualizing white *khata* scarves billowing out and then back in. Wouldn't they tickle? Or choke me?

Try again.

Changing strategies, I opened my eyes, determined to think only of the scene unfolding before me: the chanting and soft padding of feet. Novices swirling blackened teapots before pouring. The scent of juniper. Swords of sunlight dancing in blue smoke. I gazed at an ornate *thanka*, a colorful Buddhist painting fringed with silk, hanging from a nearby pillar. Soon I was wondering if I could buy one in Zanskar and take it home to hang in my office as a reminder of our time here.

Try again.

❧

Every morning started the same way.

I rose as the light began seeping over glaciated peaks, stealing past the sleeping bodies of Christine, Bodi and Taj, tiptoeing into the dark kitchen and instinctively casting about for a light switch—until I remembered, of course, there wasn't one.

As my eyes adjusted, I filled a saucepan with cold water from a brass urn, then carefully added a handful of tea leaves, a pinch of sugar and a shake of chai masala—a fragrant mixture of finely ground cardamom, cinnamon and cloves. With the flare of a match, the stove hummed to life, casting a pale-blue glow across the earthen room.

As I waited for a boil, I listened to bats in the thatch overhead, clawing their way home. Outside, gusts battered the cliffs. And from the attic, muffled footsteps and an occasional giggle.

Then Tashi Topden tumbled down the ladder. With a heavy *clunk*, the hobbit door flew open, and a blinding flash flooded the passageway. Paljor and Jigmet followed.

When the tea was ready, I ladled it into a red vacuum Thermos. Remarkably efficient, such Thermoses are common across the Himalaya, and I'd used precisely the same model at Everest base camp twenty years earlier, where it kept water scalding all day long, even at minus twenty degrees Celsius. After leaving a steaming bowl of tea beside Christine's sleeping form, I shuffled down the long earthen passageway, Thermos in hand, and emerged into the light.

The valley remained in shadow, but already the sky overhead was a vast, unbroken blue. Crowded around the frost-rimmed barrel, the monk boys were scrubbing arms, chests and faces. I left the Thermos beside them and carried my own bowl of tea down the trail, toward a large boulder that offered a sweeping view of Zanskar's central plains.

Far off—on the opposite side of the valley, and a full day's walk away—sat the ghost village of Kumik, its fields fallow and brown. Glacial meltwaters once nourished this community. But a decade ago, as the Zanskar climate began to change rapidly, the glaciers disappeared and the life-giving stream dried up, leaving the fifty-odd inhabitants no choice but to pack up and move. Instead of resettling beside another clear stream and growing barley, as had been the Zanskari tradition for millennia, the elders instead foresaw a future of selling meals to passing truckers. So they constructed homesteads alongside the dusty highway construction project. Ten years later, they were still waiting in vain for traffic to roll.

But for me, in the resurrection of first light, the world felt blessed with hope. The air was cleansed, and in the village below, I watched the tiny figures of women gathering dung and children driving sheep. The stillness was only broken by the occasional bark of a dog. And the bellow of yaks. Slowly the great, hidden valley creaked to life.

It was three weeks after our arrival at Karsha Gompa that I witnessed something unexpected—perhaps magical—at sunrise.

When the first shaft of sunlight landed on the valley floor, like a spotlight on a darkened stage, it illuminated the six-hundred-year-old monastery of Pipiting, perched atop a drumlin at the geographic center of Zanskar's plains. This extraordinary phenomenon—which I concluded could only occur for a few days each year, when the sun's trajectory was perfectly aligned with a crack in the eastern peaks—offered a physical manifestation of Zanskar's origin story.

Legend holds that the great valley was formed after Guru Rinpoche subdued a demoness and pinned her on her back, using Buddhist shrines to hold down her head, hands and feet. Finally, Pipiting, the most holy temple of all, was built atop her heart, the symbolic point upon which the universe pivots.[*]

Defying belief, the spectacle repeated itself at sunset that same day: a final shaft of sunlight piercing ragged spires to the west and lingering, as if by divine ordination, on the crumbling temple of Pipiting.

Moments later, the spotlight faded, and a purple dusk flooded the hidden valley.

❧

All of the fundamental tasks of living took longer to perform at Karsha Gompa and demanded we pay attention in a way I was not accustomed to at home.

Dishes were washed by hand in the dented pewter basin on the path outside the hobbit door. Squatting on haunches, we scrubbed and scrubbed, but with nothing but cold water and a bar of soap, dishes never came perfectly clean.

---

[*] This Zanskari legend parallels a popular Tibetan myth, in which the demoness Srin Ma, who once ruled the plateau, was subdued by King Songtsen Gampo, and pinned on her back with twelve temples, all built upon her extremities. The thirteenth temple, constructed atop her heart and meant to forever suppress her malevolent impulses: Lhasa's Jokhang.

Cooking water had to be gathered from the rusty fifty-gallon barrel, using a cracked juice jug. And before that, the barrel had to be filled, using a long, leaky hose attached to the monastery's cistern.

Living in a tiny room reminded me of living aboard a sailboat: everything had a place and needed to be stowed after each use. A whisk of twigs was used to sweep the carpets, and we crawled around on hands and knees, plucking up bigger flecks by hand.

Dust was a constant enemy. Pulverized beneath the glaciers of the Himalaya, this "rock flour" turned lakes turquoise and rivers brown. It billowed beneath feet on trails and arrived through cracks in the walls and windows, drifting like snow across our room. We were forever wiping books, toys and tables. I often awoke to the feel of grit coating my front teeth. Despite vigorous scrubbing, dust stained our clothes, and they grew steadily darker.

The "toilet" was located in a cramped closet at the end of Lama Wangyal's earthen passageway, just inside the hobbit door. Squeezing into the room was a challenge, for the ceiling was shoulder high and a tangle of homemade garden implements crowded the walls. A small hole in the dirt floor, roughly the size of a paperback, demanded accuracy. When one of my early attempts grazed an edge, Lama Wangyal grimaced and demonstrated how to rinse the fetid hole with boiling water, and then scatter fresh gravel across the floor.

While my aim improved, one challenge remained: updrafts.

The winds that raked the monastery cliffs often made it feel as if a cold blow-dryer was blowing directly upon my backside. Any crumpled toilet paper tossed into the void would inevitably come sailing straight back up, fluttering around the cramped closet like a poisonous butterfly. Eventually I arrived at a solution: wrap a few pebbles into each wad of toilet paper before pitching it. Et voila, it disappeared.

Every few days Lama Wangyal scattered a handful of straw into the abyss. And once a year, he emptied the chamber beneath, loading the "night soil" into a wicker basket and carrying it to the village fields, where it provided essential fertilizer in place of animal dung, which was burnt as fuel.

A spider's web of electrical lines was strung across the monastery in 2007, after a diesel generator was installed near the administrative center of Padum. There was even an outlet in Lama Wangyal's kitchen. But the network was notoriously unreliable, so in place of electrical appliances, we relied on more traditional measures.

When the chai masala ran out, Lama Wangyal demonstrated how to grind cardamom, cloves, cinnamon bark and fennel seed using a mortar and pestle. Christine lifted the heavy stone mortar again and again, until her forearms ached and her face was coated in powder. *Bang. Bang. Bang.* At home, the task would have been accomplished in seconds, with the flick of a blender switch.

There was a notable absence of intrusive sounds in this life. Apart from chanting, wind, livestock and the occasional boiling of a kettle, we lived in silence: no beeping phones or microwaves, no vacuums, radios, televisions, lawn mowers, leaf blowers, blenders, horns, engines, humidifiers or shavers.

And as the urgency of modern life faded, time stretched out in a reassuring way. There was a serenity to our days, a whisper of a half-remembered paradise.

Christine was happy, as happy as I could remember. At home, during the dark days of postpartum depression, she'd tried all types of healings and interventions. But no matter what she did, modern life seemed to have a way of heaping more stress on. Now, she was laughing frequently and worrying less.

"I feel like I've loosened the reins," she admitted. "I'm usually such a *should* person. I *should* do this. I *should* do that. But I'm trying not to put any expectations on myself. It's certainly not my typical way. But at the monastery, it just feels right."

When I remarked that this might just be the most peaceful period I could remember in my life, she reminded me, "We've only been here a month."

❧

The weather had been cloudless for weeks, and that night I asked Bodi if he wanted to sleep on Lama Wangyal's roof with me, under the stars. There was a long pause, and given Bodi's instinctive resistance to any change, I suspected he might refuse.

But he surprised me, suddenly blurting out, "I'd love to."

Lama Wangyal did not share our enthusiasm.

"No good, Mortub," he barked when he found us dragging our sleeping bags to the clay roof. Realizing our minds were set, he retrieved a yak-hair blanket from a steel storage trunk and spread it beneath our bags. Then he pointed to the abyss beyond our feet, a precipitous drop of more than fifteen meters off the front of the house. "Carefully, Mortub! Carefully!"

I made Bodi promise that if he needed to go pee during the night, he'd rouse me before getting up. Then we bundled up, pulling on ski hats and puffy jackets, crawling inside thin sleeping bags. After reading *Tintin in Tibet* by headlamp, we lay back and stared up at the darkening sky. Bats were already pouring from their roost, the air filled with the faint clicks of their echolocation. Somewhere a dog barked.

When the first star appeared, Bodi pointed excitedly. More and more materialized. Soon the Milky Way stretched between the horizons like a glittering splash of lime and ice.

Unable to spot Orion, the Big Dipper, Cassiopeia or any other familiar constellations from home, we used a guidebook to learn new ones. For the first time I saw Sagittarius, Capricornus and Aquarius. Scorpius hovered on the western horizon with a pair of smouldering embers for eyes—the planets Mars and Saturn.

We lay in silence with shoulders touching, and I marvelled at the infinite universe and our own human insignificance. Then a shooting star etched an ephemeral line across the southern sky.

"DAD!" Bodi screamed. "Did you see that?"

The Perseid meteor shower was nearing its August zenith, and soon flaming trajectories criss-crossed the sky. Bodi giggled and squirmed with delight.

I put an arm around Bodi and pulled him closer, but in the process, my sleeping bag caught on a jagged stovepipe. Down feathers billowed into the night like escaping moths. Catching as many as I could, I stuffed them back in and later ran a piece of duct tape over the tear. Then I cuddled Bodi in a tight spoon. Eventually he fell silent.

I was certain he was asleep, and was drifting off myself, when he whispered, "This is going to be the best night of my entire life."

9

LOST HORIZONS

<figure>⚕</figure>

If there was a schedule of events at Karsha Gompa, it remained opaque to us. Some mornings the horns sounded at 5:45 A.M. Other days, not until 7:30 A.M. Puja generally lasted an hour, but occasionally the chanting stretched on for three or four.

One chilly morning in early September, we arrived to find the assembly hall deserted. Where was everyone? Our family was milling in the courtyard, confused, when Christine spotted young Purbu from our class sprinting up a distant flight of stone stairs.

"Where is puja?" she yelled. He pointed upward and kept running.

We followed, navigating steep stairways and narrow passages, eventually arriving at a squat temple I'd never noticed before. Adding our sandals to a pile outside the doorway, we pulled aside heavy blankets and slipped in.

Rows of lamas filled the hall, which appeared ancient and cramped, with tiny windows set in thick mud walls. An army of golden statues filled the altar, the most notable a ferocious blue-faced demon wearing a crown of skulls. The six-armed Mahakala was Karsha's wrathful protective deity, and this chapel, known as Gonkhang, or "protector's shrine," was dedicated to him.

We were slipping toward the rear when Lama Wangyal spotted us and leapt to his feet. Shouting over the chanting, he directed our family toward a portal in the wall beside the altar. I felt embarrassed for disturbing the ceremony, but none of the lamas appeared perturbed.

"In, in, in!" Lama Wangyal yelled and motioned impatiently.

Pulling open a wooden trap door, Christine and I got down on hands and knees and crawled through. Bodi and Taj followed. Inside was a small chamber heaped with treasure. Shelves and cabinets housed countless relics: conch shells, silver daggers inlaid with turquoise, a brass stag carrying what appeared to be Christian angels, yak-hair boots, desiccated animal horns, and soda bottles crammed with incense sticks. A pair of skin drums hung from the ceiling, and strings of dried geraniums adorned a photograph of the Dalai Lama. A candle flickered before a small statue of Loepön Dunde, Karsha Gompa's founder.

Behind a wooden lattice lay a collection of hideous masks with bulbous eyes and bloody fangs. I was about to investigate when I felt a tap on my shoulder. One of the Lost Boys had been silently watching from the doorway, and he now explained the area beyond the lattice was a prison for bad spirits and strictly off limits. The masks only came out during the depths of winter, when the monks performed *Karsha Gustor*, a mystical 1,300-year-old dance.

Crawling back into the main temple, our family sat cross-legged against the back wall. The chanting was different from what we'd grown accustomed to, song-like in nature, with one melodic voice soaring above the rest.

Resonant throat singing, or overtone chanting, is common in Tibetan Buddhist ceremony, occurring when a singer creates two stable notes while simultaneously letting a third note flutter over top. The extraordinary sound—part diesel engine, part bullfrog—was being created by the fresh-faced but perpetually melancholy Lama Tsering Sundup, who we'd dubbed Broken Angel.

As we listened, Jimba Sonam, the broad-shouldered disciplinarian, began stalking the aisles, pausing before each lama and holding out a hand. Most shook their heads and averted eyes, but a few relented and handed the intimidating man a set of *mala* beads.

What was happening? Was the monastery in need?

I fingered my own *mala* beads. While I treasured Lama Wangyal's gift, this seemed the perfect opportunity to practise the Buddhist ideal of non-attachment. I resolved to donate them and raised my hand, but the disciplinarian had already moved on.

Eventually he spread the rosaries on a table before Lama Mortub, the monastery accountant. A thick wad of cash materialized from Lama Mortub's robes, and he methodically counted out bills, creating tottering piles atop each set of *mala* beads. Then the disciplinarian returned the rosaries to their respective owners—along with a Monopoly-like stack of money.

That evening, Lama Wangyal explained that whenever a significant sum of money arrived at the monastery—either through donation or an estate—all the monks, including novices, were entitled to a portion, the size varying according to age, stature and position.* To ensure fair distribution, ten lamas had been selected at random (those who volunteered *mala* beads) and they were responsible for dividing the monastery's newly acquired funds to an umbrella group below them.

Thank goodness I hadn't handed over my *mala* beads!

As chanting resumed, money was counted and recounted. Lamas shuffled through the aisles, demanding to see what others had received. Intense negotiation ensued. Bills were passed back and forth, some held up to the light and refused for being too dirty or wrinkled. Such monetary focus felt wildly out of place at a religious ceremony, but Bodi and Taj had other thoughts and eyed the passing bills with interest.

"Can we get some rupees too, Dad?" Taj whispered. "I think they are handing them out instead of *tsampa*."

As the commotion continued, Lama Sundup, the throat singer, retrieved a book of scripture from its cubbyhole above the altar, delicately placing the volume on a prayer table before the Head Lama. Printed by hand on long sheaves of paper and stored between wooden end plates, the 108 books of *Kangyur* are believed to be the directly translated words of Buddha. After carefully unwrapping swaths of protective cloth, the Head Lama gingerly divided yellowing sheets into equal batches, which Lama Sundup distributed amongst the lamas.

A traditional Tibetan book of scripture, with loose sheaves held between end plates of wood.

---

* Eighty-two monks were officially resident at Karsha Gompa, though many were not physically present. Some studied at the great Tibetan learning institutions of southern India. Others had been dispatched to manage land holdings in the Indian lowlands, near the village of Bodh Gaya, more than one thousand kilometers away.

Abruptly, chanting ceased, and in a cacophonous uproar, every lama in the room began reading aloud. All were reading different Sutras, of course, and it seemed yet another example of Tibetan Buddhism's admirable focus on efficiency: if an entire book must be read aloud, why not split it up and get everyone reading at once?

Taj elbowed me in the ribs.

I glanced at my watch. We'd been sitting cross-legged for an hour, and Christine was ready to leave as well. Not wanting to offend the monks, I decided to see the ceremony through to the end. Christine shook her head and slipped out, taking both boys with her.

After forty-five minutes, the reading slowed. The monks returned their pages to the Head Lama, who methodically rebuilt the book of scripture and returned it to its place in the cubbyholes.

Thank goodness. Puja was finally over. I shoved my tea bowl in a pocket and was trying to stand on sleeping legs when another book was retrieved. I sat back down. Once again the Head Lama cleaved the aging sheets into piles. Reading resumed. An hour later, they started in on a third book. Finally I gave up and limped from the Gonkhang.

Lama Wangyal did not return home until after dark. The monks had read twelve volumes aloud, he told me, looking exhausted.

The celebration marked the beginning of *yarne*, a three-month retreat during which the monks refrained from leaving the monastery. Established by Buddha, *yarne* originally took place during monsoon, and was meant to prevent monks from inadvertently stepping on insects while collecting alms. But in recent years, many monasteries, including Karsha Gompa, had begun splitting *yarne* in half, observing six weeks of retreat during summer, then another six mid-winter.

The wintertime retreat was more difficult, Lama Wangyal explained, for then the monks read all 108 volumes of *Kangyur* aloud.

❧

I was standing outside the hobbit door with Taj and Bodi when a horde of novice monks descended, breaking over us like a wave, laughing and leaping, a blur of hands and singsong voices. There was little Nima, rugged Nawang, Skarma, Purbu, RamJam, Jigmet and tiny Norgay in his brown robes and orange cap. The curious boys pushed buttons on my watch and inspected the Tintin book

Bodi held. Several hugged my legs, and I squeezed their shoulders in return, wondering what path had led them here to the monastery at such a tender age.

Abruptly, I realized Taj was in tears.

Shorter than the boisterous novices, he had been overwhelmed by the melee. So I hoisted him atop my shoulders, and as I did, the monk boys froze, mouths agape. Apparently, they had never seen a "shoulder ride" before, and as the possibility crystallized in their minds, the pack went berserk. After failing in initial attempts to hoist classmates upon their shoulders, the boys began scrambling atop a stone wall and then leaping onto others from above, like cowboys mounting a rodeo bull in the chute. They charged up and down the rocky trails, classmates on shoulders, squealing with glee and jousting. It was a miracle no one fell in the frenzy.

But even if one had tumbled and skinned a knee, they would have shaken it off and carried on, for the monk boys were practically feral in their toughness, routinely leaping from rooftops two or three times their height, tumbling down rocky slopes and whipping each other with sticks. At one communal lunch, I'd seen Purbu heave a boiled egg toward Nawang. It was meant as a gift, but Nawang didn't see it coming, and it smashed into his nose with a *thud*. But the seven-year-old didn't flinch. Instead he rubbed watering eyes, then peeled the egg and ate it.

Bodi and Taj seemed frighteningly delicate by comparison. Both cried easily and often—which distressed the lamas to no end.

"No good," the old men would tut angrily.

Even in the village, passing strangers implored our boys to stop sobbing, as if they'd never previously witnessed such a horror. Anthropologist Kim Gutschow, who spent years living in Zanskar, explains there are two words used to describe crying in local children: *nyid shrin* ("sleep crying") and *stod shrin* ("hungry crying"). Notably, there is no word for "hurt crying."

As the novice monks continued their shoulder-top battle, a filthy bandage fell from Skarma's hand, revealing a festering fingernail. Retrieving our first aid kit, I washed the area, applied antibiotic ointment, and then covered everything with gauze.

And that was how word of our healing abilities got out.

Sonam, the math whiz, appeared at the hobbit door that night, holding out a hand ravaged by warts. Christine dabbed the area with salicylic acid. The next day Tsephal quietly asked Christine to treat his own outbreak. I excavated a sliver from Purbu's foot. Jigmet wanted "headache pills." Tashi Topden had a sore throat.

When Norphal developed a cyst the size of a half-lime on his forehead, we soaked the region with hot rags for days, hoping to draw the infection out. Eventually, one of the lamas who didn't share our patience crudely lanced the boil with a nail, and for weeks afterward, Norphal wore a white rag around his head, marked with a red circle of blood—giving him the appearance of a kamikaze pilot.

"I feel constantly overwhelmed by my mothering instinct," Christine admitted. "I want to help every sick novice I see."

Most of the boys suffered from chronic sinus infections—green boogers dropping like little worms from their nostrils with every breath—and Christine soon gave away all our antibiotics. Despite her efforts, none of the boys got better, and Christine eventually realized the novices routinely tossed their antibiotics aside before the course was complete. When she asked the lamas living with the sick novices to remind them of their medicine, they just shook their heads.

"It would have been better if I'd never given out our drugs in the first place," she fumed. "I don't understand it. Why don't the lamas value health? None of these boys even know what it's like to live without a snotty nose."

One morning, we found wispy Tsephal lying on the hard floor of the puja hall, head in hands. I felt his forehead, and it was burning with fever. That afternoon, he shuffled into class looking no better and collapsed.

"Go home and rest," I suggested, but he shook his head. No matter how sick or injured, the lamas never allowed the novices to rest in bed. So instead, I sent Bodi to retrieve a couple of Tylenol from our first aid kit.

❧

"Mortub!" Lama Wangyal yelled. "Photo taking!"

We had been playing Simon Says with our class when the old monk burst in. The novices scattered, grabbing satchels and racing for the door. We followed with our own boys in hand, led by the throbbing sound of drums toward the courtyard, which was now milling with villagers.

The lamas sat in rows, wearing elaborate silken shawls, grasping a silver bell in left hand, brass *dorje* in right.* Their golden crowns were adorned with shaggy

---

* In Buddhist ceremony, the twin implements of bell and *dorje* symbolize the inseparability of wisdom and compassion, and their ritualized sweeping movements are meant to free the mind from distraction.

visors of black wool, meant to obscure the men's vision and prevent them from inadvertently glancing upward and causing Buddha to abandon the ceremony. At the very center, atop a waist-high dais, was perched the Head Lama. On the ground before him sat an immense fire pan, stacked with dung.

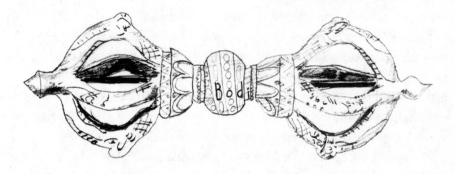

The dorje, *a stylized thunderbolt, represents the decisive moment of enlightenment, when the world is recognized for what it truly is.*

The fields of Karsha were now ripe—among the first in Zanskar, due to the village's valuable southern exposure—but no farmer would gather a single head of grain until the *jin-sek*, or fire puja, was complete. Today marked the beginning of week-long sacred rites, meant to bless the coming harvest.

Preparations had been underway for days. Barley, wheat and peas had been washed and laid to dry in the sun. Tangled boughs of juniper had been dragged into the courtyard, hacked into short lengths and bound together in bundles. *Tsampa* had been moulded into an army of small statues, painted red and adorned with elaborate flowers of yak butter.

Silence fell as Stanzin Ta'han, the young man we called the Noble Face, doused the dung with molten butter using a silver ladle, its handle as long as a shovel's. Holding a torch of flaming grass, the Head Lama leaned forward. When torch touched dung, flames leapt up. The radiant heat was so intense I could feel it across the courtyard, like summer sun on my cheeks.

A thick wooden shield was hurriedly propped up to protect the Head Lama, and as the lamas chanted, the Lost Boys delivered a stream of copper bowls to the Head Lama, heaped with barley, wheat, rice and peas. All were dispatched into the inferno with muttered prayers. Then came bundles of grass, peacock feathers and juniper. Pungent smoke drifted through the crowd.

After twenty minutes, Bodi and Taj lost interest and began casting looks at a village toddler. Wearing only a blue sweater, the boy was naked from the waist down, and rushed over to investigate. The trio were horsing around when the little boy peed on the cement beside, and our boys erupted in laughter. Nearby, even the dour monastery accountant managed a smile.

Lama Wangyal sat in the very front row. When he began motioning for me to join him, I pretended not to see, not wanting to disturb the sacred rituals. But he stood up and waved his arms overhead insistently, leaving me no choice. Self-consciously, I tiptoed to the epicenter of the ceremony and crouched beside him.

"Mortub," he whispered in my ear. "Photo taking!"

Since arriving at the monastery, more than a month earlier, I'd been reluctant to photograph the monks, particularly during puja, for it felt intrusive. But now, at Lama Wangyal's insistence, I retrieved my camera, and crouching at the back, used a telephoto lens to snap discreet images: a leathery hand, a brass *dorje*, barley seeds tumbling into the flames, tiny Norgay curled up in the disciplinarian's lap.

A back-row monk—nicknamed the Frenchman, for his flattened monk's cap was reminiscent of a beret—hooted at me. I felt horrified. Was he warning me to stop taking photographs?

But no, he wanted me to join him.

Once again, I tiptoed self-consciously into the midst of the lamas. The Frenchman made space on the carpet beside him, and I sat down. He put an arm around me and pointed quizzically at the camera. I showed him a photograph on the digital display, and his eyes widened. Yanking the camera from my hands, he showed the pictures to Lama Sundup, the throat singer, who sat beside him. Sundup promptly took the camera and pointed it around like a spyglass. Soon the camera disappeared, passed down the line between chanting lamas. Everyone wanted a turn peering through the lens.

And still, grain was heaped onto the flames.

The Frenchman lay down and put his head on my lap, squirming until he found a comfortable position. Then he closed his eyes and drifted to sleep. The half-naked toddler wandered over and pooped beside us. His red-faced father apologized profusely, hurriedly cleaning up the mess with a tissue. Bodi and Taj appeared. The Frenchman hauled Bodi onto his lap. Taj settled on mine. Christine nestled between us.

Purbu and Nima rushed through the crowd, serving milky tea spiced with cardamom. Tashi Tsering, the cook, followed, carrying a plastic wash basin heaped with sweet rice, hazelnuts and apricots, which he spooned into outstretched hands.

We were greedily eating when a violent gust of wind buffeted the courtyard. Bowls bounced across concrete. Grain flew into the air. Sparks scattered. The wooden shield protecting the Head Lama toppled over and landed with a crash.

As the wind built and the sky darkened, villagers scurried beneath the protection of a covered terrace. Peering through lattice windows, they pointed at a wall of dust racing toward us across the central plains. A great wind had clawed its way over the Himalaya and was now aimed directly at Karsha Gompa.

Standing beside me, Wang Chuk whispered, "Harvest puja always making big storm."*

The Head Lama bellowed instructions. The Lost Boys doubled the pace of their grain delivery. Offerings were dumped into the fire at a frantic rate. Butter was added in great splashes.

Then the storm hit. The sun was obliterated. Flying sand stung eyes and cheeks. Robes were torn from monks' shoulders. Burning embers swirled in the wind. The crowd scattered.

Scooping up our two oblivious boys—still happily licking rice from fingers—I sprinted alongside Christine toward the shelter of Lama Wangyal's home. Glancing over my shoulder, I caught one final glimpse of the Lost Boys, staggering through the flying refuse, sheltering plates of barley against their chests.

And in the center of it all sat the the Head Lama, tossing grain into the licking flames.

❧

There was something *different* about the tiny novice, Norgay.

To start, he wore a brown satin coat and the dog-eared hat of the lamas, while the rest of the novices dressed in maroon robes. Rarely involved in shenanigans,

---

*   A passage in *The Yogins of Ladakh* (John Crook and James Low) describes an identical Harvest Blessing puja at Karsha Gompa during the summer of 1974. In uncanny synchronicity, the text reports, "The ceremony had a marked effect on the weather! No sooner was it over, than a great sandstorm blew down the valley."

he seemed to exist on the periphery of the other boys, moving with unhurried grace and dignity. Classmates were deferential to the cherubic youngster. And senior lamas displayed unusual affection toward him, taking the small boy on their lap during puja, affectionately squeezing his shoulders when passing on the trails.

Lama Wangyal attributed the boy's diminutive size to the fact that Norgay's mother had died during childbirth, and as a result, he was raised without *pipi*, or breast milk. His father, unable to manage both farm and child rearing, had brought the boy to Karsha Gompa at the tender and unusually young age of two.

One day during class, as the young novices tumbled rambunctiously across the floor, I noticed Norgay's orange hat knocked askew. He pulled it quickly back into place, but not before I spotted an unusual port wine stain: a dark purple discoloration spreading across the scalp above the left ear. I'd heard rumours, and that evening, I asked Lama Wangyal.

Norgay's "second ear," as Lama Wangyal called it, was what first identified the infant as a possible *tulku*,* a living reincarnate of the "Ear-Whispered" lineage.† The previous Ear-Whispered incarnate, the twelfth Dagom Rinpoche, was born in Tibet but displayed a deep affinity for Zanskar throughout his life, travelling frequently to the valley and establishing a Buddhist training center. He passed away in 2006—just a year before Norgay's birth. Suspicions grew further when Norgay wandered into the assembly hall as a three-year-old and settled on a dais, as if preparing to deliver a teaching.

Tibetan Buddhists believe all living things, from ants to elephants to humans, are trapped in an eternal cycle of rebirth, known as *samsara*, which finally ends when one achieves enlightenment and enters nirvana. Most of us are reborn "involuntarily," our future lives dictated by the sway of past karma (thoughts and deeds). But a select few, generally teachers of exceptional spiritual attainment and compassion, are believed to be able to choose the place and time of their reincarnation, and sometimes even their parents.

---

* A *tulku*, or reincarnate, is believed to embody a lineage of Buddhist teaching stretching all the way back to the original master. Roughly five hundred *tulku* lineages exist across the Himalaya today, the most famous being the Dalai Lamas, living incarnations of Avalokiteshvara, the bodhisattva of compassion.

† The Ear-Whispered lineage is an ancient line of wandering yogis and hermits, a secretive group with no written records of their teachings and practices, relying strictly on an oral tradition.

Reincarnation can be a challenging concept for the Western mind, and my face must have betrayed skepticism, because Lama Wangyal led me to his altar. After using a flickering candle to light a neighboring one, he extinguished the first then asked, "Still same flame, no?"

Establishing the veracity of a reincarnate is a complex tradition. The process is often set in motion by the appearance of predictive omens: a letter left by the predecessor, visions of an oracle or even signs in nature. But conclusive identification requires the child in question to identify possessions from his former life—such as tea bowls, books and *mala* beads—from an array of similar items. Lama Wangyal told me the Dalai Lama would visit Karsha Gompa the next year and use such techniques to declare definitively whether young Norgay was a *tulku* or not.

His Holiness was identified in a similar manner.

Following the death of the thirteenth Dalai Lama in 1933, senior Tibetan lamas watched in vain for any portent of a reincarnation, but it was two years before signs began to appear. A star-shaped fungus grew on a pillar in the Potala Palace, pointing to rainbows in the northeast. Shortly after, the embalmed head of the thirteenth Dalai Lama reputedly turned to gaze in that very direction. When the temporary regent of Tibet had a vision of a small house with strange gutters, built in the shadow of a gold-and-turquoise roofed monastery, teams of lamas were dispatched on horseback to search.

Months later, a young peasant boy was discovered in Taktser village, in the far-flung province of Amdo, in precisely the described circumstances. A collection of tea bowls and *mala* beads was spread before Lhamo Thondup, and in every case, the child headed toward the possessions of his predecessor, declaring with certainty, "It's mine, it's mine."

After being taken to Lhasa to begin training, the incarnate Dalai Lama—already renamed Tenzin Gyatso—was wandering the colossal storerooms of the Potala Palace when he passed a wooden box. Pointing to it, he stated flatly, "My teeth are in there."

When the box was opened, it held the thirteenth Dalai Lama's dentures.

At home in North America, no amount of debate had ever been able to sway my skeptical views on reincarnation, but here, in the shadows of the ancient, I found myself reminded of a Sherpa saying: "Maybe true. Maybe not. Better you believe."

❧

Long after the boys were asleep, Lama Wangyal appeared in our doorway, holding a cheap DVD player, its red plastic cracked and sun-faded.

Nestled between Christine and me, he pressed the power button. The screen flickered to life, casting a faint blue light across the darkened room. Soon the distorted sound of Tibetan horns began to play, so devilishly loud that Christine leapt to her feet, frantically motioning for Lama Wangyal to turn the volume down. But it was too late. Bodi stirred. Then he sat upright.

"Oh no, oh no. I can't control everything," he screamed.

Christine gently laid a hand on his shoulder and whispered reassurances. Gradually the sobs receded. We held our breath. Bodi settled. Lama Wangyal pressed play again.

The footage was hand-held and unsteady. It followed a four-year-old boy, carried by motorcade from a remote country village to Leh's Spituk Monastery, where he was enthroned as the twentieth reincarnation of the spiritual leader Kushok Bakula Rinpoche—an immensely popular lineage believed to have descended from one of Buddha's original disciples.

Lama Wangyal, who had clearly watched these events many times, was transfixed and provided running commentary.

The *tulku*'s convoy wound through barren countryside, where throngs of adoring villagers lined the road, not unlike cycling fans at the Tour de France. *Khata* scarves were tossed in the air with such abandon it appeared to be snowing.

Occasionally the motorcade paused, and the small boy emerged to sit on a dais and receive devotees. As gifts were piled before him, his tiny hand reached forward to brush each passing bowed head. Men, women and children all wept openly. To witness such faith was humbling, and the grainy footage felt like a glimpse into a long-lost era.

But these events had been recorded just four years before our visit.

❧

Lama Wangyal was born into a world unrecognizable by any modern measure.

He arrived on the floor of a mud-brick homestead in the village of Neyrok— seven homes tucked behind a grove of poplar on the banks of the Stod River. Lama Wangyal didn't know the day of his birth or even the month, for birthdays are not celebrated in Zanskar. But he did know the year: 1953.

At the time, foreigners were forbidden from entering Zanskar. No roads penetrated the region, and there were no vehicles or even wheelbarrows in the valley. Instead, everything was carried on bent back. A cash economy did not exist, and villagers subsisted through an ancient system of co-operative barter.

When he was two months old, his parents carried their infant son to Karsha Gompa, a full day's walk away, where he received the blessings of the Head Lama. During the ceremony, he was bestowed with his name, Tsering Wangyal—*Wangyal* denoting "powerful" or "victorious," in the Buddhist sense of overcoming one's own ego, and *Tsering* meaning "long life."

Tsering Wangyal was one of eight children, but only five remained alive. "One sister extinguished," he told us, matter-of-factly. "And two brothers bye-bye." Childbirth, infection and a kick from a horse had stolen his siblings before their time.

From an early age, Wangyal understood his future did not lie on the family farm. The Tibetan tradition of primogeniture—established in the seventh century by Songtsen Gampo, founder of the Tibetan empire—dictated that the land would eventually pass to his eldest brother. Likewise, his eldest sister would inherit all the family's material wealth, in the form of a *perak* (turquoise-adorned headdress) and silver jewelery.

Because land could neither be bought nor sold, the notion of private real estate did not exist in Zanskar. And as a result, villagers viewed themselves as guardians of the land, not owners. Another notable side effect of primogeniture was that every household possessed fields of roughly similar size, allowing social equity to remain balanced for generations.

But primogeniture leaves a large number of young men without land, and in Zanskar, this was counterbalanced by both significant populations of celibate monks and the widespread practice of polyandry. Younger brothers were welcome to join the union of elder siblings. But any boy wishing to marry separately had to leave the family homestead and establish a new farm elsewhere.

Monasticism and polyandry both act as natural regulators of growth, and for more than a thousand years, Zanskar's population remained perfectly stable—critical in a land of such meager carrying capacity.

But for Tsering Wangyal it meant he had to make a difficult choice. And at the age of fifteen, after milking the cows on a chilly fall morning, he set off toward Karsha Gompa without so much as a word of farewell to his parents.

"Too little food. Too many brothers. Better me going."

On the other side of the world, Richard Nixon had been elected president; the Vietnam War continued to escalate; the first 747 jumbo jet was being constructed. And in the snowy suburbs of Toronto, I had just been born.

Karsha Gompa, the most prestigious monastery in Zanskar, was home to more than two hundred lamas at the time. It lay within sight of Neyrok village—just three kilometers as the crow flies—but to get there, Wangyal had to walk far downstream, to a bridge of woven twigs. It was dark by the time he started climbing the steep trails toward whitewashed temples.

Upon taking the vows of *genyen*—refrain from killing, lying, stealing, sexual misconduct and intoxicating substances—Wangyal was housed and tutored by senior lama Meme Stanzin. In the monastery school, he displayed an uncanny aptitude for memorizing Sutras, and within a year he'd taken the thirty-six vows of *getsul* and become a full novice.*

"School very happy time," Lama Wangyal recounted. "With my teacher, and blessing of six-armed Mahakala, I understood quick and fast all the hard book," referring to the 108 volumes of *Kangyur*.

By the age of twenty-one—considered early, even in those years—Wangyal ascended to *gelong*, or fully ordained monk, submitting to 253 vows which include such odd-seeming admonishments as not transporting wool, not tickling, not eating in big gulps, not sitting down heavily and not leaning to one side like an elephant's trunk.

It was at the same time that modernity began seeping into Zanskar.

During the summer of 1976, twenty-three-year-old Lama Wangyal was dispatched to the Pensi La pass, one hundred kilometers to the northwest, where he joined a crew of monks from other monasteries supporting the Indian government's construction of a road. That August, the monks paused and leaned against their tools, watching a vehicle creep over the rugged track. It was a police jeep, carrying two officers from Kargil, sent to investigate a riot in Padum. Two days later the men motored back, carrying several prominent community members with them for questioning.

For millennia, reaching the hidden valley of Zanskar had demanded, at minimum, a seven-day, 235-kilometer trek. That seclusion had been pierced, and the effect was like the bursting of a dike. A century of technological advances flooded into the valley. Tractors thundered over the pass, soon crushing precious

---

* The boys in our class were all *getsul*—apart from the youngest five, who remained *genyen*.

topsoil in the irrigated fields. Foreign labor arrived. A diesel generating station was built. Transistor radios brought news from Delhi. Stores sprang up, selling flashlights, concrete blocks and booze.

The young welcomed such change, but as James Crowden, a British geographer and among the first academic visitors to Zanskar, reported, "Older men and some of the more intelligent lamas foresaw problems. One man in particular summed it up neatly. 'Today we are happy, we have enough food. When the road comes, young people will want money, and we will lose our peace of mind.'"

And via the road, Lama Wangyal left Zanskar for the first time, two years later. Until that moment, his entire world—every person he knew, every home he'd visited, every path he'd walked—could all be surveyed from the airy perch of the monastery. It was a physically tangible life unlike anything we know today.

Traveling with a group of senior monks, he visited the distant Ladakhi capital of Leh, where the men attended a seven-day Kalachakra initiation hosted by the Dalai Lama.* In that time, Lama Wangyal saw his first car, heard his first foreign language, ate his first banana and watched a person speaking into what he thought was a shoe—a telephone.

Returning to the monastery, after a decade of living under his teacher's roof, Lama Wangyal began building his own home. Felling poplar trees by axe and forming mud bricks by hand, it took three months to complete the structure we now lived in: three storeys tall, connected by a labyrinth of passageways.

In the ensuing years, Lama Wangyal continued a meteoric ascendency at Karsha Gompa. By the age of forty, he became *ohm-zet*, or chant master. Three years after that, he was instated as *ghe-gheu*, or monastery disciplinarian. Then he became *lopon*, or leader-in-waiting. Finally, in 2009, at the age of fifty-six, Lama Wangyal was installed as Head Lama of Karsha Gompa, the youngest monk to hold the prominent position in over a thousand years of monastic tradition.

Stepping down after three years—as tradition dictates for all roles at a Tibetan Buddhist monastery—Lama Wangyal had settled into his role as *lazur*, recognized by every man, woman and child in the valley, when our family arrived.

---

* The Kalachakra is an ancient teaching, typically offered to large public audiences and intended to empower initiates with tantric skills necessary on the journey to Buddhahood. After it faded into obscurity, the current Dalai Lama revitalized its popularity, presiding over thirty such ceremonies, many attended by two hundred thousand devotees or more.

৺

When the movie ended, Lama Wangyal leapt up and disappeared into the adjoining puja room, soon returning with two wooden bowls.

"For you," he said, handing one to Christine and one to me. "Wanting?"

Fashioned from fine-grained wood, the bowls were polished to the color of amber. Lined with silver, they appeared ancient. Lama Wangyal told us he bought them in Varanasi, eleven years earlier, while attending another Kalachakra teaching.

"You keeping," Lama Wangyal said. "No money."

They were gorgeous, and I imagined drinking tea from them at home in Canada: talismans of our time here. Desire swelled within.

Faded price tags taped to the bases showed ten thousand rupees for one and eight thousand for the other—or roughly three hundred US dollars for both. Even in Canada, that would have seemed a lot of money for a pair of wooden bowls, but in Zanskar it represented a fortune. There was no way we could accept them as gifts.

Glancing at Christine, I opened our duffel and dug out a wad of US cash, wondering if I was being rash. I handed Lama Wangyal three crisp hundred-dollar bills, and he inspected them carefully, turning each in the light.

Then he leaned close and whispered, "Maybe me lucky man? Maybe me Canada coming?"

Norgay, the young *tulku*, believed to be a reincarnated lama,
peers from an abandoned monastery rooftop.

Novice monks in the class
room (LEFT). A communal
meal in the courtyard
(CENTER). Monks painstak
ingly creating an intricate
mandala, or sand painting
(BOTTOM).

ama Wangyal, wearing a headlamp, stands on the roof of his house.

Novice monks mill in the courtyard after class while Taj rides on Wang Chuk's back and Bodi shares his work (ABOVE). Bodi leaves an offering on a *chorten* outside Karsha village (BELOW). Christine treats Tsephal's warts (OPPOSITE TOP). Bodi and Christine sit in the village fields (OPPOSITE CENTER). Christine teaches mathematics to the junior boys (OPPOSITE BOTTOM).

The view of Zanskar valley from outside Lama Wangyal's hobbit door.

Dorjey, Lamo and Lama Wangyal in Tungri during harvest, with prayer wheels spinning in the foreground (OPPOSITE TOP). Lamo tutors Christine in the art of pulling barley (OPPOSITE CENTER). Bodi, Christine and Taj in the family bedroom (OPPOSITE BOTTOM). A team of yaks threshes barley in the fields of Karsha, with the monastery beyond (ABOVE).

A procession of lamas carries the remnants of the mandala down the winter trail, into the gorge, where it will be tossed in the village stream (ABOVE). Senior lamas wearing ceremonial yellow hats (LEFT).

A nun prepares chai and chapatti in the nunnery kitchen (ABOVE). Puja, or ritual prayers, in Karsha Gompa's ancient Labrang temple (BELOW).

Bodi, Norgay, Thurchin, Taj and Joray (ABOVE). Christine shares yarn with Skarma and Joray while the rest of the novices heave lines of wool over the parapet of the abandoned rooftop, gleefully "sky fishing" (BELOW).

Using a hand-cranked machine, Lama Wangyal sews traditional Zanskari coats for Bodi and Taj (ABOVE). The coats are presented before the long trek home and fitted with colorful sashes (BELOW).

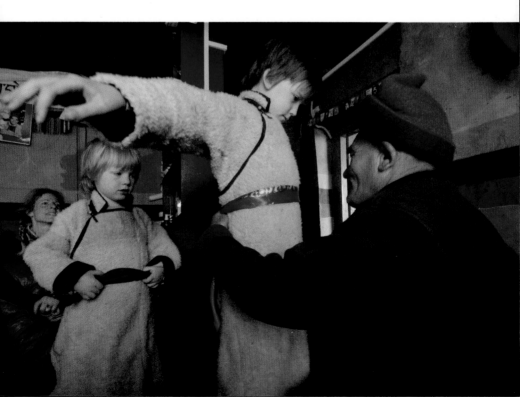

Bodi and Christine add a *khata* scarf to the offerings on the summit of the Sisar La pass (OPPOSITE TOP). Ascending one of fifteen passes on the long trek homewards (OPPOSITE CENTER). Bruce and Taj are happy to return to lower elevations after the passing of a bitterly cold snow squall (OPPOSITE BOTTOM). Bodi and Christine navigate the deep Shilla Gorge (ABOVE TOP). A family portrait on the final day of the journey (ABOVE BOTTOM).

Lama Wangyal and Taj in Delhi, while awaiting a visa that would allow the senior lama to accompany the family on a visit to Canada.

ॐ

IN THE SKY, THERE IS NO DISTINCTION OF EAST AND WEST

There is a special intensity of things at 12,000 feet in the Himalayas that brings out the gods within us.
—Michel Peissel,
Zanskar: The Hidden Kingdom

10

SEAT OF THE KINGS

I left the monastery after puja the next morning, bounding downhill toward the village, seeking a ride to Padum. The night before, Christine and I had stayed up late, whispering in darkness about Lama Wangyal's suggestion—or request—that he return with our family to Canada, to visit with us for a few months.

Years earlier, a young French woman had spent a winter living with the old monk, and his subsequent trip to France remained a highlight of his life. Photographs from that journey were plastered across the walls of our room: Lama Wangyal at Notre-Dame, at an outdoor café, in a patisserie.

If Lama Wangyal wanted to join us in Canada, we both agreed that paying for his flights was the least we could do. We'd stayed under his roof for a month already, with two more to go.

But beyond a sense of obligation, it also seemed to me like a possible way to bridge these two worlds and plant some seed of Zanskar's peace in our frenetic, distracted lives at home. Already I could imagine the robed monk and myself sitting cross-legged beside the wood stove, chanting. Or walking hand in hand through the forest. Visiting the local supermarket. The first step would be obtaining a Canadian visa, and I wanted to begin the application process immediately.

One dented car was parked in Karsha's village square. Inside, a young man in a leather jacket was fussing over the stereo system. When I approached, he rolled up the window.

So I set off by foot, intending to walk the ten kilometers to Padum. The skies were grey, and a biting wind swept down from the north. Puffy clouds stuck to mountainsides like cotton batting.

Twenty minutes later, as I neared the rusty bridge across the Stod River, a Suzuki car pulled alongside. Two heavy-set men filled the front, as if they'd been poured in. The driver pointed a thumb to the rear, where a lean farmer sat with a propane tank on his lap, next to a young school girl in braids. I squeezed between the pair.

Halfway across the barren plains, the Suzuki screeched to a halt and the young girl jumped out, skipping away across the desolation, presumably toward a distant farm. The driver popped the clutch and we roared on. We passed the Dalai Lama's official residence in Zanskar: a humble, whitewashed building with gilt roof, standing alone. Upon first visiting the valley in 1980, His Holiness declared it a vital sanctuary for Tibetan Buddhism, and he has returned every summer since to hold public teachings.

As we neared Padum, barley fields began to spring up from the rubble, which in turn gave way to a tangle of light industry: log peelers, furniture makers, propane-tank fillers and rock crushers. Beyond the carcass of a military helicopter—an Indian Mi-17 that crashed during the '99 Kargil War with Pakistan—we entered a maze of narrow alleys. Once the seat of Zanskar's king, the small town was now the valley's administrative center, home to police, heliport, infirmary and a population of one thousand.

I jumped out at the central square, where an Indian Army officer, in tan uniform and red beret, directed jeeps and tractors with a burnished baton. The milling crowds held farmers in puffy jackets, nuns in robes, teens wearing British football jerseys, dark-skinned laborers from Kerala, Kashmiri merchants and a sizable Muslim contingent, identifiable by head wraps and shalwar kameez, the baggy shirt and trousers of Pakistan.

Padum's Muslims had emigrated from Kargil generations earlier, and now comprised half of the local populace, which was an anomaly because elsewhere in Zanskar the population was almost exclusively Buddhist. For decades the two communities had enjoyed a comfortable coexistence, marked by friendship and even interfaith marriages. But in recent years, that peace had collapsed. While the origins of the dispute remain hazy—often traced to a quarrel over grazing rights—the effect had been shattering. Buddhists no longer ate at Muslim restaurants or shopped in Muslim stores. And vice versa.

Half-constructed buildings rose above the crowds, echoing with the clatter of hammers and generators. The noise and press of people felt overwhelming—which was ironic, for Padum lies as far off the beaten track as a traveller can get. Here one finds none of the trinket vendors, banana pancakes, mixed-fruit lassis or neon massage signs ubiquitous across much of Asia. In fact, I saw no other Westerners at all. But already, I missed the monastery's quiet isolation.

Wandering the main street, I discovered two bakeries, a hardware store, a medical dispensary, four restaurants and a general store, which sold prayer flags, fish-shaped padlocks and incense. The butcher's door was propped open by a severed calf's head. Three fresh produce stands carried exactly the same hodgepodge of wilting fruits and vegetables—whatever the latest truck from Srinagar had brought.

This relative abundance marked a staggering change from 1976, when visiting French ethnologist Michel Peissel reported not a single store. Instead he found a non-monetized, self-reliant society, where locals grew their own food, made their own clothes and even gathered their own herbal medicine on surrounding mountainsides. They appeared to have everything they needed, Piessel observed at the time, beyond salt, tea and metal cooking utensils—which they acquired from passing traders.[*]

After cramming my backpack with a watermelon, apples, tomatoes, cashews, fresh peas, garlic, tomato sauce, and toilet paper, I bought a handful of Center Fruit gum for Bodi and Taj, a small jar of instant coffee for Christine and a tin of brown paint for Lama Wangyal.

A Kashmiri shoeshine, sitting beneath a dirty tarp and surrounded by scraps of leather, held out a handful of dried apricots. The wrinkled fruit was the color of amber and rattled like dice in my palm. Splitting one between my molars, I found it sweet, chewy and pleasantly tangy. After handing over a small wad of rupees, I filled my pockets with the exquisite treats.

Down a nondescript dirt track, I found my objective: the Mont Blanc Cyber Cafe. A slim man named Lichten sat at the front desk, wearing aviator sunglasses and a satin jacket with *Top Gun* embroidered across the back, engrossed in a video game. Absently he motioned me through a curtained doorway to a

---

[*]   On his journey, Peissel was approached by "an old man with a pointed scraggy beard and
       weather-beaten face" seeking tea packets, who he later discovered was *Gyalpo*, King of
       Zanskar.

darkened room, where five computers sat atop a sheet of plywood, connected by a bird's nest of wiring.

I flicked one dusty machine on. It took a long time to boot, and then web pages required minutes to load. The power failed, plunging the room into blackness. Lichten started a generator, but the internet was frozen, and the satellite link had to be reset.

It took an hour to find a Canadian visa application form. When I clicked *download*, a blue bar began inching across the screen. *Estimated time remaining: thirty-four minutes.*

To pass the time, I uploaded a photograph from my camera and posted it to Instagram, feeling mildly guilty for connecting to the world beyond. Almost immediately, a comment popped up, questioning the accuracy of my caption. It came from a friend, and while the intent was surely innocent, I felt tension wiggle in my brain.

Eventually the download finished, but the computer was unable to open the file. Its software was outdated. When I asked Lichten if I could run an update, he shook his head.

"Daytime no possible. Too slow."

Instead, he promised to download the necessary software that night, when fewer users clogged the satellite network, and suggested I come back the next day to print the form. I thanked him, paid for my time, then slipped out into knife-sharp sunlight.

After waiting vainly on the edge of town for a ride back toward the monastery, I shouldered my pack and set off alone. Soon it began to drizzle. Yanking a garbage bag from my pack, I tore holes for arms and head, and pressed on.

With every step, my friend's Instagram comment wriggled in my mind. I knew it was pointless to dwell on the words, yet I seemed unable to push them aside. I tried to concentrate on my breathing, but that didn't help. The worm inside my head was feeding. If one inconsequential social media comment could send me into such a tailspin, how could anything we learned in Zanskar endure upon our return to Canada? Pulling Lama Wangyal's *mala* beads from my neck, I rolled them through my fingers, quietly repeating, *Om mani padme heung.*

Twenty minutes later, I was still battling with my attention when two middle-aged women appeared on the rocky plains ahead. Goatskins were slung across their shoulders and they carried rope lassos in their hands. The pair scrambled onto the asphalt ribbon, a stone's throw ahead of me, then turned to stare at the odd, garbage bag–clad foreigner.

"*Jullay!*" I waved.

"*Jullay! Jullay!*" they replied, waiting for me to catch up.

"Where going you?" one asked.

"Karsha Gompa."

"What doing you?"

"Shopping in Padum."

"What name you?"

"Tsering Mortub."

The women glanced at each other, then began shaking with laughter. "Tsering Mortub! Oh, Tsering Mortub!" they said over and over, until their eyes watered.

Once they'd calmed down, they introduced themselves as Torje Palma and Sherup Dolma, hailing from the hamlet of Upti, six homes tucked in the shadow of Pipiting Monastery. I came from Canada, I explained, and was staying at Karsha Gompa with my family.

"How long?"

"Three months."

"Three months?" they exclaimed in surprise. "With who staying?"

Lama Wangyal's name brought approving nods. "Very, very good lama."

Torje reached up to examine a tangle of necklaces hanging from my neck. Pointing to a tattered piece of red string, she said, "Dalai Lama."

It seemed uncanny, but twenty years earlier, the uncle of a Sherpa teammate had indeed taken that very piece of string to Dharamsala, where it was blessed by the Dalai Lama.

We walked on in silence, the women flanking me no taller than my elbows.

"One biscuit?" Sherup abruptly asked.

Rather than feeling slighted or infringed upon, I felt a pang of sadness, for I had none to share. Then I remembered the Center Fruit. Rummaging through my pockets, I held out the gum in an open palm. Sherup and Torje gingerly took one each, touching the candy first to foreheads and then hearts, before finally popping it in their mouths.

When we reached a dirt track leading toward the Stod River, the pair said farewell. They invited me to bring Christine and our boys to their homes in Upti. They would kill a sheep, they promised. On impulse, I took off two of my necklaces and held them toward the women. They refused of course, but I insisted, and eventually they accepted. Then the pair set off at a skip down a narrow lane, laughing and holding hands.

I continued along the strip of tarmac, warmed by the fleeting encounter.

As the road slowly passed underfoot, I found myself questioning a prima facie assumption I'd accepted since childhood: the conceited construct that somehow Western nations hold a monopoly over progress.

Since my first journey abroad (Pakistan in 1991) I have harbored a deep regard for all foreign lands and cultures. And over the years, I have experienced a visceral sense of loss while watching my own monolithic Western civilization spill steadily outward, shrinking differences, creating an increasingly homogenous planet—aware of my own role in this trend as a traveller. Still, I assuaged my horror at this ongoing loss of diversity with the insipid belief that somehow it was necessary; it was *progress*. It was the only way.

Perhaps this idea was kindled by the nomenclature of my youth: *First World* versus *Third World*; *developed* versus *developing*. Or by some unwitting combination of British colonialism and American exceptionalism. Whatever the case, the idea that progress flowed in one direction had long gone unquestioned in my mind.

But recently, despite the wealth of Canadian society, I had begun to wonder if we were not simultaneously growing poorer, in ways that bank accounts and standard-of-living indexes couldn't measure—time, connection and community.

Ironically, it was Canadian cab drivers who brought my attention to such growing impoverishments. Typically men—often Ethiopians, Punjabis, Somalis or Pakistanis—the majority of these immigrants, I think it is fair to say, came to Canada in search of a better life for their families, seeking education, health care, peace and security. And while they found, and appreciated, such benefits, I sensed such progress had also exacted unanticipated losses.

Frequently, if we were caught in traffic, and talked long and freely enough, our conversations would invariably arrive at reminiscences of their former homes, about warm evenings and streets crowded with familiar friends, about sharing food with neighbors and wedding feasts attended by thousands, about impromptu daily gatherings where news and gossip were shared over tea. And it all sounded so wonderful and natural—and foreign.

What human riches are we sacrificing in our endless rush toward progress? What can we still learn from the unseen, unheard cultures who today are clinging to existence, before their ancient ways are paved over? And why does "progress" only ever seem to travel in one direction? Why don't we, as Canadians, also learn and enrich our society from the ways of, say, Borneo's Penan, Arabia's Bedouin or the Zanskaris?

I was mulling such bleak thoughts as I climbed the monastery's pathways and spotted Bodi far above, silhouetted atop the abandoned roof. He was spinning, carefree. I called out, and he came running with open arms.

As we neared, he raised his head to kiss me, but then at the last moment turned away, as if unsure what to do, and awkwardly planted his lips on my shirt instead. Then he asked if I'd bought any Center Fruit gum.

"Who is the best dad in the world?" I asked, holding out the bag.

"Oh, Dad! You know that's impossible to know," he retorted with annoyance. "I haven't met every dad in the world."

❦

In Lama Wangyal's kitchen, Christine ladled curry from the pressure cooker into bowls. I could tell with a glance that she was beside herself.

"I burned the first goddamned pot," she fumed. "And now this batch is underdone. It's inedible. I'm gonna throw it out."

I stopped her just in time, and after tasting the curry, assured her it was perfectly palatable. Then I carried brimming bowls to our room, before she could intervene. Lama Wangyal was nowhere to be found—he must have chosen to eat supper with the other monks in the courtyard—so the four of us ate in silence.

Later, as Christine and I scrubbed dishes together on the path outside the hobbit door, I realized she was crying. Gently, I put my hand on her shoulder.

"I'm sorry," she said eventually, rubbing her eyes. "I just miss some basic comfort. Like a shower. A proper toilet. Coffee."

Another silence, then she added, "You try having your period over a stinky hole in the floor." We leaned against each other in darkness, bent over the pewter basin. "Don't worry. This doesn't mean I want to leave," she said. "It'll pass. I just needed to get it out."

When our knees gave out, we sat together on the rocky path. Then she asked, "Have you noticed I'm the only woman here?"

Embarrassingly, I'd never considered the situation.

"It doesn't bug me," Christine said. "I've never felt out of place. Or unwelcome. But it just dawned on me that for an entire month, I haven't talked to anyone but men. I've prayed with men. I've eaten with men. I think I'm ready for a change."

To remedy the situation, we decided to visit a small nunnery, Karsha Chuchikjall Kachod Gyrubling, which neighbored the monastery. Sharing the same cliffs—but separated from Karsha Gompa by the deep gorge of the village stream—it was the largest of ten nunneries in Zanskar, founded in 1986 and home to twelve nuns.

❧

The next morning, as dawn broke over the high peaks, I tossed Taj on my shoulders and chased Christine and Bodi down the winter trail, into the cool gorge.

We followed a concrete pathway up the far side, swept as clean as a suburban sidewalk. A small *chorten* marked the nunnery entrance, and beyond lay a cluster of tidy homes. Gardens bloomed with marigold and aster. Picket fences glistened with fresh paint. The orderly atmosphere was in contrast to the monastery, where garbage littered the trails and it was not uncommon to stumble upon human feces.

"This place is a lot newer made," Bodi whispered.

"*Jullay,* Tashi! *Jullay,* Norbu!"

A beaming woman with a shorn head waved from an upper-floor window of a small house. Moments later she burst from the front door and introduced herself as Ani Garkyid.* Her brother was a lama at Karsha Gompa—we later surmised it was Dorjey Tundup, a jolly lama we'd nicknamed the Manchurian—and he'd told her of our family.

Taking the boys by their hands, she dragged us past the temple—now crammed with scaffolding and paint tins and undergoing restoration—to an adjoining storage room, where the sound of song drifted from an open door. Inside, seven women were seated on the floor. All wore maroon robes and the orange hats of Zanskar. Two elders, with blankets pulled across their laps, were entirely toothless. The chant master bore a remarkable resemblance to the Irish songstress Enya.

The singing never stopped, but the nuns welcomed us with a round of applause and gestured for us to sit among them. A short, stout woman shuffled

---

* *Ani* is a Tibetan prefix added to the name of a nun, akin to the Catholic *Sister*.

out and soon returned with an urn of milky tea and chapattis. Taj ripped two small holes in his flatbread and held it up as a mask. The elders laughed so hard it left them breathless.

When the singing ended, the nuns broke into excited chatter. Ani Garkyid translated their questions. *Where were we living? How long would we stay? Did we go to puja every day? Had we been learning about Buddha? Were the boys healthy? Happy? How was school?*

A pot of vegetable broth arrived, along with fried bread. Singing resumed. Then came butter tea, *tsampa* and dried yogurt curd.

When puja ended, the nuns toured us around their grounds, showing century-old frescoes, a small schoolhouse, a communal greenhouse and an innovative dormitory, heated with passive solar. The women gathered at the gates to see us off. Stroking our boys' cheeks, they implored us to return again soon, and their singsong voices followed us down the mountain.

"Bye-bye, Norbu. Bye-bye, Tashi."

"I know it's pointless to say, but I kinda wish we'd stayed at the nunnery," Christine remarked, as soon as we were out of earshot. "There was something so pure about those women. Did you notice that instead of hiring Nepalis, they were doing all the hard work themselves? I think they could have taught us far more about Buddhism."

❧

On Sunday, with no class to teach, I set off toward the guest house alongside Lama Wangyal, a tin of paint swinging in hand. We found paintbrushes in a closet full of cobwebs, but they were as stiff as nails. Lama Wangyal marched to an adjoining homestead, banged on the door, and returned with a mug of kerosene. After much bending and twisting, we resurrected a pair.

Then, side by side under a scorching sun, we began repainting the guest house trim. It was challenging work, for our paint was mahogany, the walls bone white and our brushes abysmal. So it came as a great relief when, after twenty minutes, Lama Wangyal inspected my progress and happily proclaimed, "Mortub good painting man."

When I glanced at Lama Wangyal's window, I was shocked to see paint splattered all over the place, and I began to worry less about the perfection of my efforts.

Working beside Lama Wangyal reminded me of working beside my father, who died twenty years earlier in an Ontario farming accident. Like my father, Lama Wangyal could be brusque and demanding, without ever meaning ill. And as with my father, I sought his approval.

Bodi soon appeared, racing across the yard to see what we were doing.

"Can I paint too?" he asked excitedly.

"No," Lama Wangyal barked, waving him off.

Bodi ignored him. "Dad, please?"

"No!" Lama Wangyal repeated emphatically. "Too dirty." He pointed at Bodi's bright blue polypropylene shirt.

Bodi burst into tears. "Why, Dad? Why can't I paint?"

I knew Lama Wangyal viewed the issue pragmatically. Bodi would slow us down, and the elderly man wanted the job done quickly. Compounding his frustration was Bodi's insubordination, as orders were always followed obediently in the monastic world.

I understood his point of view, but at the same time, as a parent, I saw the teaching opportunity—a chance to expose Bodi to the practical skill of painting, while involving him in something beyond play.

"Please," cried Bodi.

"NO!" declared Lama Wangyal.

I distracted Bodi with a Thermos of milky tea and biscuits, feeling mildly guilty I was choosing ease over my son's best interests.

Eventually Lama Wangyal headed toward the village in search of rags, and I handed Bodi a paintbrush. As I watched him dab paint on the window trim—far more carefully and methodically than either Lama Wangyal or me—I saw a flash of my father in him. It was not the first time.

In the years following Bodi's diagnosis, I had come to a deeper understanding of my father than I'd had while he was alive. While it is impossible to diagnose a person retroactively, I am confident in saying my dad—a nonconforming, socially awkward, and occasionally prickly scientist—exhibited classic spectrum-like behavior, and likely could have fallen within the clinical bounds of ASD. Many of my father's eccentricities make sense in retrospect: his aversion to hugging, his obsessive insistence on fairness, his lack of interest in trends and fashions or anything "cool," his nitpicky arguments with friends and strangers alike.

While I loved my father unconditionally, I certainly wondered at times why he insisted on making life so difficult. But in hindsight, as the father of my own child on the spectrum, instead of feeling frustrated by his idiosyncro-cies, I am staggered by what he managed to achieve—getting married, staying married, raising three kids, having a successful career—as a somewhat geeky and nonconforming child who emerged from a British grammar school system determined to bend him to its mold, then immigrated as a teenager to the equally unsympathetic Canadian society of the '60s and '70s.

I feel grateful for the extraordinary posthumous understanding Bodi has granted me, though it seems tragic my own father never gained these insights. Unfortuntately, Asperger's research remained buried during his lifetime, only emerging into broader awareness later. While my father lived an engaged and vibrant life, I suspect he never had the opportunity to understand himself entirely—something Christine and I were determined to afford Bodi.

More than once I joked with Christine that Bodi could be a reincarnation of my father, sharing his dedication to fairness and truth, a complete lack of concern for others' judgment, and even a keen interest in the physical sciences.

Now, as Bodi reached to paint the top of the window frame, he cried out in pain.

"I can't do it," he declared and put the brush down.

"What do you mean, you can't do it?"

"I can't," he repeated. "It's my shoulder. It's frozen inside."

Then he skipped off to drink another cup of tea while I remained behind in silence, looking out over the vast valley, asking myself once again what was real and what was imagination. For an entire year before his untimely death, my father had struggled to raise his right arm overhead, plagued by a condition that physiotherapists describe as "frozen shoulder."*

---

*   Frozen shoulder, or adhesive capsulitis, is a condition characterized by stiffness, pain and loss of range of motion in the shoulder joint.

11

THE ECONOMY OF MERIT

From our perch in the monastery, I watched as patches of brown spread across the green and yellow quilt of Karsha's fields. Harvest was underway, and after puja our family ambled down to explore.

It was a glorious autumn day, and villagers dotted the fields. Some were stooped, pulling barley by hand. Others cut alfalfa with scythes. A few carried towering loads back toward the village, where alfalfa was piled on flat rooftops to be used as winter fodder, and barley was heaped in haystacks so high they required a ladder to ascend, awaiting threshing. Husks and chaff drifted across footpaths, and our boys delighted in chasing the flocks of sparrows that gorged on this bounty.

In a quiet field, a family was stacking sheaves of barley—a grandmother, two daughters and six grandchildren all close in age to Bodi and Taj—and we joined them for a time, though I suspected we were more hindrance than help. The midday sun was scorching, and soon, both our boys were red-faced.

We were returning to the monastery when we passed an elderly woman on the trail. Wearing yak-hair boots and an indigo robe, she was bent in half at the waist and shuffled beneath a towering load of alfalfa. At a tumbledown homestead, she climbed a rickety ladder to the roof, balanced precariously the entire way.

I felt an overwhelming compulsion to help the elder, and Christine—whose homesickness had dissipated as quickly as it descended—encouraged me to stay.

"You should lend her a hand. Take your time," she yelled back. "Seriously, no rush. I'll get some lunch ready."

So I waited, and eventually the ladder started to shake. The ancient reappeared, a chunky necklace swinging atop her robe, each turquoise stone the size and color of a robin's egg. She stared at me, expressionless. I pointed to the ropes on her shoulders, and then myself. She broke into laughter and handed them to me.

"Mortub," I said, patting my chest, but she shook her head, which I took to mean she spoke no English. Then, taking my hand in hers—one finger bore a silver ring so tight I doubted it would ever come off—she led me into the fields.

It took ten minutes to reach her family's land. After laying the ropes parallel on the ground, she began stacking alfalfa on top. I joined, and after we'd created a waist-high pile, the woman cinched it tight. Taking a blue shawl from her hair, she spread it across my shoulders to prevent scratching. Then she pushed me backward until I lay across the pile, and indicated I should slip my arms through the two ropes, wearing the bundle like a backpack. With great effort, I struggled to my feet. The load must have weighed thirty kilograms, and by the time I dropped it on her roof, my legs ached.

The elder spread the fragrant fodder with a wooden rake, and a hoopoe swooped in, a distinctive old-world bird with a striped crown. Probing for insects, it soon caught a spider the size of a tarantula, and throwing its head back, swallowed it in a single gulp.

We headed to the fields again, and this time villagers hooted at our passing. The elder waved but said nothing. What on earth were they yelling? *Who is your new husband? It's a shame he is so ugly. Can I borrow him when you are done?*

Yaks were now returning from the *doksa* (summer grazing lands), and we passed one surly beast tethered to a post by a wooden nose ring. A flap of hide had been torn from his rump, perhaps in a mating battle, and the festering wound reminded me of Tibetan lore, where in times of hardship, nomads were rumoured to peel a flap of skin from a living yak, hack off a smidgen of meat, then press the skin back in place and carry on.

Soon I was again staggering toward the elder's homestead beneath another heavy load. As I walked, I mulled the difference between "working" and "working out." Living in a modernized society, where most physical labor has been stripped from my life, I often resort to lifting pieces of metal in air-conditioned gymnasiums, or spend hours pedalling bikes that go nowhere. I remembered the confusion on a Sherpa's face when I'd explained such training. All that effort, he seemed to be thinking, and nothing accomplished?

By the third load, I was dizzy.

By the sixth, my calf was twitching like a sewing machine. The elder offered me a bowl of sweet black tea, and I doubted I had ever tasted anything so delicious.

It took nine loads to clear the field.

As I prepared to leave, the elder took my hands and pressed them to her forehead. We'd worked side by side for three hours and never shared a word.

❦

I was dozing in our sunlit room later that afternoon when I became aware of an odd sound—a soft thrumming that rose and fell in intensity.

What could it be? A machine? Helicopter? Chanting?

"Can you hear that?" I asked Christine, who sat across the small room, repairing underwear with a needle and thread. She nodded, and as we listened, the sound was abruptly silenced. Then something flickered above my head, and the sound started again.

It was a fly, caught in a web!

As the fly thrashed, struggling to escape, a dark spider materialized from the recesses of the curtain and began inching closer. With a leap, it began bouncing back and forth over the fly, as if on a trampoline, trying to land a sting.

"Look! Look!" we both exclaimed, and the kids leapt up from their Lego.

"Wow," whispered Taj. "That's so awesome."

"It's trying to sting the fly," Bodi whispered. "Oh no. I don't want the fly to die. But I don't want the spider to starve either."

Soon the spider scored a lethal hit. The fly twitched violently as life ebbed. Quickly entombing its prey in silk, the spider dragged the fuzzy coffin back toward its lair, hidden somewhere in the curtains.

At home I would have swept away the cobweb without hesitation, but now I paused, for the spider seemed to be fulfilling an important function by keeping the fly population in check. Besides, I knew Bodi would have been apoplectic.

So I left the arachnid in peace and dozed off, dimly aware that somewhere overhead, a plump spider was munching on a fly.

❦

When the monk boys finished memorizing all twenty-six verses of "*A* says Ahhh," we held an impromptu celebration. We called every boy to the blackboard in turn, where they led the class through the song, pointing to each letter as they went. Over and over and over, the class sang the same song. I worried it might become boring, but oh no, the boys loved every minute. Even the surly teenagers acted out the parts with gusto: arms chomping like an alligator's mouth, legs kicking like a kangaroo. When Norgay's turn came, I hoisted the tiny *tulku* aloft so he could reach the blackboard, and the class erupted into applause when he finished.

In English, we began studying opposites (big versus small, high versus low) and played a lot of Simon Says, which was highly competitive and occasionally ended in scuffles.

In math, the senior boys mastered three-digit multiplication and began long division. The junior boys were struggling with even simple addition, so Christine built a cardboard abacus for each, using *mala* beads and string. The youngsters loved these new tools and progress came quickly.

We established two special days of the week; Friday Fun Day, when the boys all drew, and Saturday Story Day, when Christine and I read aloud to the class.

Concerned that Wang Chuk might not approve of art lessons in his classroom—I suspected traditional subjects, such as mathematics and science, were held in higher regard by the monks—we tried to circumvent censure on the first Friday Fun Day by asking the boys to sketch a Buddhist symbol. We explained it could be anything they wanted: a mandala, a *dorje*, a thousand-armed Avalokiteshvara. After receiving construction paper and pencil crayons, the monk boys fidgeted uneasily and did nothing. Eventually Norphal explained they needed something to copy. It appeared these boys had never drawn from imagination before.

So we sent them off to wander the monastery, scanning lintels and frescoes for inspiration. Over the coming hours, an astounding variety of drawings emerged. Some boys were gifted artists, while others produced barely recognizable stick figures.

When four o'clock rolled around, we gathered in a circle and Christine held the drawings aloft, one by one. The class broke into an ovation for every picture, and I stuck a shiny silver star on each—which the boys adored—before taping the artwork to the mud walls. At last the barren chamber was beginning to look like a classroom. When Wang Chuk ducked in to brew tea, he pulled up short with a look of surprise, and I could have sworn a fleeting smile passed his face, but he said nothing.

With each passing week, the novices produced more and more art. Color swept across the walls. Christine and I always brought objects for the class to sketch: a miniature prayer wheel (the type seen on Zanskari dashboards), a tea bowl, Lama Wangyal's potted geranium.

One Friday I pulled a Captain America action figure from my backpack and introduced the superhero as "Captain Canada." The monk boys, knowing no difference, exploded with delight, but Bodi was appalled.

"That's not right, Dad!" he shouted. "It's not Captain *Canada*. It is Captain *AMERICA*."

I tried to explain that our family came from Canada, so calling the figurine "Captain Canada" was meant to be fun, but Bodi was inconsolable.

Meanwhile Wang Chuk began joking with Taj. "You Kapitan Karsha! You stay here. You no go home."

"No way, José!" Taj jeered. "I'm Captain Canada."

"Captain America," Bodi screamed.

"Kapitan Karsha!" Wang Chuk insisted.

And so it went, as the monk boys feverishly drew.

❧

Another fly was caught in the spider's web. I lay on my back and watched as the spider emerged from hiding and inched closer. Then the fly broke free, and the spider retreated.

Buzzing back and forth across the pane, the fly was soon ensnared again, and this time the spider approached more quickly. The fly went berserk as the final showdown commenced, and I found myself silently rooting for the spider. Soon it landed a fatal sting and was dragging its meal away, when Lama Wangyal strode into the room. Entranced, I pointed toward the unfolding drama.

Without hesitation, the old monk began delicately pulling the web down, thread by thread, as if unpinning a curtain. The spider, its meal forgotten, zipped frantically this way and that, until Lama Wangyal gathered it in one hand, along with the web, and held the mess toward me.

"No good, Mortub," he said, shaking his head and pointing to the dead flies. "Too much."

I followed him down the earthen passageway and out the hobbit door, where he gently shook the spider into rose bushes. Then, still chanting, he brushed his hands and disappeared down the path.

❧

A traveling pharmacist arrived the next morning. The bespectacled man wore a collared shirt and tie, and made annual visits to all Zanskari monasteries. I found him in the courtyard, surrounded by a group of senior lamas.

Lama Norbu, the senior *lopon* and next in line to become Head Lama, shifted nervously as a blood pressure cuff was attached to his skeletal bicep. Upon receiving a thumbs-up, the seventy-seven-year-old beamed with relief. Nonetheless, he was handed a package of foil-wrapped pills, just like every other lama. When I asked the pharmacist what the pills were for, he replied, "Good health."

The majority of the monks certainly appeared to be in good health, remaining lean and strong into their advancing years, able to walk for hours on end, often at a blistering pace. The local villagers appeared equally healthy.

For generations, communicable diseases had been what felled people in this remote valley: diarrhea, tuberculosis, cholera, parasites and infection. Thankfully, medicine capable of treating such maladies arrived in the mid '70s, following the construction of the road.

But other illnesses lurked in modernity's wake.

Within years of adopting a modern lifestyle, traditional societies unfailingly suffer an epidemic of previously unknown, non-communicable diseases—heart attack, stroke, diabetes and cancer—all caused by skyrocketing consumption of salt, sugar and fat.

This was the fate that awaited our novices.

But who was I to worry? The same fate awaited me. And my own boys, along with the majority of our family, friends, neighbors and co-workers. And anyone else eating a Western diet. Although we rarely pause to consider it, we are all killing ourselves slowly with what we eat.

Perhaps in Zanskar it just felt more poignant—for in the crossroads of our family's visit, the villagers, monks and novices still grasped the last vestiges of a traditional diet, even as the seeds of disease were being sown around them.

❧

The next morning, we found the lamas congregated in the courtyard again. Many sported freshly shaven skulls. As Bodi, Taj and I neared, we spotted Jimba Sonam, the monastery disciplinarian, running a blue disposable razor over Wang Chuk's glistening noggin. Nearby, Stanzin Ta'han, the Noble Face, kneaded a basketball-sized lump of *tsampa*.

When Bodi and Taj sprinted off in pursuit of a butterfly, he glanced up and murmured, "Your babies so cute."

The sharp-faced young man had never spoken to me before, or even nodded in recognition, and when I asked what he was doing, he gestured to a row of small *tsampa chortens*. "Daily days, my responsibility is making *jarden*."

Glancing around furtively, he held his thumb and forefinger close together and whispered, "I have only little power."

Every morning, he and his partner—a blushing teen with milky skin—fashioned four hundred *tsampa* balls for puja, all perfectly symmetrical. But today was different, Ta'han explained. They would make one thousand balls, to mark the annual celebration of *Kalzang Tongchet*, the puja of a thousand offerings. As we spoke, he explained, other members of the Lost Boys were lighting a thousand candles in the assembly hall.

Ta'han was twenty-one years old. He'd arrived at Karsha Gompa at age seven and, after showing great scholastic promise, had been dispatched to Gyuto Monastery, in distant Dharamsala. But his studies had recently been cut short when his father fell ill.

I asked if he would return to Gyuto when his father was better, to complete his *geshe* studies, but he glumly shook his head. "Not possible. No big money for me."

We sat in silence for a time, then he asked, "Good jobs in Canada possible?"

I stammered, unsure how to respond.

"If I visiting, job possible?" he clarified.

"Maybe," I stumbled.

Ta'han asked for my journal and carefully entered details of his Facebook account. He hadn't used it for three years, he told me, but suggested we could keep in touch that way. I said that would be lovely.

Leaning close, he whispered, "Do you want to see Dode?"

"Yes, of course!" I stammered. "Please."

Dode—pronounced do-dee—was the nickname of Dorje Rinchen, a fifteenth-century Buddhist reformer who spent his later life teaching at Karsha Gompa.

Following the lama's passing, his mummified remains had been sealed inside a silver-plated *chorten* in the assembly hall.

During the tumultuous days of the Partition, when India and Pakistan were cleaved apart in 1947, a rogue brigade of Pakistani soldiers pillaged Zanskari monasteries, carrying away anything of value—including the jewel-encrusted silver sheets covering Dode's *chorten*.

But now an effort was underway to restore the funerary monument. The *chorten*'s four-hundred-year-old framework had been disassembled and the timbers refinished. Now the monastery was raising funds to purchase silver sheeting; a sign near the entrance to the assembly hall sought donations from tourists. In the meantime, Dode's remains had been stashed somewhere at Karsha Gompa.

After I rounded up my boys, Ta'han led us into the assembly hall, where the altar was already ablaze with a thousand yak-butter tea lights. In a darkened corner, beyond the scripture cubbyholes, was a box draped in silk, roughly the size of a washing machine. Ta'han pointed to a hand-written sheet of paper on the wall beside it, which read, NO SNAPS PLEASE. I nodded, and then with a flourish, he pulled the fabric aside.

Inside was a clear Plexiglas box, holding what appeared to be a golden statue of a cross-legged man, arms folded, sapphire eyes staring toward infinity. It took me some time to comprehend we were actually looking at the mummified remains of Dode, for his face had been thickened with plaster and painted gold, making it appear like every other Buddhist statue across the Himalaya. But protruding from the disintegrating robes beneath were blackened arms and legs, thin bones supporting a gossamer of desiccated skin like ridgepoles in a tent.

"Whoa," Bodi burst out. "A gold-faced man. That is so cool."

"Is he real, Dada?" Taj whispered, and I nodded.

The lama's dark fingers gripped a wooden bowl, identical to the tea bowls used in puja today. "That Dode's cup," Ta'han explained. "Him using daily days."

We stared in silence, until Ta'han finally let the fabric drop back in place, and rushed back out to the courtyard to continue his chores, leaving us alone in the flickering light of the assembly hall.

Curious, we explored the sea of candles on the altar, where offertory plates were buried beneath *khata* scarves, barley grain, *kusha* grass and soiled rupee bills. In a small adjoining chamber, we found life-sized statues of Buddha and his disciples, gold-plated and inlaid with gems. The 108 books of *Kangyur* occupied cubbyholes in the wall. And two yellow-cushioned daises, which I'd never noticed before, stood at the very front of the hall, higher even than the Head Lama's seat.

The lower dais of the two was reserved for the monastery's abbot, Ngari Rinpoche,* who resided in Dharamsala. The other—closest to the altar, and highest of all—waited for the Dalai Lama. A similar seat awaits him in every Tibetan Buddhist temple, in every country around the world.

A small black-and-white photograph balanced on the cushion showed the Dalai Lama as a young man. It was taken around the time Mao Zedong summoned the youthful leader to Beijing, famously sharing his assessment that religion was poison, while hinting at his future designs on the Tibetan Kingdom. The man in the photograph, wearing horn-rimmed glasses and looking like a university graduate, surely sensed the rising darkness that would engulf his country. Yet his peace appears unassailable.

What an extraordinary leader the Dalai Lama has proven to be, I mulled, guiding his people through times turbulent beyond imagination. Even as he enters his eighth decade, the man remains indefatigable, insisting he is just a simple monk—despite navigating a relentless schedule of public appearances and meetings with world leaders. He still rises at 3:30 A.M. every day and meditates for four hours.

Remembering my boys, I glanced about and found the pair peering into the cubbyholes holding ancient scripture.

I gazed back upon the empty seat. It was hard not to wonder what fate would await Tibetan Buddhism upon the death of this great man. The Chinese government will unquestionably attempt to interfere with the identification of a

---

* Ngari Rinpoche, the Dalai Lama's younger brother, is often referred to by his secular name, Tenzin Choegyal. Like his famous sibling, he was discovered to be an incarnate as an infant, and spent his youth in the Potala Palace. Fleeing Tibet with his family at thirteen, he continued his Buddhist training in Dharamsala, but eventually grew disillusioned and traded in his monk's robes for paratrooper fatigues in the Indian Army, taking up smoking and dismissing Westerners who flocked to Tibetan Buddhism as fawning groupies. He returned to Dharamsala later in life to work for the Tibetan people as a reformer, and now lives in a small apartment beside the Dalai Lama, acting as his translator and private secretary.

reincarnation.* To protect against that possibility, the Dalai Lama has declared his successor will not be born in either Tibet or China. And recently he has begun floating an even more revolutionary idea: Perhaps the institution of the Dalai Lamas has outlived its usefulness?

His Holiness has pledged to consult with Tibetan high lamas in the coming decade to evaluate what will be best for future Tibet, but the possibility exists that he will be the last in a line of *tulkus* stretching back to 1391, all believed to be incarnations of Avalokiteshvara, the bodhisattva of compassion.

I was still gazing at the youthful man in the photograph when Tashi Tsering, the cook, appeared by my side, wearing a leather motorcycle jacket with silver zippers at the cuffs. His head was freshly shaved, and after rounding up Bodi and Taj—who had been ordering and stacking rupee bills on the altar—he placed an arm across their shoulders, then asked me to take a photograph. Afterward, he inscribed his address in my journal, and I promised to send him a copy.

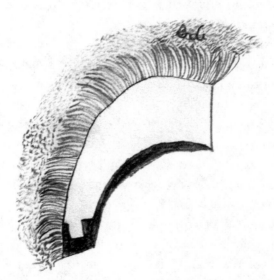

The distinctive ceremonial yellow hat of Tibetan Buddhism's Gelugpa sect.

---

* Following the death of the Panchen Lama in 1995—whose spiritual authority is second only to the Dalai Lama—Tibetan lamas identified six-year-old Gedhun Nyima as the reincarnation. Chinese authorities swiftly took the boy into custody, along with his family, and they have never been seen again. When Beijing identified another *tulku*, it left the ancient lineage in disarray and under threat of collapse.

Soon lamas wearing ceremonial yellow hats began streaming in. Christine appeared, back from a successful mission to buy eggs in the village. Unrolling a carpet, we sat together—Taj in Christine's lap, Bodi in mine. Milky tea was served, and for a sublime moment, I wanted for nothing.

❧

Christine woke up the next morning with itchy eyes. By dinnertime, globs of mucus clung to her lashes. Her eyes were so red it appeared as if she'd smoked a bag of weed. There was no question: she had pink eye. But unfortunately, our well-stocked first aid kit held no antibiotic eye drops.

Before leaving Canada, our family doctor had warned of a global eye drop shortage. Seriously? Such things happened? After canvassing pharmacies across the province, and finding none, we admitted defeat. And now we desperately needed some. It seemed improbable that Padum's small dispensary might carry anything suitable, but I promised to go in search the next morning.

But Lama Wangyal had other plans.

A car would arrive before dawn, he explained, to carry us both to his home village of Neyrok, where he would perform a puja. I told him I desperately needed to go to Padum in search of medicine, but he waved off such concerns.

"First puja. Then Padum."

I glanced at Christine, with her clogged eyes, and she shrugged.

The next morning Lama Wangyal's heavy footsteps woke me, banging down the ladder. "Oh, Mortub!" he cried. Moments later the hobbit door swung open. Leaping into clothes, I grabbed my backpack and raced after him. The old monk floated down the steep trails, and I struggled to keep pace.

We joined a group of lamas milling by the monastery gates in first light, all bound for satellite villages to begin the season of home puja, a process whereby local households accrue merit by hosting—and paying dearly for—elaborate prayer ceremonies. A column of headlights appeared on the central plains, bouncing toward us, climbing the dusty switchbacks toward the monastery.

Lama Wangyal ushered me toward a white pickup truck. Two monks hopped into the cab before us. Old Sonam Wangchuk, who was stout, large-eared and heavily wrinkled. And beside him, younger but larger-eared Thukstan Chosphel. (Privately I nicknamed the pair Yoda and Baby Yoda, long before Baby Yoda debuted in *The Mandalorian*.) Lama Wangyal crammed in beside the pair.

With no space in the truck, I clambered over the tailgate, joining a wiry farmer in collared shirt, jeans and gumboots. We shook hands, but when I spoke, he waved me off.

The truck spluttered to life, then set off at a frantic pace downhill. A loose tire careened around the box and the farmer and I struggled to avoid it, crouched low, knees pounding up and down like shock absorbers. In the village, school children swarmed the truck, all seeking a ride to Padum. Our driver shook his head, and instead, two nuns hiked up their robes and crawled over the tailgate.

"Mortub, Mortub!" they beamed in recognition. "Where Norbu? Where Tashi?"

Before I could answer, the engine roared again and we raced off across the plains. Dawn was spilling over the eastern peaks, and with wind caressing my hair, for a fleeting moment, a sense of teenage immortality returned.

The truck bounced to a stop on a lonely section of road, and the nuns leapt out, carrying on by foot. We veered off the main road, jolting across boulder-strewn plains and splashing through shallow streams, eventually arriving at a constellation of six whitewashed homesteads tucked behind a thicket of poplars, on the banks of the Stod. This was Lama Wangyal's home, Neyrok.

In the largest homestead, a Zanskari woman was preparing butter tea using a wooden churn, known as a *gurgur*. A chunky turquoise necklace bounced as she worked, and her dark hair was tightly pleated. Probably no older than forty, she possessed a face creased from sun and wind, and eyes the color of the summer sky. For a fleeting moment, I thought of Christine—still suffering at the monastery.

"My sister's baby," Lama Wangyal introduced us. "Padma."

Sitting on the floor, Lama Wangyal began mixing milk, water and barley flour in a copper bowl, creating an immense ball of *tsampa*. After adding yogurt, sugar, cinnamon and yak butter, he rolled the mixture into a long snake while Baby Yoda sliced off pieces, molding them into *chorten*-shaped statues, with flared bases and pointy tops. Yoda stretched out beside the pair and fell asleep.

A nearby wall displayed the family's cookware: shelves lined with brand-new copper pots, kettles, pressure cookers, ceramic cups, saucers and plates—so many I couldn't imagine even a busy restaurant would need them all. Taped to another wall was a poster of Albert Einstein. Beiside it, a framed photograph showed a group of Zanskari businessmen in the middle of a muddy field, with *khata* scarves draped around their necks, huddled around the Dalai Lama. The pickup driver—Padma's husband, Tashi—stood amongst them.

A daddy-long-legs crawled into the *tsampa* bowl, and Lama Wangyal returned it to the floor gently, as if he were handling a kitten. Padma appeared with a Thermos of tea, head bowed low. She soon returned with bowls of *zorro*, a delicious porridge of whole-grain barley, flavored with butter, salt and sugar.

With fingers submerged in a basin of cold water, Lama Wangyal and Baby Yoda molded decorative flowers from yak butter, using them to adorn the statues.

After an hour, Baby Yoda nudged Yoda awake. Lama Wangyal handed me a tray of *jarden* and I followed the men up one ladder, then another, to the family's puja room on the top floor.

Lama Wangyal settled on a cushioned dais. Despite being the youngest of the three monks, he was also the most senior. Yoda and Baby Yoda flanked him on the floor. I sat against the opposite wall.

There was no definitive start to the ceremony. Rather, it spluttered to life, like an old diesel engine. Lama Wangyal fiddled with a peacock feather in the spout of an ornate brass kettle, sitting on the altar before him. He began to chant. He stopped. Then he started again, and the other two joined in. Then they all stopped and began looking around frantically, as if searching for something. What on earth did they want?

Pillows! I finally understood they wanted pillows, to support their backs.

Leaping up, I retrieved several from a distant corner. Next Yoda wanted a blanket, grunting in thanks when I handed him one, pulling the wool high across his shoulders until only his bald head and large ears emerged. Comfortable at last, the men leaned back and began chanting in earnest.

Lama Wangyal poured a slick of oil onto a silver plate, tracing complex patterns with his finger. He sent a spray across the carpet, smeared his cheeks, patted oil atop his skull, and finally, took a sip. Then the plate was passed to Yoda and Baby Yoda, who both performed the same ritual. Finally the oily plate came to me, and Lama Wangyal waved impatiently. *Get on with it!*

Reluctantly, I dabbed a bit of oil across my cheeks, spread some in my hair, and then raised the plate to my mouth, only to discover (with considerable relief) it was not oil after all, but rather saffron-infused water.

Chanting continued. One hour passed. Then two.

Occasionally Yoda grunted—a signal he wanted his butter tea refilled—and I leapt up to retrieve a Thermos. Padma appeared regularly, bringing fried chapattis, curried vegetable greens, *tsampa* and a clear broth containing chunks of yak and doughy dumplings.

Eventually Tashi strode into the room, wearing a blue suit and tie. He was departing for Padum, he told me, where he worked as a government clerk. It was time to go. Before slipping from the room I turned and bowed to the lamas, but not a single one looked up.

The three men wouldn't move for hours, chanting late into the night.

❧

Padum's medical dispensary lay on the outskirts of town, tucked amid a row of cinder-block shops selling fabric. The pharmacist, a reed-thin man hailing from the Indian foothills, retrieved three different types of antibiotic eye drops from a closet. I tried to decipher the ingredients, but they were listed in miniscule text that was impossible to read, so I bought all three. Total damage: seventy-eight rupees, or about a dollar and thirty cents.

Next I dropped by the Mont Blanc Cyber Cafe, hoping to complete Lama Wangyal's visa application. But Lichten, the owner, had not yet downloaded the required software.

"Connection very slow," he shook his head. "Maybe tonight possible?"

At a roadside tea stall, I drained several cups of sweet, milky chai while trying to hitch a ride. But cars were infrequent. I was striding home across the plains when a pickup lurched to a stop beside me, Hindi pop music blaring from inside the cab.

"Get in," shouted the teenaged driver, wearing a Yankees ball cap sideways.

He pulled his seat forward, and I squeezed onto the rear bench. A crumpled man wearing aviator glasses and a leather jacket sat in the passenger seat. I guessed he was the teenager's father. The pair were headed to Pishu, a village beyond Karsha.

The truck raced on at a breakneck pace. Dust devils danced across the plains. The cab smelled of liquor, and the passenger sipped from a bottle concealed inside a red plastic bag. Eventually he turned and asked my name.

"Mortub," I told him, and he scoffed.

"Calling you Mortub in Canada?"

The man appeared incensed and hammered me with questions. What did I know about Buddhism? Why did I pretend I was a Buddhist? Where did the name Mortub come from?

"Lama Wangyal," I admitted flatly.

"Oh," the father nodded, taking his sunglasses off and turning the music down. "Very good lama man. Sorry."

He didn't need to apologize. I imagined it must be hard for locals not to feel resentment toward foreigners like me, all apparently wealthy beyond imagination, crowding into puja halls, wearing beaded bracelets and T-shirts emblazoned with *Om mani padme hum*, buying trinkets and taking pictures and then disappearing—every one of them carrying home some romanticized vision of the valley, the Shangri-La they wanted to believe in.

On we sped, across the barren plains. Groups of uniformed school children were walking toward distant homes, hand in hand, and the pickup always slowed, allowing youngsters to toss backpacks over the tailgate and then wriggle aboard themselves. Soon more than twenty stood crammed in the back. I glanced at them through the rear window, and they waved in unison. Not one was older than ten years of age.

As the truck swerved and bounced on toward Karsha, the children swayed like a grove of poplars in the wind.

❧

Christine was waiting for me, and tried all three medications the moment I returned. One stung her eyes like hell and she tossed it aside. The other two didn't hurt, but didn't appear to help either, for the next morning her eyes were just as red and clogged with pus.

We were discussing what to do in the early hours, when Lama Wangyal bellowed from upstairs. "Angmo! Oh, Angmo!"

Christine's face went pale. "Oh my god. I think he might have found one of my tampons on the trail."

"What?" I asked incredulously.

Yesterday, she told me, she had stumbled upon a used tampon while walking the monastery trails. How appalling, she thought. What type of tourist would toss such a thing aside?

Then it dawned on her that it was the same type she had brought from home. Next came the horrific realization that the tampon was hers. Winds must have stolen it from Lama Wangyal's open-sided outhouse and carried it out onto the slopes. Mortified, she had scooped it up and dashed off.

"Oh, Angmo!" Lama Wangyal called again, more insistently.

"Wish me luck," she said, shuffling from the room and climbing the ladder toward his room.

Five minutes later, she was back, grinning.

Lama Wangyal had not discovered any incriminating evidence. Instead he wanted to pray for her eyes.

"He blew and blew and blew on them," she told me between giggles. "Spit went everywhere. Then he rubbed his *mala* beads back and forth across my face like he was scrubbing a pot. The crazy thing is they'll probably get better now. And we'll never know if it was the medicine or the spit that did it."

Minutes later Lama Wangyal's footsteps thundered down the hallway. Leaping up, Christine raced after the lanky man. It was her turn to accompany him for a home puja.

When she returned that evening, her eyes were clear.

12

THEY WERE THE LUCKY ONES

"Bruce!" Christine's shout sent a chill through me as I explored a catacomb of ancient dormitories, collapsing structures clinging to steep cliffs below the assembly hall.

I eventually spotted her on the abandoned rooftop, waving frantically, and my first thoughts went to the boys. Neither was with her. What had happened? Sprinting toward her as fast as I could, my lungs heaved and my legs felt heavy in the thin air.

"Is everything OK?" I gasped when within earshot.

"No. I mean, yes, everyone is OK. But Sonam Dawa is here. He's been waiting to see you for over an hour."

Our former guide sat on a pallet in our room. He leapt up and extended a hand as I rushed in, but I pulled him into an embrace, for we hadn't seen each other since arriving at Karsha Gompa ten weeks earlier. The quiet man, wearing a blue track suit and bearing the same sad eyes, had spent the summer constructing a guest house on the outskirts of Leh. He was visiting Zanskar for a few days to harvest potatoes on his family farm.

I'd forgotten how fluent Sonam was in English and peppered him with questions about life at the monastery, local traditions and Zanskar's history. Lama Wangyal joined us, bringing a plate of yak jerky and fried bread. The two men knew each other, and chatted as Christine and I prepared our boys for bed.

Eventually Sonam stood, brushing his hands. "OK, we go now."

It was a statement, not a question.

Apparently, Sonam had asked Lama Wangyal if he could take our family to his farm, an hour's drive away. The timing couldn't have been worse. Our boys were hungry, it was almost their bedtime and even the slightest change in routine could cause Bodi to break down, so I suggested we visit Sonam another time.

But Bodi interrupted. "What are we waiting for? Let's go."

Sonam clapped him on the back, and before Bodi's unexpectedly laissez-faire attitude could ebb, Christine and I quickly stuffed sleeping bags into a duffel.

As Sonam's white pickup bounced away from the monastery, Bodi and Taj sat with arms around each other in the back seat, giddily making funny sounds. Shortly after, both were asleep, mouths ajar.

An hour later, we crossed the Stod on a bridge of steel girders. Ahead, tucked in the shadow of menacing peaks, lay the tiny village of Shegar.

❧

Almost thirty years before our visit, during the winter of 1988, a severe storm dropped more than a meter of snow on Rimalik Range. As strong winds loaded the slopes further, the snowpack became dangerously unstable.

Shortly after midnight on March 8, what sounded like a gunshot rang through the barren mountains. As the fracture propagated, thousands of tons of snow were released, accelerating down a narrow gulley, gaining speed and momentum. Far below, directly in the avalanche's path, sat the tiny village of Shegar.

The snow brought complete destruction. Every homestead was buried. Forty villagers perished in their sleep, and all livestock was lost.

But miraculously, three villagers survived.

A husband and wife—lying together in bed and buried beneath four meters of snow—endured for three days, eating fermented grains of barley (the residue in the bottom of a cup of local beer) while a shattered chimney delivered whispers of air. A neighboring nun survived under similar circumstances. Rescuers wept when they discovered the survivors, for they believed they had been digging for bodies. *

---

* The trio never fully recovered, and the man wandered homelessly for years, viewed by many as a crazed yogi.

Spring revealed the extent of the devastation. Every house, stable, field, stone wall and irrigation canal was gone. The precious topsoil, cultivated over generations, was lost too, buried beneath tons of rocky debris.

Only a handful of Shegar residents were absent from the village that fateful night—including Sonam.

"I was very young then," Sonam explained as we drove on in darkness. "Just seventeen."

After finishing his third year of high school in Delhi, he had ridden trains and buses northward, racing over the Shingo La with school chums. Not until reaching the village of Kargiak did he sense something was amiss.

"Everyone looking funny. But no one saying nothing."

Finally, an elder took Sonam aside and tearfully explained his village was gone. Destroyed by avalanche. Among the dead: both his parents, four grandparents, seven brothers and sisters, two uncles and three aunts. All gone.

One uncle survived. The army colonel, who paid Sonam's school tuition, was stationed on the Pakistan front at the time. He had sent Sonam a letter bearing the tragic news—but the headmaster inexplicably never delivered it.

So when young Sonam arrived in Kargiak, he suddenly found himself alone in the world, without parents, home, possessions or money.

And he did the only thing he could: he kept on walking, toward the rubble.

❧

We arrived at dusk, bouncing down a valley stained with sadness, toward four homesteads tucked in a protected grove of willows.

Headlights revealed Sonam's wife, Tolma, on a stool outside their whitewashed homestead, milking a cow—a striking woman with high cheekbones, dark eyes and a wide mouth. Sonam explained their marriage had been arranged by his uncle, who, in the years following the avalanche, had assumed the role of Sonam's father. The couple's youngest daughter, three-year-old Norzing, clung to Tolma's knees.

Inside, we sat cross-legged on the kitchen floor while Tolma brewed tea. Bodi drew in his journal while Taj played hide-and-seek with Norzing—despite sharing no language. Sonam delivered Christine and me each a glass of Amrut whisky.

"Made in India," he said proudly. "Much better than China."

The amber liquid burned my throat, and I felt myself melting into the carpet. Time seeped by. More Amrut arrived. I was aware of Taj and Norzing chasing a spider. Bodi was talking intently with Tolma, but I couldn't catch the words. I glanced at my watch. It was 9:30 and dinner was nowhere in sight.

Such a moment may sound simple—chatting with friends, dinner slightly delayed, kids playing happily on the periphery—but in seven years of parenting a child on the spectrum, I could not recall anything vaguely similar.

"Is this really our family?" Christine whispered, leaning into me. "It can't last. We are going to pay for this."

Eventually Sonam tramped out to the garden with a flashlight gripped between his teeth. I joined him, gathering potatoes, onions, radishes and cardamom for dinner. He showed me a sun-bleached yak skull, perched atop a stone wall nearby. It had been killed the previous October by a *shen*, or snow leopard, among the world's most endangered, and elusive, cats.

"Many *shen* coming, every fall time," Sonam told me, a reminder of just how wild Zanskar remained.

Tolma prepared lamb curry, and we devoured it by the bowlful, drizzled with tangy homemade yogurt.

"Do you know how yogurt is made, Mom?" Taj asked, and Christine shook her head. "Well, first the cow eats milk and fills its stomach. Then it goes poo. And that's yogurt." He was dead serious.

It was past midnight when Sonam fell asleep with Norzing in his arms, sprawled across the kitchen floor. Tolma shepherded our family to an adjoining bedroom. After hauling fuzzy pyjamas onto the pair, we read each a quick story. Then I searched for a light switch. But there wasn't one. The bulb that burnt above our heads was wired directly to the main line, flickering on and off as service came and went. That wasn't going to work for our boys, so I cautiously unscrewed the bulb, mindful of bare wires stapled to ceiling logs. The room plunged into darkness.

❧

I awoke to the sound of a torrential downpour. Then the tang of bovine urine flooded the room, and I realized a yak was pissing outside an open window by my head. Tolma was already up milking cows under a slate sky. Two steel buckets of frothy milk were set on the fire to boil.

Later, Sonam and I led the cows to pasture, winding through a scrub forest—though we didn't so much "lead" the cows as drag them by nose rings, which one would think must hurt like hell, but nonetheless, the cows resisted every step of the way. After tethering the animals to wooden stakes, we set off to gather alfalfa, for there was no sense in walking home unburdened. A few other villagers were already there, cutting fodder that sprouted amid the rubble of the abandoned village site. Sonam showed me exactly where his family's fields once lay.

"Where was your home?" I asked.

Sonam pointed to a grassy rise nearby. Red and blue prayer flags fluttered from a solitary pole on its crest. A pond rimmed with brown reeds sat nearby, and a gull squawked noisily at our approach, but otherwise everything was still. Sonam explained that he and his siblings waded these waters as children.

"We always remember that day," he eventually said. "Each year I bring lamas here to praying."

I gazed up toward spectral peaks above, their summits obscured by cloud.

"The first avalanche came at noon," Sonam said. "But it was small and didn't reach the village. Because people had lived here for hundreds of years, they thought they were safe. So no one left. Then the big avalanche came at midnight."

After a long silence, I asked, "Do you feel sad when you come here?"

"Not anymore. I used to feel very sad, for a very long time. But not now. It's just my life."

A chunk of mountainside as large as a suburban home had come to rest nearby, and tucked in its lee was a small stone shack. I wouldn't have noticed it if Sonam hadn't walked over and opened the door. Inside, an old man sat beside the embers of a dung fire, roasting a charred leg of lamb. Sonam said a few words. The man grunted. We stepped back out.

Not until we were hobbling homeward, beneath towering loads of alfalfa, did Sonam explain the wizened man was his uncle—the same uncle who had served in the army, had given Sonam money for schooling and had arranged his marriage.

"He likes the old ways," Sonam said, as if to explain why he hadn't introduced me. "These days he not so happy. Too much changing."

I asked Sonam what he thought about the changes sweeping Zanskar, and he chose his words carefully.

"When I was young, people were very friendly. If they saw you in the fields, they would invite you for tea and insist you come, no matter what. If there was a wedding, they would physically force everyone in the village to attend. And make you stay late in the night.

"Today, no one invites friends for tea. And if they do, it's not coming from the heart. It's out of obligation. And they hope you'll say no, because they are busy. Everyone is busy. I'm busy. Everyone wants to buy mobile phones and fancy clothes and televisions. They want to join the upper class."

"Do you think people are happier now?"

Again, Sonam paused.

"Twenty-five years ago, people were very happy. They were fit. Both in body and mind. Zanskar was isolated in those days, so life was simple. Just learning about the Buddhism. And living in nature. Nothing else. People had lots of kids to help on the farms. Often there wasn't enough to eat, so some boys had to go to monasteries. They were the lucky ones, getting good education and good power. But to your question, yes, I think all people were more happy then.

"I remember being a young boy, playing outside my home with other children. We would watch the old men and old women of the village, sitting by the irrigation canal. All day talking, spinning wool or carving *mani* stones. They were happy. Every piece of clothing was made by their own hand. They didn't care about another world. Just Zanskar. They were at rest. Mind at rest. Body at rest. They were the lucky ones. Now people in Zanskar never at rest."

It was hard to imagine those with materially so much less than we enjoy today being the lucky ones. But I understood what Sonam was saying, and again I found myself wondering why modern progress couldn't seem to coexist with ancient peace. Why have we allowed so much of what brought us joy in generations past to seep from our lives? Collateral damage in the search for more? More of what? We walked in silence for a time.

"Today, families have less children. Two, maybe three. And parents have a different mind. If they have money, they send their kids to private schools outside Zanskar. Not to the monasteries. There is still a strong faith in the villages, but it's weakening. Less boys are become monks."

I asked Sonam if he thought Zanskar's monasteries could survive.

"Today, there are two ways for a boy to become monk. The first way is rare. A boy completes his schooling and then decides on his own, say at age fifteen or sixteen, that the monastery is where he wants to spend his life. Studying Buddhism. This is a very good route.

"Second way is pressure. Monks visit families every year and demand a boy be given. If the parents say no, monks refuse to do home pujas and no longer bless the fields, which is very bad for that family. So family always gives a child. But these boys are young, seven years or less. And so they aren't ready for such a big choice."

I thought of the novices in our class.

"Because *gompa* schools no good anymore, these young boys fall behind. By the time they realize *gompa* life is not in their heart, it's too late. The only thing they can do is become a taxi driver. Or a shopkeeper. The boys in the monastery today are the unlucky ones."

As if to illustrate his point, we passed a young man wearing a red ILLINOIS BASKETBALL hoodie on the trail. It was Sonam's nephew, Tenzin Choldin, who had been forced to join the Bardan monastery at age twelve. Three years later he ran away.

"Now what?" Sonam shook his head. "No schooling. No job. No future. Just passing his life. Very sad."

"For the *gompas* in Zanskar to survive, they must once again become institutions of high learning. But I don't think that will happen. Today, the lamas and monk boys, they are just drifting through life, doing nothing."

❧

Down a darkened hallway in Sonam's house was a puja room. The simple wooden altar held shelves of scripture, a brass *dorje* and bell, and a small statue of Buddha.

"These were only things to survive the avalanche," Sonam told us. "They were my father's."

In the spring, after the snows melted, the altar stood alone, untouched, amid a field of rubble. The books of scripture, Sonam explained, had come across the mountains from Bhutan, more than five hundred years ago, their hand-painted letters containing flakes of gold. He showed us a wooden printing block, used for making his family's prayer flags.

"Fifty years ago, every household in Zanskar making their own prayer flags. Today, they come by truck, from factories in China."

I turned the dark wood in my hands, the exquisite detail speaking of time and passion no longer common. Sonam told me it had been carved by his grandfather, who perished in the avalanche, sleeping beneath this very altar.

❦

Sonam was a busy man, with ambitious dreams.

The trekking company he'd started after college was celebrating its twentieth anniversary. He'd just finished building a guest house in Leh, and next summer, he planned to construct six tourist cottages on the banks of the Stod River. He was thinking of starting a rafting company. And he'd recently purchased three fallow fields from a neighbor, where he would plant potatoes come spring.

"The soil very good. Potatoes very easy to grow. Every day I see empty trucks leaving Zanskar. They should be carrying my potatoes, no? I will make too much easy money."

Sonam's iPhone was constantly buzzing. And little Norzing, who hadn't seen her father for three months, constantly fought with it for his attention. But he often brushed her aside when she crawled onto his lap, scrolling through messages instead.

❦

We were eating a breakfast of paratha—curried potatoes fried inside dough, served with a homemade salsa of tomatoes, onions and coriander—when three monks in robes appeared at the door. Sonam had sent the trio a text, inviting them to join us on a climb to the deserted Tselakche temple, on the cliffs behind his home.

The shortest of the men wore a down vest and red baseball cap, and said he came from Karsha Gompa, but I'd never seen him. He explained he lived in Padum during summers, where he managed the monastery's hotel, and only returned to Karsha when the snows fell.

The second monk was a *geshe* at the renowned Tashi Lhunpho monastery in southern India. He was in Zanskar visiting his brother, the third monk. That man, with a craggy face and stern air, was a *geshe* also, at Stongde Monastery, situated across the valley from Karsha. He stooped to pull our boys into a tight embrace, and I could tell at a glance they trusted him.

Tolma immediately brewed tea for the three monks and began preparing a meal of rice and dal. Suspecting the boys would climb more slowly, our family set off while the men ate, suggesting we'd meet them along the way.

The small monastery was perched atop a high band of cliffs, and we wound our way toward it, following faint livestock paths over rocky slopes. After two breathless hours, we emerged beside a squat temple surrounded by crumbling *chortens*.

The brush at this elevation was already turning mustard and crimson with the frosts of autumn. Dappled pools of sunlight drifted lazily up the Stod River, and far below I could see three maroon dots moving quickly across the scree.

Bodi scrambled atop a boulder to wait, sitting in the lotus position with closed eyes. While many in today's society seem to crave distraction—earbuds in gymnasiums or subways, phone calls while driving, scrolling through texts on the toilet, televisions in the background—our son instinctively abhorred it, and in this, he shared an uncanny parallel with the Buddhists.

"There is a lot going on in there," Christine whispered. "Sometimes I'll find him sitting quietly and ask him what he's doing, and he says, 'Oh, just praying.' Earlier today he walked straight into Sonam's living room and introduced himself to the monks without prompting. That's new—and exciting."

Sonam soon arrived with the monks. Unlocking the temple door with keys hung from his neck, he led us down musty hallways, past barren dormitories, to a small puja hall with an eight-hundred-year-old *chorten* rising in the center. Books of scripture still rested in cubbyholes, and the silk-covered altar was adorned with silver bowls and bronze statues. Finding a brass kettledrum tucked in a corner, the craggy-faced lama from Stongde hoisted Taj upon his lap, and the pair happily hammered out a chaotic rhythm.

Bodi spotted rupee bills tucked behind photographs of famous lamas, and asked if he could leave some of his money too.

"Of course," Christine told him. "I'm so proud of your generosity."

As youths, Sonam and his brothers stayed at the temple every summer along with other children from Shegar, learning to write and read in ancient Tibetan, the language of Buddhist scripture.

"Twenty-eight monks once lived here," he told us. "And many, many goats. Maybe fifty, or more. The garden was so beautiful then. Growing so much vegetables and flowers. This place always had a special feeling. Very powerful lamas would visit, bringing beautiful *thankas* and statues from far off places.

But these things are all gone now. It is bad luck that we have not preserved this history."

Up a shaky set of stairs we found a balcony overlooking the valley. All three monks pulled smartphones from their robes and snapped selfies of themselves with our boys on their laps.

✲

Sonam and I were leading his cows home when Hindi pop music broke the silence—a ring tone.

Sonam glanced at his phone but didn't answer. "Lama Wangyal," he muttered.

The phone rang again. Shaking his head, Sonam picked up.

I could hear Lama Wangyal barking in the background. Sonam yelled back into the device, as if the increased volume might help his words traverse the distance. After more shouting, Sonam hung up.

"What did he say?" I asked.

"He said bring family home now. But what is the rush?"

Sonam clearly wasn't ready for us to leave and suggested we ignore the call. Instead we should eat dinner, and he'd drive us home to the monastery the next morning.

Christine agreed. It was late, and our boys were exhausted. Sonam tried to call Lama Wangyal, to advise him of our plans, but the cellular network was down. I felt like a naughty teenager, staying out past curfew.

Hours later, the red glow of tail lights appeared outside. Christine thought she saw a silhouette of a monk in the passenger seat, and guilt washed over me. Sonam hid the bottle of Amrut whisky under the table and ran outside.

But it wasn't Lama Wangyal. Just a friend from Kargil, visiting his uncle. The whisky reappeared.

13

ALONE

Sonam dropped us at Karsha Gompa the next morning, and as we wearily dragged our duffel bags up the steep paths, I felt resentment building toward Lama Wangyal. Why had he called late at night and ordered us to return to the monastery? I suspected he would be annoyed by our disobedience, and momentarily wondered if he might have done something vindictive, like locking us out?

But the hobbit door swung open as we approached and Jigmet scrambled out, late for class. Breathlessly, he explained that Lama Wangyal had left the monastery at dawn. When I asked how long he would be gone, Jigmet sprinted off with a shrug and a wave.

Waiting on the carpet of our room was a bag of expensive treats: noodle soups, spicy Indian snacks and lollipops for the boys. I felt overcome with guilt. Lama Wangyal had only wanted to bid farewell to our family.

๛

Lama Wangyal never allowed the novices to visit our room—that was a privilege reserved for him alone—but with the strict disciplinarian away, Tashi Topden, Paljor and Jigmet began appearing at our door routinely.

"I think they miss their dad," Bodi commented, and I realized that until that moment, he had thought Lama Wangyal was the novices' father.

We were pleased to have the monk boys' company, but their presence in our room also proved stressful, for they were curious about everything and tried to disassemble whatever they laid their hands on: camera, headlamps, tripods, battery chargers. A Lego scene that had taken Bodi weeks to build was ripped apart in seconds.

Tashi Topden was particularly troubling. Ribbons of yellow snot dangled from his nostrils as he wandered our room in search of food. Everything went into his mouth: bubble gum, an entire bottle of chewable vitamin C, my pen, Lego mini-figures.

The novices seemed to live in a state of perpetual hunger, and with Lama Wangyal away, we heard them rustling about in the dark kitchen at night, nibbling on crusts of bread, gobbling leftover rice, pocketing apples.

One morning, Christine stumbled upon the trio in the hallway, a dusting of white powder covering guilty faces. What on earth had they gotten into, she wondered?

Later that day, we discovered our entire bag of milk powder was gone, eaten spoonful by spoonful.

❧

At communal lunch, Skarma sat alone, bent forward until his face rested on the concrete. Christine checked his forehead and found it aflame with fever.

She was leading Skarma toward the water barrel when he spewed lentils everywhere. The other novices swarmed, snickering and trying to push over their sick friend. Christine shooed them away angrily. Lama Norbu, the senior *lopon*, ordered Skarma to class. Instead, Christine snuck him home. Within minutes, the young boy was sleeping.

Tashi Topden soon appeared at our door, sent to investigate. Blocking the entrance, Christine shooed him away. Other novices arrived, racing into the room and shaking their sleeping friend, unleashing a flurry of questions. Eventually Christine locked the hobbit door. Skarma puked violently throughout the day and night, unable to hold down even a sip of water.

The next morning, Wang Chuk visited, probing the sleeping boy's belly, then sniffing a pot of vomit beside the bed. He explained that a special puja would be held that day in the neighboring village of Yulong, and "Skarma must coming."

I gently suggested Skarma should stay in bed and rest. A heated discussion erupted between Wang Chuk and Skarma, who was now awake. Eventually Wang Chuk stormed out.

By afternoon, color began returning to Skarma's cheeks. He sat up and nibbled at a piece of bread. Soon he was nestled between Bodi and Taj, flipping through storybooks. When I popped a set of headphones over his shaven head, playing ambient music from Enigma, a look of profound joy—and trust—passed over his face. And in it, I glimpsed, for the first time, the betrayal that our departure would feel like to these boys.

❦

For generations, the emerald fields surrounding Karsha—a fertile blip in a sea of rock and dust—had provided everything five hundred or so local villagers needed to survive.

Gazing upon the patchwork of crops from a boulder outside Lama Wangyal's, I was reminded of astronomer Carl Sagan's words upon viewing an image of Earth from space: "Look again at that dot. That's here, that's home, that's us. On it everyone you love, everyone you know, everyone you ever heard of, every human being who ever was, lived out their lives." And so it was with every village in Zanskar—a cosmos unto itself.

But just how big were those fertile fields?

Estimating the size of a plot of land is difficult, at least for me, and I'd been contemplating this quandary for weeks when I recalled a simple surveying method that might yield an answer.

Peter Hopkirk's *The Great Game*—a classic account of cat-and-mouse confrontations between Russia's Tsarists and Britain's Raj across the shadowy lands of Central Asia during the nineteenth century—describes a group of highly capable Indian spies, known as "pundits," trained in methods of reconnaissance and espionage. Dispatched on foot over the Himalaya by British Intelligence, these brave souls spent years disguised as pilgrims in sensitive borderlands, where if their true purpose was discovered, certain death would follow.

Among the pundits' camouflaged survey instruments was a prayer wheel fitted with a hidden compass, a wooden stave concealing a thermometer (altitude was determined by the boiling point of water), cowrie shells filled with liquid mercury (used to set an accurate horizon) and a collapsible sextant hidden beneath the false bottom of a travelling chest. But the most essential tool the pundits carried was a set of *mala* beads—specially modified to hold one hundred beads instead of 108.

Each man had been rigorously trained to maintain a precise stride, no matter what terrain was encountered—uphill, downhill, rocky, grass or snow. By slipping a single bead between their fingers every hundred paces, these spies were able to measure great distances with uncanny accuracy.

Nain Singh, the most famous of this under-recognized cadre, covered more than two thousand kilometers on foot, eventually reaching the Forbidden City, and returning from Tibet with cracked skin, sunken eyes and a scalp ravaged by lice. His measurements of latitude, longitude and altitude pulled back the veil on the high plateau, an act for which he was awarded the Royal Geographic Society's Gold Medal.

Sadly, the pundits kept no notes beyond geographic measurements, so little is known of their exploits. But their simple surveying tools remained in my mind, and I realized if I wanted to take a stab at measuring Karsha's fields, I could walk their perimeter while using my *mala* beads to record strides. Christine and the boys did not share my enthusiasm—instead they called me a geek—so I set out alone, *mala* beads in hand, leaving the others to watch over Skarma.

In the village square, two dilapidated trucks were being loaded with barley. Music played over tinny speakers, and children chased goats. Tsomo, our young friend from the guest house, spotted me and ran to my side. "Hello, *Aba*," she said in a husky voice, and I tousled her hair.

Then I set out, slipping a bead through my fingers with every step—but my fingers couldn't keep up with my feet. So I started again, this time slipping one bead for every two steps. Soon the noise was behind, and with beads counting strides, my mind was free to wander. Gradually I fell into a sort of meditative trance.

A redstart accompanied me along the stone walls, skimming ahead, ducking into crevices, then darting out again. We travelled together for some time, heavy-footed human and flitting bird, enjoying the autumn warmth. I passed red-throated skinks warming themselves on rocks, performing what appeared to be countless push-ups. A well-camouflaged family of chukar, a species of partridge, scattered at my passing. At the farthest margins of the village fields, I stooped to pocket a flat green stone inlaid with a cross of quartz—a perfect gift for my Anglican mother. The tang of the decaying poplar leaves came on the wind, transporting me in a flash home to Canada.

It took an hour to circumambulate the fields, and as I followed the creek back toward the village, I passed women whapping sudsy clothes against smooth boulders. Two naked boys hauled a bleating sheep into the frigid waters. Another group pushed a bicycle rim with sticks. Little feet pattered behind me, and seven-year-old Phuntsok caught up, his face streaked with blood. I asked gently if he was okay, and he nodded. Apparently a sheep had crashed into him.

We climbed back toward the monastery in silence, holding hands, until Phuntsok spotted a green ball lying on the rocky slopes and dashed off to retrieve it. It was a toilet float, and he held it quizzically toward me. How it ended up on the slopes of Karsha Gompa I couldn't imagine, but as I struggled to explain how the contraption worked, I realized Phuntsok had likely never seen a flush toilet before. Growing bored, Phuntsok heaved the ball back down the slopes.

Later that evening I did the math.

A counter string on my *mala* beads revealed I'd completed 17.25 rotations of the rosary, meaning I'd taken 3,726 strides and traveled a distance of 2.9 kilometers.* Simple arithmetic revealed that the village fields covered roughly one hundred hectares (250 acres), a trifling amount of arable land.

In North America, the standard diet requires 3.25 acres of land per person, meaning those fragile green fields could feed just thirty souls. But for centuries, here in Karsha, a population of five hundred had sustained itself on nothing else.

❧

Lama Wangyal returned four days later. I heard him fumbling at the hobbit door and quickly yanked the headphones off Skarma.

"Lama Wangyal," I whispered. "Look sick!"

The old monk strode in, and after hugging the family, headed directly to Skarma's bed. He tore the blankets aside, but Skarma was a good actor and now appeared to be on death's doorstep. After prodding his belly and yelling questions, Lama Wangyal threw the blankets back over him. He returned with a bowl of apples.

"For Skarma?" Christine asked.

"No!" Lama Wangyal said, looking appalled. "For Tashi and Norbu."

---

* The accuracy of the pundits' method was confirmed upon my return to Canada, when a satellite image yielded 2.92 kilometers as the circumference of the village fields.

I was often saddened by the contrast between how the Karsha monks treated our boys and how they treated the novices. As we munched on the bounty, I glanced down at the pallet beside me. One of Skarma's eyes was peering out from under the blanket. I winked. It winked back.

Later, I managed to sneak a precious apple from the kitchen. But when I brought it to Skarma's bed, he'd vanished.

❦

Lama Wangyal had been away visiting his youngest sister, Lamo, in the village of Tungri, some ten kilometers distant. He returned from her farm with two turnips the size of footballs, a bucket of yogurt, a rotting leg of yak and a sack of *tsampa*.

"Very, very good *tsampa*," he declared.

It had been milled that morning, by stone rather than machine, and he urged me to sample it. I did, finding the dough to be velvety, nuttier and richer than anything I'd tasted before. I made a second bowl, then a third, amused by the idea that I might be becoming a *tsampa* connoisseur.

Before departing for evening prayers, Lama Wangyal instructed our family to eat the yogurt he'd brought back for dinner. And by that, he meant the entire bucket.

At home, the idea of consuming twenty liters of yogurt in a single sitting would be abhorrent. Even if we had that much yoghurt in our fridge, we would ration it slowly over days, eating some for breakfast, putting a dash in salad dressings, using it for smoothies, perhaps mixing in a spoonful with berries for dessert. In the end, we'd probably throw some away. But Zanskaris operate differently. In the absence of refrigeration, they'd eat yogurt to the exclusion of everything else, in grotesque, stomach-stretching quantities, until it was all gone.

Apprehensively, I cracked open the bucket. A pungent whiff of fermentation wafted out, and a layer of yellowish whey floated atop the thick yogurt. There was no way we could eat it all, certainly not at once. But over the coming days, we did the best we could, adding the tangy mixture to cereal, feeding it to the boys for snacks, and even eating it with jam before bed. Still, we hardly made a dent.

When Lama Wangyal discovered the bucket tucked in a dark corner of the kitchen, still half full and starting to spoil, he charged into our room, shaking the evidence before my face. "You no eat? Why? I told you, eating!"

I had no answer.

The following evening, Lama Wangyal declared he was going to prepare a special dinner: yak *momos*, or steamed dumplings.

I was delighted. Since our arrival seven weeks earlier, we'd subsisted on an entirely vegetarian diet—apart from meager meat in communal lunches—and I was beginning to wonder if my perpetual sense of fatigue might be due to a lack of iron and not the high altitude. But my enthusiasm for the meal diminished when I saw the flank of yak, hanging from a nail in the earthen kitchen. Covered in bloody hair, it looked mummified and smelled rancid.

"Dead six months," Lama Wangyal beamed.

Soon a thudding reverberated through the house. Lama Wangyal sat on his haunches in the kitchen, raising a cannonball-sized rock overhead and then slamming it down upon gristle, tendon and bone, over and over and over. Eventually the yak dust was mixed with water, butter and curry to form a paste.

Next, Lama Wangyal rolled out a layer of crepe-thin dough, cutting circles using the lip of a cup. After popping a dab of meat into each, Lama Wangyal deftly pinched the edges together. Within minutes, he had produced a hundred or more identical dumplings, which he piled inside a five-level aluminum steamer.

Soon, a plate of *momos* arrived in our room. Lama Wangyal watched as I popped the first one in my mouth. It smelled like roadkill at the height of summer and tasted no better. I gave a hesitant thumbs-up. Lama Wangyal beamed, then turned to the watch the others.

"Ketchup might help," I coughed.

Christine retrieved the precious bottle we'd brought from Manali. Dousing a *momo* in ketchup, she took a nibble and gagged.

"Very good, Lama Wangyal!" she smiled, unconvincingly.

"What do you mean!" Bodi screamed, spitting out his. "It tastes disgusting."

"*Shhhh,*" Christine and I hissed.

"The *momos* taste disgusting. You know they do."

He didn't intend to be rude, but unaware of implications, his truth was always searing.

"Good, Norbu!" Lama Wangyal clapped, clearly not understanding. "*Zo! Zo!*" (Eat! Eat!)

Then he left to cook more *momos*. Immediately Christine dumped her bowl onto mine, followed by Bodi and Taj's. I stared at the pile in resignation.

Lama Wangyal returned, and seeing the three empty bowls, laughed. "Good, Angmo! Good, Tashi! Good, Norbu!" But he was not as impressed with my efforts. "Mortub bad eating man. *Zo! Zo!* Mortub."

Soon another steaming load of yak dumplings arrived.

"*Momo, momo!*" Lama Wangyal clapped, heaping more in all our bowls.

My eating marathon continued into darkness. Christine and the boys watched merrily from the sidelines, snacking on concealed crackers and apples.

❦

The sound of rock striking bone sent a wave of resignation through me.

We had been eating yak for days, in soups, curries and dumplings. Shards of bone and gristle crunched between teeth, and the rancid tang was so pervasive that it drowned out every other flavor. By now the odor oozed from my pores and permeated our clothing.

Brimming bowls of *thukpa* (or "local soup" as Lama Wangyal called it) arrived. It was the second batch of the day, and no one was hungry. We stared dejectedly at the bowls. I gagged down a spoonful, which left fat congealed on my stubble. When Lama Wangyal sat beside Taj, the tiny boy farted. Christine looked mortified, but Lama Wangyal clapped.

"Good, Tashi! Good *brrr, brrr.*" The passing of gas appeared to have enlivened the old monk.

"No *thukpa* in Canada, no *brrr, brrr.* Now much Zanskar food eating. And much *brrr, brrr* coming."

While Christine and I choked down our soup, the boys serenaded us with a joyful chorus of "*Brrr, brrr. Brrr, brrr.*"

When the soup was finished, Lama Wangyal dashed off toward the kitchen.

"Now I *momo* making. And everyone much *brrr, brrr.*"

14

THE GREAT SINS

Discipline in the classroom was a constant challenge. Our lessons often disintegrated into chaos, the monk boys shouting and shoving, stealing pencils from classmates and throwing textbooks over the cliffs outside. Christine was more tolerant of such behavior, confident we were still having a positive impact on the lives of the novices despite the bedlam. But as the weeks passed, I grew increasingly frustrated.

One particularly bad afternoon, I had had enough. Gathering the boys around the blackboard, I furiously scratched out a list of rules:

MR. BRUCE'S RULES
No Hitting
No Throwing
No Yelling

The novices diligently copied the list into their notebooks. Years of monastic schooling had made them excellent copiers. Of course, they didn't understand a word, so slowly and methodically, I explained each rule.

"No hitting," I said, then pretended to bonk little RamJam on the noggin, which elicited a round of laughter. "None of this. Understand?" The class nodded.

Then I threw a piece of chalk, which rattled off a wall. "None of this either!" The boys nodded. A few shifted nervously.

Yelling was harder to clarify, for I was already yelling, and even trusty Norphal seemed unable to translate the word. Eventually I screamed at the top of my lungs, "NONE OF THIS!" Twenty-one pairs of wide eyes stared at me in shock. It might have been the first time I had the entire class's undivided attention.

If anyone broke these rules, I explained, they would sit alone on the pathway outside for five minutes. But even as I turned back to the blackboard, I saw Tashi Topden crack Nawang over the head with a ruler. So off Tashi Topden traipsed to sit alone on the trail. It was going to be a long road.

Every day, we started class by reviewing these rules, and after just a week, we added a fourth.

It came when I witnessed Purbu spearing Phuntsok in the stomach with a pen, causing him to collapse. I knew there was a good chance Phuntsok had struck Purbu first, or stolen his books, for the young boy often antagonized classmates, but regardless, the incident saddened me. In this quasi–*Lord of the Flies* environment, cast adrift from parental love, constantly cold and hungry, these boys needed each other. Besides, they were supposed to be training as bloody Buddhists. So I gathered them around the blackboard again and solemnly added a fourth classroom commandment:

Be Nice

Then I gave an impassioned lecture about the importance of caring for each other. Flooded with emotion, I explained they were beautiful boys, every single one of them, and they were in this journey together, and they needed to watch out for each other, to help each other, to love each other.

I don't think anyone understood a word.

❧

A week later, Wang Chuk swooped into the classroom carrying a fragrant pot of sticky rice seasoned with coconut, apricot, cashews, almonds and dates. The novices quickly aligned themselves on the carpets with cupped hands held before them, and the gruff monk packed a snowball-sized lump into each. After devouring the treat, the boys raced out and dragged us with them, explaining an important puja was about to begin.

In the assembly hall, we found the lamas seated in silent rows, wearing their tall, ceremonial yellow hats. The Lost Boys wandered amongst them, distributing brass cymbals and silver bells. Two enormous skin drums had been hung from the ceiling, and a row of *tsampa* statues adorned the altar: colorful demons, deities and an unusual portrayal of Buddha himself.

Earlier in the week, a village elder had undergone stomach surgery in New Delhi, and now a puja was required to bless the man's recovery. After consulting astrological calendars, today had been deemed the most auspicious date.

Glancing around, I saw everyone was present: the lamas, the novices, the cooks. Even the Nepali laborers, who all had white *khata* scarves tied across their mouths. At the end of the ceremony, these men would carry the *tsampa* statues outside, and the *khata* scarves were to prevent anyone from accidentally breathing on Buddha.

Wang Chuk quarrelled good-heartedly with a plump lama beside him about whether cymbals should be held horizontally or vertically. Norgay the *tulku* caught my eye and waved. Butter tea was served. Drummers tested mallets. I took a deep breath and focused on the flow of air through my nostrils—in and out, in and out. Ta'han swung a silver box that billowed juniper smoke. A yellow banner flapped beside an open window.

Then the chant master led off.

Crooked sticks pounded on skin drums, and cymbals crashed. Chanting filled the room. As the astonishing throat singing of Lama Sundup soared above all, the instruments and voices seemed to meld into a single wondrous throbbing, as eternal as the mountains.

Suddenly the heavy fabric covering the door was thrown aside and light flooded the room. A group of tourists staggered in. "We haven't missed anything, have we?" demanded a curly-haired woman in oversized sunglasses.

During our months at Karsha Gompa, we'd occasionally encountered tourists on the monastery paths, but for the most part they arrived by bus, took a hurried peek around and then vanished again.

With nowhere to sit, this group crowded into the central aisle. A young German man pulled a camera from his pack and began taking close-up photographs. Lama Sundup waved him off, but to my amazement, the man ignored him. Another woman held an iPad close to Lama Ishay's face, without even acknowledging the ancient *lazur*'s presence.

I felt a surge of resentment.

While part of me wished we could have enjoyed the ceremony in peace, I knew our family held no special claim over the monastery. No, what really irked me was the insensitive use of cameras.

Photography raises many dilemmas for the modern traveller. If I yank out a camera, will I make my subject uncomfortable? If I wait, will I miss something? Do I really need a photograph of this? Or would it be better to just sit and observe? Will the presence of my lens alter events or separate me from the experience?

Of course, everyone answers such questions differently but, until recently—at least in my estimation—unsettling photographic situations seemed isolated. But the recent advent of social media seems to have changed all that, creating an urgency to document every detail of a journey. Images often appear to hold more currency than the experience itself, and this hunger is inciting increasingly disrespectful behavior.

No one in the tour group would have approached an elderly stranger on the street at home—much less in a cathedral—and pushed a camera to their face without first asking permission. So why did it feel okay here?

Perhaps I was being unnecessarily ornery? Lama Sundup was already laughing again, and none of the other lamas appeared perturbed. Who was I to judge? Even if I wasn't taking photographs, I was still etching these moments into memory—wasn't that just another form of memento I would take home?

A crescendo of drumbeats shattered such brooding thoughts. The yellow-hatted lamas leapt to their feet and swept down the aisles, picking up and carrying away everyone else, like flotsam.

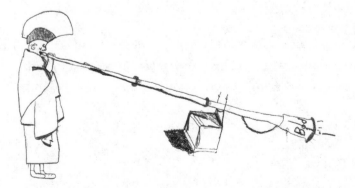

The dung-chen *is an enormous brass horn common in Tibetan Buddhist ceremony, which produces a deep, resonant wailing, often likened to the singing of elephants.*

Outside, Ta'han hoisted a banner high overhead and led a procession toward the rocky slopes. The Nepalis followed, each cradling a *tsampa* statue in their arms. Lama Sundup came next, hoisting a skin drum. Norphal played a *gyaling*, an ancient oboe-like instrument encrusted with coral and turquoise. Changchup blew into the *dung-chen*, an immense brass horn that produced haunting moans.

Beyond the assembly hall, everyone gathered around the Head Lama, who blessed the *tsampa* statues one final time. Then they were heaved down the mountainside, smashing to bits on the rocks below—a reminder of the impermanence of all things. Choughs quickly swooped in for a free meal.

Hours later, our family was playing tag with the novice boys when Lama Wangyal appeared and once again dragged us all to the assembly hall. Just a handful of senior lamas remained, along with the young German photographer, who sat beside us on a carpet. Tea was served. Chanting resumed.

I couldn't help but notice the young German man wore a Gore-Tex jacket and pricey altimeter watch, and as he prepared to leave, I leaned close and reminded him there was a donation box by the door. Perhaps it was unwarranted.

"Fuck off," he hissed. "I've already donated."

Later, as the ceremony wound down, the monastery accountant held aloft a handful of crumpled bills from the donation box that day. It totalled 120 rupees (two US dollars).

Lama Wangyal later told me the puja—paid for by the family of the sick farmer—cost fifty-four thousand rupees (920 US dollars).

❧

Bodi and I set out to climb a ridge rising above the nunnery. The surrounding slopes were dotted with wild rose, and when I mentioned the brilliant red hips contained a fantastic amount of vitamin C, Bodi paused to inspect the shiny fruit.

"You can eat these?" he asked incredulously.

"Sure. Wanna try?"

"Yes! I'd love to."

Harvesting rosehips has always seemed like a waste of time to me, hardly worth the effort required to garner a few nibbles, but Bodi's enthusiasm warmed me, and I plucked a few ripe fruits, cracking them between my fingers, carefully scraping away the seeds that lined the skin. Decades ago, someone warned me the inner fuzz could induce a fearsome cough, but I can't confirm the rumor, for I've never experimented. Now I handed Bodi a tidbit of flesh, no larger than a grain of rice, which he popped into his mouth.

"Oh, I love these," he said, rapturously, and began stuffing his pockets. "A snack for later."

Then he skipped away up the path as butterflies tumbled on the wind overhead, their gossamer wings the color of the summer sky. We were nearing the nunnery when Ani Garkyid's voice rang out, "*Jullay,* Norbu! *Jullay,* Mortub!"

She was weeding a vegetable garden, and beseeched us to pause for tea. I was about to decline, concerned Bodi might melt down—visiting the nunnery wasn't in our plans—but he happily agreed, "Oh, yes please."

We sat together in the shade of a willow, sipping milky tea and nibbling from a bowl heaped with apricots, almonds and raw sugar crystals. A toothless elder joined us, and Bodi held the bowl of snacks toward her, but she pointed to her barren gums.

Later, when we'd skipped out of earshot, Bodi said, "Maybe that's why they are called nuns? Because they got none teeth."

I grew fonder of these warm women with every encounter, impressed by their resourcefulness and enthusiasm, which they maintained despite enjoying just a fraction of the prestige—and patronage—accorded to their male counterparts.

Himalayan Buddhism has a dismal record with gender equity that stretches back to the time of Buddha himself, who reluctantly admitted that women could attain enlightenment, but declared after, "a nun that has been ordained a hundred years must bow down to a monk ordained for only a day."

The nuns' motivations appeared unquestionably pure to me—they had devoted their lives to Buddhism for reasons of faith alone—but in the complex economy of merit that drives Himalayan village life, a lama is regarded as infinitely more virtuous than a nun. As a result, monks are paid handsomely to perform pujas while nuns must labor in village fields just to meet their basic needs, rising in the darkness to perform morning puja, and only praying again after sunset.

As a result, many nunneries teeter on the edge of subsistence, while neighboring monasteries accumulate and enjoy vast fortunes. Of course with such affluence comes inevitable vices: greed, corruption and sloth.

"Men will be men," is how Sonam Dawa later explained such murky behavior to me.

"It's the same all over the world," Christine added with a sigh. "Why should the monks be any different?"

As Bodi and I continued our climb, my mind drifted to the Dalai Lama. If this extraordinary man, who had shepherded Tibetan Buddhism through unthinkable trials, were to leave the world with one final, revolutionary act, it would surely be declaring his intention to reincarnate in a female form—for if anyone can keep the flame of Buddhism alight in the Himalaya through the difficult years ahead, it would surely be the nuns. *

We followed livestock trails up rough, crumbling slopes. Clouds of locusts scattered beneath our feet, paper wings snapping as they flitted away. Only a nubbin of brush remained here, and the herds had long since passed to higher grounds.

We passed a water-smoothed boulder, larger than a mobile home, and I wondered how on earth it had come to rest alone on those slopes. Perhaps it had been deposited by glaciers? Or carried by outwash from icefields above? Whatever the case, it was a reminder that these mountains were still young and being shaped by cataclysmic forces.

We reached the top of the ridge an hour later, only to realize that it wasn't the top, for higher ridges rose beyond, stretching toward the horizon like corduroy. But this was good enough for today. A small barricade of stones—ankle high and shaped like a coffin—showed where someone had taken shelter during a stormy night. Bodi and I settled beside it, snacking on the rosehips carried in his pockets. Spiders darted through pebbles, and an aggressive male locust put on a spectacular mating display, attempting to copulate, unsuccessfully, with every passing female.

The sky was overcast, and the great valley appeared mute, as if sketched in pastel. Dust devils skittered across the plains below. The two great rivers, the Stod and the Tsarap, reflected the sky like veins of tarnished silver.

Amid all that desolation, a few scattered patches of green showed where villages stood. And beyond, forlorn peaks of ice and rock marched to the horizon. From this high perch, I could see for the first time what Zanskar really was: a

---

* The status of Tibetan Buddhist nuns has been improving under the current Dalai Lama, and in 2016—two years after our visit to Zanskar—a group of twenty nuns was granted, for the first time, a *geshma* degree: the highest level of Buddhist scholarship, equivalent to a *geshe* for monks, or a doctorate in the West.

fragile life raft bobbing amidst one of the most inhospitable landscapes on the planet.

I took a deep breath. Then another. Bodi sat beside me, perfectly still. With time, my thoughts settled. And without trying, I knew, in some odd way, I was meditating.

For years, I had glibly asserted that for me, "meditation" took the form of physical activity: biking, paddling or skiing. And while the intensity of such experiences certainly brings focus to the moment, it wasn't a frame of mind I was able to replicate elsewhere, at will.

But things were starting to change.

❧

When a group of French benefactors arrived at Karsha Gompa, they were housed in the classroom, and our lessons moved to a storage room above the kitchen. Dusty furniture was piled along one wall and cubbyholes lined the other. The boys sat on carpets, which Wang Chuk helped me drag up from the assembly hall. How long would we be stuck in this room, I asked, but he didn't know. Maybe a day? Maybe a month? Why did it matter?

One sunny afternoon, when Lama Wangyal asked Christine and Bodi to stay behind and polish statues on his altar, Taj and I arrived to find the make-shift classroom empty. We stood hand in hand in the doorway, wondering why everyone was late for class. Then I heard a giggle coming from the cupboards. The doors were locked, but eventually I coaxed one open, finding eight small boys tangled inside. Others were hidden under chairs and behind boxes. It took an exasperating amount of effort to get the group seated.

When I was finally ready to teach, I discovered the blackboard had disappeared. Thankfully I carried a sheet of laminated paper in my backpack, which I used as a tiny whiteboard.

My plan for the day was to discuss the five Ws (Who? What? When? Where? Why?) but none of the boys seemed to understand these words. I looked to Norphal for translation help, but he had vanished. Changchup, the second-best English speaker, was absorbed with a phone he'd found in the courtyard, left behind by a tourist. When five junior boys began wrestling, I broke them up and separated them among the older boys, but it did no good. Bedlam reigned. Losing my patience, I tossed the laminated whiteboard to the floor.

Everyone froze.

I was overcome with embarrassment. Had I blown the respect I'd struggled so hard to earn? What had happened to my carefully cultivated inner peace? In Zanskar, *schon chan*, "one who angers easily," stands among the worst insults, and losing one's temper is an act rarely forgotten.

It didn't matter. My efforts at exerting some semblance of control over the classroom had been futile, and having lost all heart to teach, I coolly told the boys to retrieve their workbooks. Soon they were sitting with heads down, copying sentences they didn't understand.

After five minutes, I calmed down. Not wanting to give up, I tried again.

"*What* is this?" I asked, holding up a pencil. "What? What?"

Hesitantly, a few responded. "Pencil?"

"*Where* is the pencil?" I asked, putting it on the floor. "Where?"

"Floor," someone yelled, and for the first time, I felt like I was getting somewhere.

I put the pencil behind my ear, and asked, "*Where?*"

Then on a table. "*Where?*"

Slowly the class began to perk up, and with it, my sense of hope.

"*Who* has the pencil?" I asked excitedly, dropping it in different boys' laps.

"Skarma has the pencil! Sonam! Phuntsok!"

I raced up and down the line, trying to ingrain these basic words. The older boys could not be restrained, shouting the answers aloud even when I was asking a junior boy.

After an hour, we moved on to mathematics, and I scrawled individual problems for each boy in his own notebook. They loved this and scuttled off to quiet corners where they sat with pencils in mouths, staring at their questions as if they contained some special magic—just for them. I was still writing out questions for the final boys when the first ones returned and started crowding around, throwing their notebooks on top of the pile while I worked, trying to get me to grade their work.

"No jumping the queue," I reminded them gently, sliding their notebooks to the bottom. Many still jostled for position, but a few lost interest and began playing tag.

I didn't see Wang Chuk enter the room, but I heard him. The gruff man screamed, though in their excited state, the boys didn't notice. Or they chose to ignore him. Charging into the fray, Wang Chuk grabbed Purbu by an ear and threw him to the ground. Then he reached to the rafters and extracted a long, thin stick. With a powerful swing, it snapped across Changchup's legs. The tall boy, still playing with the phone, ran off laughing. Wang Chuk next tried to rip a toy car from Nima's hands, but the seven-year-old refused to let go, even while being beaten.

Eventually, the dust settled. The school administrator had prevailed. The boys sat quietly on their carpets. Silently placing the stick back in the rafters, Wang Chuk left without a word. As my math lesson continued, I wondered if Wang Chuk thought I was a lousy teacher. Was his outburst meant to be a demonstration of appropriate discipline? Was it his way of saying, "Okay, Captain Canada, here is how it's done"?

Despite my best efforts, the classroom dissolved into pandemonium again, and by the time four o'clock finally arrived, my short-lived hope had evaporated. Packing up our supplies, I trudged wearily out the door with Taj in hand.

Wang Chuk was crouched on his haunches outside, tossing balls of *tsampa* to waiting choughs. I squatted beside him, ashamed of my inability to control the class. But he shook my hand eagerly, as if it were the first time we'd ever met, and then pulled Taj onto his lap. Apparently the mayhem of the day had washed over him without notice.

But not me.

I returned to Lama Wangyal's, mired in depression. It felt like I was floundering, and our efforts to make a difference in the lives of these novice monks was nothing more than an illusion—the well-intentioned but ill-conceived desire of a foreigner.

Christine disagreed, pointing out that if we could make a positive impact on just a single boy, that would be a success. "Look at your progress with multiplication tables. And think how much English they are speaking. Some barely knew a word when we arrived."

Grudgingly, I admitted she was right.

But I remained disheartened, moping around our room. We'd left Canada five months earlier, and for the first time, I felt homesick. I was tired of banging my head on ceilings. I was tired of being watched everywhere I went. I was tired of being dirty. I was tired of spending more time disciplining the novices than teaching them.

I found myself fantasizing about the simple pleasures of home: a warm shower, clean sheets, a cheeseburger, Saturday night hockey. My brain felt starved, and I yearned to read a magazine, listen to the news or even just aimlessly surf the Web.

"You're in the depths of it," Christine sympathized. "Be patient. It'll pass."

Her despondence had lifted weeks earlier, and she was at peace again. "We only have a month left. You should make the most of it."

❧

I was brushing Taj's teeth under a starry sky when the hobbit door swung open and Lama Wangyal burst from the house, braying like a donkey.

Two novice monks had been lingering in shadows nearby, unbeknownst to either Taj or me. Lama Wangyal began furiously whipping one across the face with a stick. What the fuck? I was horrified and remained frozen, not wanting to watch but unable to turn away.

The thrashing continued, but the boy never flinched. Or cried out. Instead he pulled his robes across his face and stood his ground, as if leaning into the wind. In the darkness, it was impossible to tell who was suffering such a beating. (Later I would learn it was shy Paljor, who apparently had skipped puja to visit his family in the village below.) Eventually, both monk boys dashed into the house, and Lama Wangyal followed, still roaring.

Not one of them had noticed Taj and me standing nearby.

I felt sick. Thankfully Taj appeared oblivious to the drama, and dashing inside, he kissed Christine goodnight before crawling into his sleeping bag. Soon he had drifted to sleep.

As shadows filled the room, I explained to Christine what I'd witnessed. She'd observed a similar interaction in puja, when young servers had failed to appear with tea on time.

"I try not to place unrealistic expectations on the monks," she admitted. "They are only human after all. But still, beating a kid in the face with a stick seems wrong."

It sure seemed pretty damn un-Buddha-like to me.

I'd never been inclined toward corporeal punishment. And raising Bodi—with his sensitivities, extreme reactions and occasional public meltdowns—had shifted my views even further away from unbending discipline and toward compassion.

As I lay in bed, watching a stain of moonlight spread across the ceiling, I felt as if something had cracked inside me. A line from Peter Matthiessen's *Snow Leopard* floated over and over through my head: "The great sins, so the Sherpas say, are to pick wild flowers and to threaten children."

NOTHING LASTS FOREVER BUT THE EARTH AND SKY

Conditions like autism, dyslexia, and attention-deficit/hyper-activity disorder (ADHD) should be regarded as naturally occurring cognitive variations with distinctive strengths that have contributed to the evolution of technology and culture rather than mere checklists of deficits and dysfunctions.

—Steve Silberman,
NeuroTribes

15

THE GODS WITHIN

I lay before the sunlit windows, lazily reading, when Lama Wangyal banged through the hobbit door. He strode past our room without a word, his footsteps fading up the creaking ladder.

Since I'd witnessed his beating of Paljor a week earlier, the old monk had seemed unusually curt. He no longer visited Christine and me at night. Nor did he poke his head into our room each morning to say *jullay*. While I'd come to terms with the incident, and felt no animus toward the old monk, I wondered if he had perhaps been aware of my presence during the incident. Did he feel embarrassed? Or maybe he was simply fed up with our family's noisy company. After all, we had been crammed into his tiny home for two months, practically living on top of each other.

Just then, Lama Wangyal bellowed, summoning me to his room, "Oh, Mortub! Oh, Mortub!"

I scampered up the ladder, worried the end of our welcome might be drawing nigh. Was he going to ask us to leave? Maybe suggest we move down to the guest house?

Instead, as the door to his small room swung open, Lama Wangyal held a traditional Zanskari robe toward me. "For you," he beamed. "From dead person."

How vastly unattuned I remained to the events and moods unfolding around me at Karsha Gompa.

Made of purple hand-carded wool, it was musty and worn—and, to my eyes, beautiful. Lama Wangyal explained he had bought the robe that morning, when the personal effects of a deceased villager were auctioned for the benefit of the monks.

Remarkably, it looked large enough to accommodate my tall frame. I slipped my arms into the sleeves and it fit perfectly, the heavy fabric hanging to the floor. My fingertips discovered a scattering of barley grains in the depths of a small pocket. Lama Wangyal cinched a fuchsia sash around my waist, and then stepped back to admire.

"Good, Mortub," he said. "Very good."

I loved the robe, and in that moment, overcome with emotion, I was certain I'd cherish it for the rest of my life.

"Cold coming soon," Lama Wangyal grimaced.

Then he waved me away, settled on his mattress, and began to chant.

❧

The next morning, I pulled on the heavy robe, revelling in its warmth as I brewed tea and then slipped outside. The Nepalis were working nearby, shoveling gravel through a screen. Leaning on their tools, they greeted me with a chorus of "*Namaste daju bhai!*"

"*Namaste daju bhais*," I shouted back.

The air was perfectly still. Far below, a flock of sheep flowed like milk down a narrow village lane, driven by two skipping boys. In nearby fields, farmers burnt slash, and beside the stream, shadowy women washed clothes. An occasional laugh floated up. Across the valley, a dusting of fresh snow clung to scabby foothills. And above, Himalayan giants smouldered purple in the gathering dawn.

Could a person ever tire of this view?

❧

Whispers began to swirl that the monks were creating a harvest mandala—a fantastical and highly complex painting made from colored sand. So after class I set off with Bodi and Taj to investigate.

Karsha's original and most ancient temple was Labrang, a fort-like structure situated just inside the lower gates. Home to the monastery's granary, the temple held the stockpiled barley taxes collected from local villagers, alongside tariffs of butter and firewood. Sacred relics were secured in a dungeon-like vault, including a tooth rumored to have come from Buddha's own elephant and the seventeenth-century robes of the Panchen Lama.

Beyond a door framed by crooked posts, and thick yak-hair blankets, we entered a barren hall, roughly the size of a school gymnasium. Silken banners of red, orange and yellow hung from the low ceiling, and a two-storey statue of Buddha rose behind the altar. Since it was too tall for the room, a hole had been cut in the ceiling, through which the head poked out into sunlight. Frescoes adorned the mud walls, dating from the fifteenth century. Sadly, recent rains had damaged much of the imagery, leaving it slumping, like molten wax.

"Oh, Norbu! Oh, Tashi!"

The Lost Boys were sprawled across the floor in a far corner. Lama Mortub, the monastery accountant, lay amongst them. Ta'han rose creakily, pouring us cups of sweet, milky tea and offering fried bread.

Eventually Lama Mortub beckoned us, and we followed him to a large sheet of plywood, resting waist-high on boxes. A complex design had been sketched in chalk across the plywood's surface, and copper bowls lay scattered around it, filled with colored sand in every hue and shade imaginable. A few strands of sand swirled outward from the center, like worm trails on a beach. This was the start of the mandala.

Lama Mortub climbed carefully onto the platform, followed by three young proteges, and the quartet settled cross-legged on the periphery. The mandala was perfectly symmetrical, divided into four identical quadrants, and each man was responsible for one.

Without words, they began to work.

After studying a blueprint, each artist searched for the needed color. If a precise match could not be found, it was created by mixing sands together like paint. The sand was then poured into a long, narrow metal funnel known as a *chak-pur*, and by running a rod over the funnel's serrated surface, fine-grained sand flowing from the spout, the monks were able to "draw" with sand.

The work was painstaking, for correcting a mistake would be impossible. Attempting to nudge even a few errant grains could induce a catastrophic unravelling. So the men took their time, steadying their forearms on piles of small pillows and rehearsing every stroke. When at last ready to apply sand, the artists took a deep breath and entered a stillness reminiscent of meditation.

Each worked at his own pace and rhythm, and slowly a splendor of motifs bloomed: scepters, flames, flowers, castles and thunderbolts. Occasionally, after a particularly intense session of sand painting, one of the monks would shake his arms. Or throw a head back with closed eyes. But no one got too far ahead of the others, and there was unity to their progress.

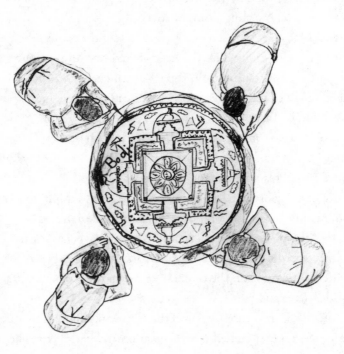

Four monks at work on a mandala. The fantastical sand painting
is meant to represent the physical universe, acting as a reminder, in
its destruction, of Buddhism's core tenet of impermanence.

A support team hovered on the periphery, retrieving anything needed by the artists: another pillow, more sand, a cup of tea. Slowly, the mandala inched outward.

Taj and Bodi watched for a time, and I prayed neither would sneeze. Eventually the pair lost interest and drifted off to investigate the altar. Finding a scattering of rupee bills, Bodi asked if he could run home and get some of his own money to give Buddha.

"Of course," I said, and he dashed off.

Soon he was back, huffing and puffing, with a hundred-rupee (two-dollar) note. Painstakingly he balanced the bill atop a silver plate. Then he spun and spun, and spun some more.

The clinical term for such behavior is stimming—an unconscious means of self-soothing, or controlling anxiety. All of us "stim" to some extent, whether we know it or not: tapping pencils, twirling hair, pacing while talking on the phone. But those on the autism spectrum tend to stim more frequently, and more gregariously, to the point that it can interfere with life.

As I fondly watched my son, he laughed and spun and giggled—and then accidentally knocked over an immense candle, plunging the temple into darkness. Only the hole in the roof, above Buddha's head, provided a glimmer of daylight.

"No problem, no problem," came the soft voice of Lama Mortub.

A flashlight snapped on. Ta'han tossed me a lighter. Soon the room was bright again. After setting the candle atop the wooden crate, I scraped up the hardening wax.

Before chasing the boys outside, I surprised myself by bowing, ever so slightly, to the golden statue rising before me. The gesture was wholly unexpected, but in the moment, felt perfectly right.

❧

Dark clouds poured into the valley the next morning, engulfing the peaks. Surrounded by mountainsides, it felt as if we were living in a box—with the lid closed.

When it started to drizzle, tarps of blue, yellow, white and orange were hastily dragged across haystacks in village fields below, leaving them looking like fairy-tale mushrooms. By evening Karsha Gompa was shrouded in mist, and I wandered the trails of that shadowy world, my purple coat whipped by winds.

Strong gusts raked the cliffs that night, and droplets splattered against windowpanes by my face. I lay awake, hoping Lama Wangyal's roof could withstand the deluge. A thunderstorm passed frighteningly close, and Bodi cried out. As I comforted him, lying forehead to forehead, I could hear Lama Wangyal chanting upstairs.

❧

The storm passed after three days, leaving wispy clouds trailing from mountainsides like *khata* scarves.

Eager to stretch our legs, our family set out for a walk after puja. The village streets were crowded—locals emerging as if from hibernation. Tarps were yanked from haystacks. Drying clothes fluttered along fences. Toddlers splashed in ditches. A merlin hunted over plowed fields. Even the swallows celebrated, feasting on a banquet of freshly hatched insects.

The stone-walled laneways were clogged with bleating goats and sheep that had returned from the summer *doksa*.* We were particularly mindful of the yaks, grazing on a stubble of barley and alfalfa left behind after harvest. Increasingly aggressive with the approaching rut, they snorted and crashed headlong into one another, the earth shaking with their collisions.

Wandering with no particular destination, we all paused to marvel when Taj spotted a caterpillar the size of a small banana. Nearby, in a muddy meadow, barefoot women were stomping out flat platforms the size of parachutes. After the sun dried these circular pans, teams of yaks would be attached to a central post and driven in circles, threshing barley seed from chaff beneath their hooves.

On the way back to Lama Wangyal's home, we stopped at Labrang, so Bodi and Taj could show Christine the mandala. An astounding amount of progress had been made, the sand now almost reaching the edges of the plywood. After working for six days straight, the artists were exhausted and had entered a trance-like state, glancing up briefly before returning to their work. Thankfully, the end was in sight.

"Maybe tonight finishing." Ta'han slurred his words.

When we returned home, Lama Wangyal presented Christine with her own Zanskari robe, which he had bought at another funeral auction. She too was deeply touched by the gift—though being less nostalgic than I, suggested in private the coat might not make the return trip to Canada.

"I can't imagine wearing it in Kimberley," she laughed. "Seriously, Kirkby, why do you want to take yours home? It'll just end up in the bottom of a closet."

---

* Zanskaris don't differentiate between sheep and goats, keeping the animals in the same herd and referring to them to by the same name: *ra luk*, which literally means "goat sheep" in Tibetan.

But I couldn't imagine letting go of Lama Wangyal's gift. I suppose it symbolized all of Zanskar's intangible gifts to me: a peace I didn't yet entirely understand, and was scared of losing.

But here, for the time, the robes felt perfect to us both. And later that evening, we were wearing them—huddled close, gazing over the moonlit valley—when a disharmonious racket echoed across the mountainside.

Horns! On and on they wailed.

We raced inside, worried the clamor might have roused our boys, but Bodi and Taj slept soundly. Christine was ready to crawl into her sleeping bag, so I set out alone to investigate.

Following the racket down darkened pathways, I spotted four silhouettes standing atop the Labrang roof. Tsephal and Paljor were blowing into brass *gyaling*, fingers hopping indiscriminately up and down the jewelled instruments. Beside them, Norphal and Changchup blustered into a pair of enormous *dung-chen*, the flared bells resting on the parapet. The mandala had been completed, and the boys were summoning Guhyasamaja, the great Gelugpa protector. His temporary home among the grains of sand awaited.

The tangled music was a signal to the village, the valley and the entire universe that tomorrow at sunrise, ancient rites would begin.

❧

Horns sounded again at daybreak. Rousing the boys, Christine and I pulled on puffy jackets, grabbed tea bowls and raced outside. The monk boys stood on the roof of Labrang, joyfully blowing into their ancient instruments.

Inside, we found the prayer hall empty. An elaborate yak-butter statue stood on the altar. Three feet tall and as delicate as lace, it had taken the Head Lama a week to craft. The mandala was hidden from view by four *thanka* paintings. I unrolled a carpet and we huddled together at the back, boys tucked between Christine and me.

Eighty-two-year-old Lama Ishay was the first to arrive, shuffling down the central aisle with robes dragging behind him. Other senior lamas followed, all wearing ceremonial yellow hats. Monk boys raced amongst them, stocking feet sliding on the wooden floor like ice skates. The disciplinarian prowled the aisles, an orange hooded robe hanging from his shoulders and a hardwood staff in hand. Lama Norbu, the Joker, paused before our family and playfully pretended to kick Bodi and Taj. Then he turned to the great golden Buddha, its head buried in the ceiling, and dropped to hands and knees, prostrating three times.

As the first shaft of direct sunlight penetrated the hall, shining on Buddha like a spotlight, the chant master's voice rang out. Singsong chanting grew, crested, subsided, then erupted again. Butter tea was served. Paljor distributed shiny biscuit packages, fried bread and sweet cinnamon rice. Ta'han shuffled to the central aisle and recited scripture while throwing rice in the air. But he must have been mixing up the words, for Wang Chuk corrected him continuously. Eventually he slunk back to his seat, head hung low. Then more butter tea. And more chanting.

I was trying to imprint the marvellous scene into my mind when I became aware of a faint tickling on top of my head. The sensation stopped, then started again. What could it be? Suddenly suspecting a spider, I whipped a hand across my scalp. But my fingers found a warm hand?

Standing over me, tears of laugher streaming down both cheeks, was Changchup. While waiting to serve another round of tea, he had been gently pulling on a strand of my hair.

Glancing around, I realized the entire congregation was watching with glee. Even the Head Lama was bent over in hysterics.

❧

For six straight days, a celebratory puja was held in Labrang. On the seventh day, the mandala was destroyed.

First, the lamas gathered in the courtyard, under a scorching sun. Robes were draped over bald scalps. Christine and I tucked our boys in the shade of a rose bush. The monastery's dog, a ferocious-looking black mastiff—said to be the reincarnation of a less-than-holy monk—was chained to a tire nearby, melting into the concrete.

A fire pan was stacked with dung, doused with butter, and the pyre lit. The Head Lama heaved rice, barley and peas into the flames. As Lama Sundup delivered an endless train of offertory plates, he probed the depths of his nostrils with a finger. Nose picking is perfectly acceptable in Zanskar: farmers, businessmen, grandmothers and children alike never hesitate to plunge a finger in mid-conversation. It is understandable, for dust and parched air can lead to horrifically crusty snot, and I often awoke feeling as if a hazelnut were lodged up my nose.

The ceremony dragged on. Taj dozed off. Tashi Tsering, the bowlegged cook, doled out rice. Wang Chuk corralled the novices and led the class around the fire with trumpets, conch horns and cymbals blaring. The burly disciplinarian fell asleep with his mouth wide open.

My thoughts settled on my breathing, and as I gazed across the barren valley—a landscape devoid of physical distraction, resting under a dome of depthless blue sky—I understood Zanskar as the physical manifestation of a meditator's mind.

One breath in. Another out.

A blue sky metaphor is often employed in meditative teachings. When storms descend upon our lives, as they inevitably do, we tend to focus on the clouds—problems, conflict, anxiety, distress, depression—forgetting that the blue sky is always there, but hidden from view, somewhere above. Like an airplane breaking through the clouds, meditation is meant as a conduit to that peace, accessible to anyone at any time.

One breath in. One breath out.

Maybe this is why a culture of peace and meditation flourished on the Tibetan plateau, because the landscape provides a constant reminder of where the mind could be. Whatever the case, in that moment, a stillness descended such as I have rarely known. It was as if my thoughts drained out into the grand valley. I became part of it. And it part of me. The borders between the physical and spiritual blurred; the land, the monks, the peaks, all one.

I have no idea how long this state of supreme relaxation lasted; it could have been minutes or hours, but it was interrupted by everyone leaping to their feet and running toward the Labrang. Feeling disoriented, I chased after them.

Inside, the silken drapes concealing the mandala were yanked aside. The Head Lama blessed the creation a final time, and by extension the entire Zanskar valley. Then he raised a brass *dorje*, and with a slash, destroyed it.

My heart sank to witness the destruction of such gorgeous artwork, but the surrounding monks appeared unmoved. Some hardly paid attention.

Using a whisk, Ta'han quickly swept the sand into a pile, the once-brilliant colors reduced to a uniform drab purplish brown. The sand was then deposited in a copper urn. Horns blared again, and the congregation surged outside. Ta'han set off down the winter trail, copper urn held overhead.

Nearly everyone else—forty monks or more, along with Christine and our boys—slouched off toward the village, where a truck laden with loudspeakers had arrived, and an outdoor Hindi dance party was underway.

I followed a handful of senior lamas into the depths of the gorge. Beside a shady pool, Lama Norbu, the senior *lopon*, lit a bundle of incense as thick as a forearm, using the smoke to purify the surroundings and each member of our group. Sutras were chanted as the Head Lama waded into the splashing stream and emptied the urn.

A stain spread across the pool, purple fingers slowly reaching downstream. Crouching on the banks, the lamas sipped the murky water with cupped hands, then splashed it over shaven heads. Wang Chuk dabbed a wet finger to my forehead, then held cupped hands to my lips—and in that water I tasted the mountains.

A passing shepherd raced to retrieve an empty soda pop bottle from his rucksack, and quickly filled it from the stream as the symbolic universe, built over the course of an exhausting week, washed away.

16

LIFE IS THE CEREMONY

We had been at the monastery for two months when Lama Wangyal hurried into our room one evening. Christine and I were reading by headlamp.

"Packing! Packing!"

A jeep would arrive at first light, he explained, to carry him and us to his sister's homestead, in the village of Tungri. How long would we be away, I asked? What about teaching? But I got no answer; Lama Wangyal's footsteps were already fading down the earthen passageway.

It was pitch-black when he pounded on our door the next morning.

"Oh, Mortub! Going now!"

I glanced at my watch. It was 5:45 A.M. The jeep had arrived early. Leaping up, Christine and I shook the boys and began stuffing sleeping bags into duffel bags. Taj refused to get out of his pyjamas. Bodi was in tears, searching fruitlessly for a lost piece of Lego.

"Hurrying!" Lama Wangyal yelled from the hall. His footsteps faded and the hobbit door slammed. We stumbled after him, Taj in pyjamas, Bodi sobbing.

A dilapidated Toyota pickup waited at the monastery gates. Tossing our duffel into the back, our family crammed into the rear of the cab: Bodi on my knee, Taj on Christine's. Lama Wangyal took the front seat. The vehicle lurched away into a crimson dawn.

Instead of following the main road south toward Padum, our driver veered west, bouncing along a dirt track in the shadow of the Zanskar Range. Soon we left Zanskar's central plains and entered a narrowing valley leading toward the headwaters of the Stod. The land grew increasingly rugged, the steep mountainsides dotted with shattered boulders the size of cars. Amid the rubble, I spotted an eagle hunting.

An hour later, the green fields of a village appeared. The pickup jolted to a stop beside a whitewashed *chorten*. Lama Wangyal leapt out, grabbed his bag and set off, maroon robes vanishing down a narrow trail. I shrugged, and the driver shrugged back. Dragging our duffel from the back, we took the boys in hand and raced after the monk, following muddy paths along the edge of irrigation canals.

We found Lama Wangyal outside a two-storey whitewashed homestead with traditional ochre-trimmed windows and a flat roof. A flagpole, draped with sun-bleached prayer flags and topped with a yak tail, signalled that all sixteen basic volumes of *Kangyur* were housed within. A humble garden held carrots, radishes, onions, cardamom, potatoes and peas. Lama Wangyal pounded on the door, but no one answered. Pressing his ear to the wood and hearing nothing, he retrieved a key from underneath a wash basin.

Beyond a pungent stable, concrete stairs led up to the family quarters: four empty bedrooms, a cold storage room (crammed with sacks of grain, barrels of barley beer and buckets of yogurt) and a windowless kitchen, where kettles and cauldrons hung from hooks above a dung-burning stove.

Lama Wangyal immediately began cooking dal in a pressure cooker, while our boys amused themselves by spinning a pair of squat prayer wheels, neon in color and the size of turntables. When the food was ready, the old monk packed it into a wicker basket. Then together we set off in search of his sister.

The pathways were bustling, and everyone bowed to Lama Wangyal. He questioned a few, and all pointed north, toward the outer village fields. Twenty minutes later we arrived at a small plot of golden barley, roughly the size of a suburban lawn. Crouched, and pulling grain by hand, were Lama Wangyal's sister, Lamo, and her husband, Dorjey.

Lamo squealed upon spotting our boys. Her brow was streaked with mud, and two greying braids emerged from beneath a knit beanie. Wearing a purple jumper and baggy harem pants, she chased the giggling pair with her tongue sticking out.

Dorjey, her husband, rose more wearily. Wearing soiled jeans and a red polo shirt, he was a lithe man. Veins snaked across his taut biceps. A tightly cropped moustache was the only sign that he was a *havildar*, or sergeant, in the Indian Army—currently on leave to help with harvest.

Two elderly women emerged from the field of barley, both wearing homespun robes and necklaces of turquoise. One was Dorjey's mother. (Dorjey's father, we were told, was in a nearby field, peeling logs.) The other woman, introduced as Doda, stared at us blankly, toothless and mute. Sewn to the brim of her floppy orange hat were a silver pendant, a picture of the Dalai Lama and a child's plastic sea star. She evidently was developmentally delayed in some way, but here she was in the fields, working alongside everyone else, contributing to the community.

All of them—Lamo, Dorjey, his mother and father and Doda—were members of the same *paspun*, a tightly bound group of households who supported each other at times of birth, marriage and death, and who worked co-operatively during the busy seasons of harvest and planting. As a social institution, the *paspun* is unique to Zanskar, and every family, in every village across the entire valley, belongs to one.

It now became clear why Lama Wangyal had dragged us here. Our family had been recruited, at least temporarily, to join Lamo's *paspun*—which suited Christine and me just fine.

Work paused while we unpacked the wicker basket in the shade of sea buckthorn bushes. Bowls of steaming dal and rice were quickly dispatched. Flatbread was washed down with a jug of *chang*.

Chang, or fermented barley beer, is a collegial, congenial drink I was familiar with from my time among the Sherpas. Milky and mildly alcoholic, it confers a glowing cheerfulness unlike any other libation I have known. Best of all, being rich in vitamin B, it rarely induces a hangover, which is a good thing, for *chang* is impossible to refuse and is often consumed in vast quantities. Dorjey used yarrow to flavor his brew, and the result was pleasantly crisp, not unlike hops in an ale. Under a warm sun, Lamo filled our cups again and again. I was soon dizzy, and lay back in the grass, idly chewing fragments of bloated barley that floated atop the opaque liquid.

Eventually Dorjey rose and stretched arms skyward; it was time to return to harvest. Lamo was reticent to accept our help—she urged us to return to her home and relax—but Lama Wangyal insisted she demonstrate the process of pulling barley. Crouched on her haunches at the edge of the golden crop, she gathered a handful of stalks—about the thickness of a shovel handle—and with a jerk, yanked them free of the ground. After shaking precious topsoil from spidery roots, she methodically stacked the sheaves in a thatched pattern behind her, meant to protect the ripening ears from scavenging birds.

Christine and I set to work beside her, shuffling sluggishly forward as we wrenched barley out, one handful at a time. Within minutes, my knees were throbbing, so I sat directly down in the dirt and scooched along on my bum. My hands soon ached. Christine quietly chanted as she worked—*Om mani padme hum, om mani padme hum*—which thrilled Lamo.

"Good, Angmo! Good!" she clapped.

Bodi and Taj floated twigs down irrigation ditches, and later chased a pair of lambs. When Taj found a dead bird, he proudly carried it over to show us, not yet tainted by the grown-up dread of touching dead things.

An hour passed, and our progress felt indiscernible. An eternity of golden barley stretched ahead. And this was only one of Lamo and Dorjey's seventeen fields.

After another round of flatbread and *chang*, Christine took the boys back to the house, while I began a job that would consume me for days: carrying load after load of pungent alfalfa to the roof of Lamo's homestead—the very task I had assisted the elderly woman in Karsha with.

Alfalfa, considered a secondary crop and used as winter fodder, is grown around the periphery of the barley fields, tucked into a thin strip of arable land. The green leafy plant had been cut days earlier by scythe and rolled into crude bales, roughly three feet long and a foot in diameter. Now dried in the sun, these bales could be picked up and moved without falling apart, an ingenious technique that circumvented the need for twine.

Using a pair of rope lassos, Dorjey bound six such bales together. I lay back on the pile, slipped one arm through each rope, and then struggled to my feet. Although the alfalfa on my back was not crushingly heavy, perhaps thirty kilograms, it was physically immense, almost the size of a refrigerator. The bottom of the bundle hit me in the calves and the top wobbled overhead. Dorjey gave a thumbs-up, and I set off toward his home.

The narrow pathways were crowded with livestock: donkeys, cows, yaks, sheep and *dzo* all grazing on a dusting of husks and chaff.* As I squeezed past

---

* Across the Himalaya, yaks are routinely crossbred with domestic cattle, producing hybrids that are larger, stronger and more productive in both milk and meat. The male offspring of such pairings are known as *dzo*, and female *dzomo*.

these animals, their warm flanks pressed against my thighs. Many attempted to steal nibbles from my load, and I was forced to spin this way and that to protect my cargo.

It took fifteen minutes to reach Lamo's homestead, where a wobbly ladder led to a barren mud roof, about the size of a tennis court. After dropping the alfalfa beside an outhouse-shaped structure in a distant corner—the family chapel—I headed back to the fields.

Dorjey was nowhere in sight, so I gathered a second load myself, lashing together seven bundles. The next trip I took eight. And then nine, which proved to be my limit, for the load must have been approaching fifty kilograms and threatened to burst from the lassos with every step.

One hour of exertion faded into the next. Thistle fluff floated on the afternoon air and clouds of locusts rose from my feet. Others wriggled against the small of my back, emerging from the load I carried. A flock of small birds took flight with a frantic beating of wings, flying away in unison like a spill of ink crossing the fields.

I slipped into a trance-like state, taking delight in the simplest of details: the weathered face of an elder, slumping fence lines, a young boy's hand stroking the flanks of a horse, glittering sunlight upon an irrigation ditch.

A line of reapers sang as they swung sickles, the freshly cut alfalfa at their feet the iridescent green of a jungle snake. A man in a tweed jacket drove two yaks, a rudimentary plough tilling rich loam behind. Then toothless Doda appeared, shuffling along beneath a load of peas, dragging a skinny horse with her.

It seemed every person I passed was either muttering mantras or running *mala* beads through their fingers. A few elders spun prayer wheels, balanced against hips. At lunch I'd even noted Dorjey reciting snatches of scripture amid lulls in our conversation. Every activity held the opportunity for devotion. And all of these actions—the mantras, the prayer beads and spinning prayer wheels—were really just meant as anchors to the present moment, as a reminder: I'm right here, right now, doing this. There seemed to be no separation between life and religion in these fields. Life was the ceremony.

Outside Lamo's home, Bodi and Taj were sword fighting with walking sticks. On my next trip, I spotted them beside the communal water pump, helping an elderly woman draw water. I waved from beneath my load, and they waved back.

As the final vestiges of light seeped from the western sky, Dorjey met me on the roof, holding up a weary hand—we were done for the day. I felt shattered, and absolutely filthy, my body caked with dust and grass.

In the dim kitchen, Lamo prepared *momos* by candlelight. Beside her, Bodi and Taj spun the colorful prayer wheels. Dorjey demonstrated how the wheels could be accelerated to a fantastic rate by placing a single finger near the middle of each. The boys were thrilled and kept the bright platters spinning for hours. But whenever their attention faded, as it invariably did, someone else would rise from the carpets, despite bone-weary exhaustion, and start the prayer wheels going.

Lama Wangyal studied a worn pamphlet he had received at a *Kalachakra* initiation, covered with annotations and highlights. Lamo peered over her brother's shoulder. Noticing my gaze, she patted his shoulder. "My teacher for Buddha."

Dorjey leaned against a wall with a glass of what looked like black tea in hand, listening to news from Delhi on a transistor radio. His mother sat cross-legged nearby, spinning wool on a bobbin. Dorjey's father, wearing camouflage fatigues and a purple fedora, rested beside her, log-peeling machete sheathed on his belt. Doda slept on a carpet near the stove.

Elders in Zanskar are accorded great respect, participating in all spheres of life, continuing to live alongside their family throughout their lives. When no longer able to perform physical labor, they still contribute meaningfully, watching grandchildren and telling stories, sharing their vast repositories of information and history.

"*Zo! Zo!*" Lamo commanded when the meal was ready.

She proceeded to feed us as if we might be leaving at any moment, on a long journey over high mountain passes, possibly not eating again for days. Perhaps it was an impulse seared in the collective Zanskari unconscious.

"*Thukpa! Thukpa!*"

Dorjey encouraged the boys to slurp the soup greedily, and they were so eager to engage in this noisy behavior that they overlooked the pervasive yak taste and happily complied. Afterward, Lamo prepared butter tea using a traditional *gurgur*, in which she churned tea, butter and salt, creating a purplish infusion the thickness of mushroom soup.

"*Cha! Cha!*"

Much later, Dorjey placed a glass of clear black tea before me. Feeling parched, I took an enormous gulp, only to discover it was rum.

"Army liquid!" he beamed, pleased to have someone to share in his scorching drink.

❧

Zanskaris describe the size of their farmland by the number of days it takes to plough. A large field might be a "two-day field," and a small one a "half-day field."

By this measure, Lamo and Dorjey owned—or more accurately, were guardians of—a ten-day farm, which by Western measure covered roughly five acres. This was typical: approximately one acre per working member of the household, for beyond that, land was of diminishing return. And until recently, Lamo and Dorjey's four children had provided critical assistance during the intensive seasons of planting and harvest.

But two years before, their eldest daughter had married and moved to Stongde village, some thirty kilometers distant, where she was now busy raising an infant son of her own. And earlier that fall, their other three children had left home to attend school—two middle daughters studying nursing in distant Jammu and a twelve-year-old son attending private school near Padum. While this was good news for the family, it left Lamo and Dorjey facing a crisis: could they manage the demands of harvest?

Their neighbors—a middle-aged couple whose children had also recently left home—had given up farming and sold their fields to an Indian multinational corporation, something unthinkable just a decade before. Those fields were now tended by migrant workers, who didn't contribute to any *paspun*. Meanwhile, the parents had built a roadside shack and were struggling to make a living hawking soda pop and deep-fried snack packs to passing truck drivers from Srinagar.

It was a familiar pattern seen across Zanskar, where more and more children were moving on from rural life, and a society that had existed for thousands of years was dissolving within the space of a generation.

For now, Lamo and Dorjey clung to the past, which was the reason Lama Wangyal had brought us to lend a much-needed hand. The pair had been working non-stop for three weeks already, and an enormous amount of work still remained. Six fields of barley had yet to be pulled. Ten tons of barley and peas needed to be carried to threshing circles. (Pea flour is routinely added to *tsampa* to stretch supplies.) An equivalent weight of alfalfa was required on their roof. There were carrots, potatoes and radishes to be dug, and piles of yak dung to be collected.

Despite the enormity of the task, neither Lamo nor Dorjey appeared rushed or stressed. They worked at a pleasant pace, pausing frequently to talk to neighbors, enjoying unhurried meals together.

❦

Our family slept in a small, carpeted room across from the kitchen, beneath shelves of copper pots, brass kettles and pressure cookers. A framed picture showed Dorjey's father in military regalia, commemorating his participation in three wars as a member of the famed Ladakh Scouts.*

After reading to the boys, I crawled into my sleeping bag, exhausted. A waning moon cast ghostly light across the room, and from beneath us came the rustling of livestock. I was drifting toward sleep when Christine mentioned she had a headache.

Hours later, I awoke to the sounds of violent retching. In the darkness, I could see Christine hunched over a pot that she'd pulled from the wall overhead.

At dawn, she puked again. Afterward, we lay together, discussing what to do.

I suggested I spend the day watching the boys, giving Christine time to recover. But that would mean I couldn't help with harvesting. And we both knew Lama Wangyal would be profoundly disappointed, because, as we had observed, Zanskari monks don't muster much sympathy for the sick and expect children to fend for themselves. Christine urged me to continue working and leave the boys with her. I said I'd carry a few loads and then check back.

In the earthen hallway outside, Dorjey was sprinkling the earthen floors with a watering can to control dust. Lamo followed, swinging a pewter incense box billowing with blue smoke, spiritually cleansing the home. Soon after, both hustled out the front door without a word, and I chased after the pair, grabbing a piece of fried bread as I went, concerned I wouldn't last long on an empty stomach.

I shouldn't have worried. I had only just settled into the routine of carrying alfalfa when the sun crested the peaks, and the crowded pathways emptied. Zanskaris like to perform the hardest physical labor during the blessedly cool hours near dawn and dusk. And then they eat.

In Lamo's kitchen, a breakfast feast was readied: curried vegetables, steaming chapatti, a cauldron of *thukpa* soup, *tuktuks* (barley dough cooked in a modern sandwich maker), and *chemik*, a Zanskar-style salsa made with peppers, salt, coriander, carrot, onion and tomato.

---

* Nicknamed the "Snow Tigers," the Ladakh Scouts are among the Indian Army's most decorated units, specializing in high-altitude mountain warfare. Tasked with patrolling the sensitive borders with Pakistan and China, the regiment has been deployed in every major combat operation since the Indo-Pakistani War of 1965.

Christine was feeling better, but nonetheless, Lamo dragged me to the village doctor, seeking "head medicine." We found a slim young woman, wearing cat-eye glasses and a blue head scarf, weeding a potato patch outside a collapsing stone building. Barbed wire was strung across open windows, and a rusty hand-painted sign read in English, MEDICAL AID CENTER, TUNGRI. The immunization records for every village child were posted on the wall inside, along with an Indian government poster warning that non-communicable diseases could be prevented by a healthy lifestyle. It seemed an unnecessary message here. The blue-scarfed woman rummaged through her desk, then held out a cardboard box overflowing with pills in foil wrappers. "You needing?" she asked.

I flipped through the assortment and took ten acetaminophen tablets, then pulled a fold of rupees from my pocket. The doctor shook her head. "From the government. No price."

Back at home, Dorjey was preparing to lead his livestock to pasture. The family owned one immense *garmo,** three *dzo,* two *dzomo,* a milk cow and two tiny calves—which Dorjey petted as affectionately as one would a dog. While Dorjey hauled the reluctant *garmo* at the front of the procession, I trotted at the back, whacking the derrière of any animals that paused to nibble grass.

We navigated a maze of narrow footpaths, and on those crowded trails, everyone we passed gazed upon me with befuddlement. A few shrieked with laughter, and I tried to imagine what they said to Dorjey. *Watch out, there is a foreigner following you. Can I rent him for a day when you are done?*

Upon reaching previously harvested fields, we pounded wooden stakes into the earth and tethered each animal by a nose ring, allowing them to graze on the nubbins that remained. Then I once again set to work carrying alfalfa.

As I stumbled back and forth between fields and homestead, I encountered the same villagers over and over, staggering toward their own homesteads beneath immense loads: young mothers, stooped elders, school girls in uniform, a government clerk in suit and tie, an affable trekking guide in a puffy jacket.

---

*   The male offspring of cow-yak hybridizations, known as *dzo,* are sterile. But the female offspring, *dzomo,* are not. And when *dzomo* are hybridized, a complex lineage emerges, with each variant holding specific values to a Tibetan farmer. A *dzomo*-yak crossbreed yields *gar* (male) and *garmo* (female). A *garmo*-yak crossbreed produces *gir* (male) and *girmo* (female). *Girmo*-yak crossbreeding gives rise to *lok* (male) and *lokmo* (female). And the cycle stretches on for several more generations.

Many laughed when they spotted me, but it was always a generous, welcoming laughter. Some even greeted me as Mortub, though we'd never been introduced. Others hollered unintelligible questions: *Are you lost? Why are you carrying alfalfa? Are you out of your mind?*

"Lama Wangyal," was my response to all queries, and it appeared to explain everything.

The women all had their faces covered with shawls, eyes peering through just a thin crack, though not a soul in the village was Muslim. It was for sun protection. Throughout Asia, dark skin is considered unattractive and stigmatized as a sign of labor. I'd seen skin-bleaching creams in the Padum pharmacy, which seemed both sad and ironic, knowing how many light-skinned North Americans lay in the sun for hours, hoping to shade their skin darker. It must be human nature, to yearn for different versions of ourselves.

By early afternoon I'd finished the alfalfa and set to work rolling freshly cut pea vines into bales. It was sweaty work, but I was not alone, for a gang of masked wagtails followed me: slender birds with black and white plumage that gobbled up insects exposed beneath the shifting crop.

Christine ambled past the field where I worked. She was feeling better, she told me, and on her way to continue pulling barley.

At dusk, I heard the voices of our boys. They came skipping along the trail to gather me, Bodi holding Dorjey's hand, Taj with Lamo. A clattering of rocks revealed goats scampering on nearby cliffs, while above, the first stars had been revealed.

❧

So it continued, one warm autumn day flowing into the next, exhaustion and joy ebbing and swirling.

On the third morning, a fresh dusting of snow coated the surrounding peaks. Crouched beside an irrigation ditch, splashing icy water on my face, I listened to the hysterical braying of a distant donkey. Plumes of smoke billowed from behind a grove of nearby poplar. Suspecting the smoke indicated that a field was being razed, I took Bodi and Taj to investigate.

Instead, we found a gang of road workers from southern India, faces hidden behind rags, melting tar over a bonfire. They were paving the dirt track that led into town.

The next morning, the road workers had disappeared, leaving behind their rusty drum caked with tar. Lamo hurriedly dragged it home. She would use the barrel, she explained, for milking the *dzos*.

"I can't imagine any positive benefits for the family's health coming from this," Christine whispered. But she held her tongue.

Generally Zanskaris waste nothing, and there is no such thing as a garbage can in their homes. That which cannot be eaten is fed to animals. Or used as fertilizer. Dishwater is either drunk by livestock or splashed across gardens. Cans, jars, shampoo bottles and even juice boxes become domestic organizers, holding everything from toothbrushes to seeds and spices. Apricot kernels are crushed, and the resulting oil used for lubricating prayer wheels. The rotten grains of barley found floating atop *chang* are dried and saved for snacks. Even old T-shirts, too threadbare for another patch, will be filled with earth and used to reinforce slumping irrigation channels.

While it is easy to romanticize traditional village life, I think it is fair to say the people of Tungri seemed, by and large, content. They certainly appeared happier than those living in Padum, just twenty kilometers away—a place of business, and busyness, where one found fewer smiles and more stress, where for the first time in memory, the unemployed loitered on street corners, already left behind by the false promises of a modern world that had no place for them.

❧

Later that night, with the boys snoring beside us, Christine and I held a hushed discussion. It may have been the exhaustion speaking. Or perhaps our imminent return to Canada—now less than a month away. Regardless, we both knew the time had come to discuss autism with Bodi.

Somewhere on the other side of the world, a team of film editors and producers was sifting through thousands of hours of footage detailing our family's journey. Whatever story they cobbled together, it would undoubtedly include Bodi's diagnosis. And neither of us wanted Bodi to learn about autism for the first time while watching the television series.

"What do we say? And how do we say it?" Christine moaned. "I feel so ill-prepared."

We both wanted to ensure Bodi's introduction to autism was positive. It had taken us years to digest the implications. How would our precious seven-year-old absorb such news? How could we tilt the scales away from shame and embarrassment, toward acceptance and pride?

Our counsellor had advised against any formal *Son, we need to talk* moment. No stilted diatribe, like the time my father had awkwardly explained the use of condoms before I left for university. Instead, she suggested we simply begin touching on the subject of autism in our conversations, gently and repeatedly, as if it was the most natural thing in the world.

"Best to keep it simple the first time," I reminded Christine, suspecting academic explanations were already churning in her head.

"Easier said than done."

"I can try," I offered, then added, "You should be there of course."

We lay in silence for some time. Christine's breathing slowed, and I thought she'd drifted to sleep, when she abruptly said, "I don't want to wait anymore. Let's have the discussion as soon as we return to the monastery."

❧

On the fifth morning, I rose to find Lamo frying dough in a pan of sizzling ghee. She handed me a glass of hot water, for Zanskaris, like many Asian cultures, hold great faith in its restorative effects, and the sight of our boys guzzling cool water from their bottles was a horror.

What would the day hold? Would we carry more peas? Pull more barley?

After nibbling on fried bread, Dorjey handed me a set of lassos, and we were headed out when Lama Wangyal appeared in the doorway, backpack slung over his shoulder.

"Bye-bye now," he announced.

A flash of disappointment shot through me. So soon?

The simple life we had glimpsed felt oddly familiar, as if I had lived it before, and some part of me wondered if I could have been content to stay here forever. But the truck was waiting. So Christine and I hurriedly stuffed clothes and sleeping bags into the duffel. Dorjey lifted both our boys at once, holding one in each arm. Lamo placed *khata* scarves around our necks.

"*Tujay-chey, tujay-chey,*" she whispered again and again. "Thank you, thank you."

It had ended so abruptly—work left undone, the rushed goodbyes. As I stooped under the low doorway, I glanced back one last time. Silent tears spilled down Lamo's cheeks.

17

NATURE'S SMUDGED LINES

The monk boys spotted us as we climbed the steep pathway leading toward the monastery, and came tumbling to greet us, screaming our names. After rubbing peach-fuzz heads, we climbed back up together, hand in hand, sharing news. At lunch, Tashi Tsering winked and ladled extra rice into our bowls. In class, Wang Chuk squeezed my shoulder with a grin. It was wonderful to be home.

Snatches of distant drumming floated through the classroom window, so after class I scrambled down to the village to explore.

The fields were teeming. Women, many with infants in arm, sat on yak-hair blankets, sharing food. Men leaned against stone fences, drinking *chang* while children scampered underfoot. Teams of yaks waited patiently, harnessed seven abreast to central poles in the flat mud pans, while sweating *paspun* members— elders, children, men, women, teenagers—heaped sheaves of barley around them.

Finally, with a whistle from their driver and the snap of his stick, the enormous animals surged forward. Saliva streamed from nostrils as they thundered in circles around the pole. The driver trotted behind, singing a harvest song and holding a small wicker basket, ready to catch any falling dung before it hit the grain.

Occasionally the ropes connecting nose rings became tangled, and the yaks were called to a halt while the mess was sorted. Then, with another snap of the stick, they were off again, around and around. More and more barley was tossed beneath hooves, until it lay belly deep. At intervals, the great yak teams were led aside and the crumpled stalks were swept away, leaving behind a precious residue of grain.

After it was swept and shovelled into waist-deep piles, women hurled the golden grain skyward using wooden rakes, a warm wind separating chaff from grain in plumes that drifted downwind.

❧

The next morning, as puja horns sounded, Lama Wangyal announced he was leaving for Leh on monastery business. He would be away for a week, perhaps more. And then he was gone.

Soon after, Jigmet raced past our doorway, gleefully declaring, "No you teaching today!"

"Why?" I shouted as he scampered down the earthen passageway.

"Lady in Karsha dead," he yelled back. "Today burning."

Then the hobbit door slammed, and I heard his feet galloping off, down trails.

We decided to follow. Led by the sound of chanting, our family shuffled tentatively down the cliffs toward the dusty village, where a splash of crimson stood out—a rooftop packed with monks. We didn't want to intrude, but Wang Chuk spotted us and began waving frantically. Scaling an unsteady ladder, we found a celebration underway.

More than fifty monks, novices and nuns were seated on one side of the clay roof, and opposite them was a group of farmers, short men with tanned faces and calloused hands—members of the deceased's *paspun*. All were simultaneously reading different pages from *Bardo Thodol*, the Tibetan Book of the Dead, their words offering guidance to the departed soul, urging her not to fear the demons she would meet in the afterlife, but instead to turn toward the pure white light.

We tried to slip toward the back of the gathering, but Wang Chuk would have none of it, and motioned for our family to sit at the very front. Seating at any public gathering in Zanskar reflects status, and guests are inevitably encouraged to accept excessively prestigious positions. I pointed toward the back again. Wang Chuk looked horrified, indicating we belonged at the front. Everyone seemed to enjoy our lighthearted dispute. Eventually a compromise was reached, and our family settled amongst the novices.

Immediately a young man rushed over, wearing jeans and a neon T-shirt emblazoned with the words YOU LOOK GOOD TODAY, serving us milky tea and deep-fried bread. The novices had been served earlier, but were now empty-handed, so I ripped the bread into pieces and passed it down the line of novice boys. They refused of course, but two could play the game, and soon all were munching happily.

The midday sun was hot, and Christine eventually slipped away, taking the boys with her, to wade in the village stream. I understood, but chose to stay, oddly enthusiastic about sitting cross-legged and doing nothing.

Beside me, young Nawang draped a corner of his robes over the top of my head to protect it. Prayer wheels spun. *Mala* beads slipped through fingers. Colored flags snapped in the wind.

An hour later, four stocky men in tattered jackets clambered up the ladder, with thick wads of cash in their hands. Payment for the funeral rites was quickly distributed amongst the monks and nuns, using the *mala* bead method. After much haggling, cries for change and a steady shuffling of bills, everyone appeared satisfied.

Platters of rice, dal and curried veggies were then distributed. YOU LOOK GOOD TODAY followed with a blistering chili sauce, refusing to take "no" for an answer. Young Norgay, the *tulku*, elicited a great cheer when he requested a second dollop. Chanting resumed, and I focused on my breath, letting *mala* beads slip through my fingers.

Sometime later, Lama Sundup tapped my shoulder. "Let's go."

The rooftop was emptying quickly as monks streamed down the ladder. In the narrow laneway below, the deceased lay atop a litter of wood, wrapped in linen. For three days following death, the body had remained in the family home, while female members of the *paspun* washed it and carefully prepared it for cremation.

Now, as lamas chanted, the Head Lama sprinkled saffron water over the shrouds while weeping nuns draped *khata* scarves. Five women, daughters of the deceased, emerged from the homestead, prostrating themselves before the enshrouded body, touching the shoulders and head. "*Tussi loma, tussi loma,*" they cried. ("Like falling autumn leaves, the leaves of time.")

The disciplinarian gently pushed them toward the house. "*Tserka macha.*" Don't be sad. But they slipped past him, placing more *khatas* on the body before finally tearing themselves away, fingers reaching behind them as they left.

Then a group of men hoisted the litter to their shoulders and set out on a dirt track leading away from the village, toward rocky plains in the east. A long procession of monks and nuns followed, forming a crimson river that wound across the barren land. At the end came a white pickup truck, piled with wood.

Waves of heat rose from the plains, and dust swirled. Christine and the boys had probably returned to the monastery by now, and I momentarily wondered about going to get them, but decided against it, for the sun was still crippling.

Half an hour later, out of sight of the village, the procession halted before a barren hillside, blackened in places by fire. Gathering an armful of firewood from the truck, I followed monks and villagers uphill, along a trail strewn with charcoal and fragments of bleached bone.

Burial is impractical in the arid Himalayan landscape, where graves are difficult to dig and nothing decomposes. So Tibetan Buddhists have long relied on other rituals for disposing of their dead—all of which represent the return of the body to the essential elements of fire, water, earth or wind. Sky burial—dismembering of a corpse upon a mountaintop; scraps left for carrion birds—is frequently depicted in popular media, but only rarely practiced, in isolated regions. In exceptional circumstances, the dead may be wrapped in linen, weighted down with stones and tossed in a river. But cremation, or "burning" as the monks called it, remains the most common method of committing a body across the Himalaya—even in Zanskar where wood is rare.

As the litter was hoisted atop a pyre, the monks chanted. Conch horns blasted. A storm of rice was hurled skyward. Then, without another word, everyone turned and began walking back to the village, leaving the men of the *paspun* to tend to their business in private.

An hour later, as I climbed the steep steps toward Lama Wangyal's house, I spotted a column of blue smoke rising in the east, dissolving into the endless blue.

❧

Our family sat together in our small room, sunlight flooding in the windows. I played with the words over and over. What should I say? How could I start? Finally, I just blurted it out.

"Bodi, have you ever heard Mom and Dad using the word *autism*?"

"Nope," he replied, without glancing up from his Lego.

"Everyone is different. Some people have dark hair. Others have red hair. Or blond. Some people, like you, have blue eyes. Others have green. One way isn't better than the other. It's just different."

Oh god, it already felt so stilted.

"So we all exist on a spectrum, like the different colors of the rainbow. And autism refers to a group of people who see the world just a little bit differently than most."

Bodi was looking at me now. Had he heard Christine and I talking about ASD before? He was an astute boy.

"When we say someone is on the autism spectrum, it might mean they don't like loud sounds. Or they might be bothered by tags in their clothing. Many don't like changes in plans. Some find it hard to play with other children. Or to look in their eyes. Some don't like wearing shorts. Some spin to calm down."

I paused, unsure what to say next. Finally I asked, "Does that sound like anyone you know?"

"Yes," Bodi said, looking down and fidgeting with his Lego. "Me!"

My heart was hammering.

"Autism can mean a lot of different things. Some people struggle to talk. Others like to flap their arms, like a bird. You have just a touch, and we used to call that Asperger's. Or Aspie for short. Now we just call it being on the spectrum."

Although Asperger's syndrome had recently been removed from common usage,* our counsellor still suggested using the term "Aspie" with Bodi in a lighthearted, almost joking manner, to prevent his diagnosis from feeling like a stigma or burden. As in, "Oh Bodi, that is the Aspie in you talking!"

Bodi stared at me, and I felt a wave of emotion.

"We love you so much, Bodi. Autism is just a small part of who you are, and of course, we love it too. But it means you will have some challenges that your friends might not—little things, like getting annoyed when people aren't precise. If someone says it's 3:20, when it's actually 3:23, that can frustrate you. And it might be hard for you to play with other boys and girls at times. But it's

---

* In the fifth edition of the *Diagnostic and Statistical Manual of Mental Disorders* (the primary authority for psychiatric diagnosis), published in May 2013, Asperger's syndrome (AS) was removed as a separate diagnosis and placed under the larger umbrella of Autism spectrum disorder. The move was controversial, and the World Health Organization still recognizes AS.

important to remember that being an Aspie brings lots of good things. You are very sharp. You spot details most others miss and understand things in a way that many others don't. You are very honest. And you care for others. You are a great friend."

I glanced at Christine, and she nodded. That was enough for now.

I asked Bodi if he had any questions, but he shook his head and returned to the Lego.

A stillness settled on our room.

❧

Despite modern prevalence, and hints of widespread historical occurrence, Autism spectrum disorder is only beginning to be understood.[*] And public awareness lags woefully behind.

The story begins in the late 1930s, when a young Viennese clinician named Hans Asperger noted a group of aloof, awkward, and socially removed young patients, who all displayed remarkable abilities with math, language, and memory. He affectionately dubbed these boys his "little professors" and identified a surrounding constellation of behaviors he described as "autistic psychopathy"—"autistic" derived from the Greek word for self, *autos*, because such children seemed happiest when alone.

Notably, Asperger considered autistic psychopathy to be part of a spectrum we all exist on, and went so far as to characterize the condition as an extreme variant of intelligence. He implored colleagues to never give up on similar cases, confident that if such children could be taught to harness their skills, immense capacities would emerge.

But Asperger's research was cast aside as Nazism swept Europe, buried in favor of extermination and sterilization programs designed to eradicate "deviant" children, including those with autism, cleft palate, cerebral palsy, schizophrenia, and physical disabilities.[†]

---

[*]   While retrodiagnosis is not possible, many great historical thinkers are now posthumously recognized as displaying classic ASD indicators, including Einstein, Tesla, Jefferson, and Michelangelo.

[†]   Asperger was long viewed as a hero in the autism community. However, recent evidence has emerged showing that the Austrian pediatrician referred patients to child euthanasia programs of the Third Reich, a revelation that has cast a shadow on his legacy and ignited a fiery debate about any future use of the term *Asperger's*.

Meanwhile, in North America, a different interpretation of the condition began taking hold—one far less accommodating. Child psychiatrist Leo Kanner had noticed young patients who appeared to inhabit private worlds, capable of amusing themselves for hours with ritual behaviors such as arranging toy cars in sequence or banging on the floor. Apparently happiest when left alone, these children often threw violent tantrums at the slightest changes in their surroundings. In an uncanny parallel, Kanner also dubbed the condition *autism*.

But unlike Asperger, Kanner perceived autism as an incurable and devastating mental deficiency, advocating that autistic children be sent to asylums and suffer forced sterilization. In his cold view, those affected by autism could never contribute to society in a meaningful way and were capable only of menial tasks, such as garbage collection, floor scrubbing, and ditch digging.

Causing even further damage, Kanner squarely placed the blame for autism on parents, suggesting the condition arose from a lack of household warmth, spawning the term "refrigerator mother." The bestselling book *The Empty Fortress* by Bruno Bettelheim (1967) went so far as to suggest "the precipitating factor in infantile autism is the parent's wish that his child did not exist." The *New York Times* painted an equally bleak picture, describing autism as "an illness, a suicide really, of the soul," and psychologists routinely prescribed tough-minded, physically punishing therapies aimed at reining in a child's unusual behaviors—severe techniques that to my mind seem akin to training a dog.

This dismal outlook would persist for decades.

As recently as 1989 (when I was twenty-one years old and studying engineering at Queen's University) my hometown newspaper *Toronto Star* described autistic children as nerds, incapable of friendship, who could burst into tears for no reason "like stroke patients who have suffered brain damage." In 2001, respected epidemiologist Walter Spitzer pronounced autism "a terminal illness . . . a dead soul in a live body."

It is numbing to think this was the professional opinion of autism spectrum disorders just six years before Bodi was born.

But thankfully, a revolution is now underway.

It began quietly, in the late 1970s, when British psychologist Lorna Wing began questioning Kanner's long-held assumption that autism was rare and always apparent at birth. Converting a London railway hostel into a school, Wing and her colleagues began seeking children who displayed traits reflective of Kanner's autism, but on a more diverse continuum. Within months they were overrun with applicants. And nearly half of those had been born symptomless, experiencing developmental setbacks in early life.

Drawn to Winston Churchill's concept that "nature never draws a line without smudging it," Wing began to postulate that instead of being a singular condition, Autism existed on a spectrum. "All the features that characterize Asperger's syndrome," she wrote, "can be found in varying degrees in the normal population."

In other words, we all carry bits and pieces of autism within ourselves.

Wing launched a determined campaign to transform the medical understanding of autism, persuading colleagues that diagnosis was not *categorical* (yes or no) but *dimensional* (what type?). Conscious of the stigma carried by Kanner's term *autism*, she proposed a new diagnostic model, where a gamut of shades and hues were contained beneath the broader umbrella of *autism spectrum*.

But it was Steve Silberman's 2001 article in *Wired* magazine, "The Geek Syndrome," that launched a quantum shift in public understanding. Silberman meticulously detailed how brainiacs and high school outcasts, who once played *Dungeons & Dragons* in their parents' basements, were now congregating in Silicon Valley, overtaking companies like Facebook, Apple, and Google, and refashioning the modern world in their image. His groundbreaking book *NeuroTribes*, published in 2015, argues powerfully for a broader acceptance of all those with cognitive differences—it is a book that has profoundly influenced my understanding of autism, as described in these pages.

Suddenly autism had become more visible, seen in movies, television series and books. Healthy role models began to emerge—scientist and activist Temple Grandin, actors Dan Aykroyd and Daryl Hannah, professional surfer Clay Marzo—autistic individuals who were living successful, creative, engaged lives.

But despite such advances, the unvarnished truth remains that those on the spectrum face a maze of daily challenges that go beyond anything I could ever imagine.

❧

"Bruce!" Christine screamed. "Come here!"

She was outside the hobbit door, and from the tone of her voice, I knew that something either incredibly good or terribly bad had just happened.

"Come, come, come!" she yelled as I rushed down the dark passageway. Outside I found her and the boys staring toward the sky.

"Birds!" she gushed. "Big birds. Overhead. Hundreds of them!"

I assumed it was a gathering of choughs, for they were now congregating in great flocks with the approach of winter. But in a glance I knew it wasn't choughs. What were they, though? My eyes strained to recognize the silhouettes.

Golden eagles!

The raptors were descending on the monastery in outrageous numbers, swooping along cliff faces, soaring out over the open valley. I had never seen anything remotely similar, and counted over a hundred before losing track. More and more continued to appear, drifting over the summits above us. Were they harbingers of the coming winter?

The boys were beside themselves, jumping and pointing.

"I wish Lama Wangyal could see," Bodi shouted.

The old monk had been gone six days, and we'd received no word of when he might return.

"Maybe he can see the eagles from where he is?" Taj suggested. "He's got good eyes."

Bodi scoffed.

A group of Japanese tourists came limping down the steep path from the assembly hall. But rather than admiring the eagles, they turned their cameras upon us. And to be fair, we must have presented a curious sight—four filthy, blond foreigners, giggling and pointing upward.

We stayed outside—Christine and I with arms wrapped peacefully around each other—until the convocation melted to dots over the central plains, eventually disappearing beyond ridges to the south.

A feeling of raw wonderment remained with me for hours.

❧

Two days later, Lama Wangyal reappeared—an imposing figure striding up the trails.

Our class had been quietly working on mathematics when Changchup leapt up and began frantically pointing. It was lucky he'd spotted the old monk, for I'd left the house padlocked. And Christine was away shopping in Padum.

Lama Wangyal always insisted we lock the hobbit door, even if we were gone just for a few minutes. "Maybe bad people coming."

"What bad people?" I asked once. A bad lama? The Nepali workers? Villagers?

"Yes," Lama Wangyal smacked his lips with an inhale. "Bad men."

I immediately dispatched Bodi with the key. He'd bought the old monk a gift (chocolate bar) and drawn a picture (Buddha) for him, both of which he was eager to deliver. I watched from the window as Taj chased after him, little legs churning down the dusty trail.

When class ended, I ducked out, excited to greet Lama Wangyal myself. Shuffling bent along the dark passageway, I bumped into Christine, who had just returned from Padum with a backpack full of supplies. She was wrapped in a bear hug with Lama Wangyal, and upon spotting me, the old monk pulled me close and kissed my face. His rough stubble brought a flood of memories; he was the first man to kiss me since my father died, twenty years earlier.

Lama Wangyal had returned from Leh with a trove of treasure: burlap sacks of onions, apples, dried apricots, cashews and Chinese noodles. He'd also bought our family a pressure cooker, the same type he owned.

"Now you making Zanskari food in Canada, and much *brrr, brrr*," Lama Wangyal clapped.

His laughter turned into a coughing fit that left him hunched and gasping for air. Christine asked if he was sick, and he pointed to a sun-faded photograph on the wall. It showed him presiding over an outdoor puja as the Head Lama. Looking more closely at the photo, I realized his body was skeletal.

"When me Head Lama, too much sick coming," Lama Wangyal wheezed.

At the time, he had been taken to Leh and hospitalized. The treatment was so expensive that Lama Wangyal had been forced to sell two of his yaks, liquidating what in local terms was a fortune. There had been several remissions in the years since, each treated with a regime of injections.

When I tried to ascertain what his sickness had been, the lama's explanation was opaque. Lama Wangyal shuffled into the puja room and returned with a cardboard box overflowing with syringes and vials.

"You needling me, OK?"

"Sure," I agreed, somewhat reluctantly.

Years earlier, during a wilderness first aid course, I'd injected saline into the shoulder of a classmate, but I was no expert. Lama Wangyal wasn't concerned. Mixing a sachet of white powder with a vial of yellow liquid, he filled a syringe and handed me the needle. Then he peeled himself like an onion, pulling off a mustard vest, orange fleece and eventually a red collared shirt. Dropping to his knees and hoisting robes, he revealed a pair of perfectly hairless buttocks.

"Slowly, Mortub," he commanded, for it was a large injection and, given too quickly, could hurt.

Holding the syringe like a dart, I placed my wrist on his butt cheek and with a quick flick, slid the needle deep into his gluteus. Gently, I depressed the plunger. Lama Wangyal probed his derrière for a bump, a sign the injection had been administered too quickly, and finding none, happily declared, "Mortub very good injection man."

We were sipping tea when Lama Wangyal pulled a newspaper-wrapped parcel from his backpack. "In Leh, I buying you *thanka*."

Weeks earlier I had asked Lama Wangyal if it was possible to buy a *thanka*, one of the ornate Buddhist paintings framed with silk and seen hanging in the assembly hall. Instead of answering, he asked for the exact time and place of birth for each member of our family. I assumed that was his polite way of saying no. But unbeknownst to me, after consulting scriptures and performing complex astrological determinations, he had commissioned four *thankas* to be painted by a well-regarded artist in Leh, each depicting Buddha in a pose considered auspicious for our individual births.

Now he unrolled the paintings, hanging each over the pallets where we slept. "This for Tashi. This Norbu. This Angmo. And Mortub."

The *thankas* were stunning. Both Christine and I were overcome.

"You buying *thanka*, too much money," he explained. "Tourist money. But me, no problem. Little money. Lama money."

The four paintings had cost eight thousand rupees in total (two hundred US dollars), and I reimbursed the old monk immediately. Before departing our room, he declared that he would perform a blessing puja in the coming days.

"*Very* important," Lama Wangyal said, as if an unblessed *thanka* was of no use at all.

❧

The next day after dinner, Lama Wangyal arranged eight silver bowls on the low table in our room. A *damaru* was unwrapped. (This small traditional drum, with garnet-encrusted handle, had two pieces of coral attached by strings and created a racket similar to stovetop popcorn when twisted quickly.) A book of scripture appeared along with a silver bell and *dorje*.

Lama Wangyal began to chant, and our boys snuggled into his lap, one on each side. Saffron was added to water. The *dorje* and bell wove. An hour passed. Four *tsampa* statues—ascending in height like matryoshka dolls and eerily reminiscent of our family—were smashed on the cliffs as a reminder of impermanence. The puja reached a crescendo, and Lama Wangyal began tossing handfuls of rice toward the *thankas*, the grains pattering off the paintings like rain on a window.

"How are we ever going to clean all of this up?" Bodi whispered gleefully in my ear.

Christine pointed to Taj, who had fallen asleep beside her. "One landed on his forehead. And another on his heart. It must be a sign."

Then it was over. The scripture was restacked between wooden plates; the *damaru* placed in its velvet-lined case; the silver bowls polished. Lama Wangyal disappeared.

After we tucked the boys in, Christine and I crawled quietly on hands and knees across the carpet, cleaning up rice by headlamp.

"You looked so shocked when he started tossing rice," Christine laughed. "I'm almost certain Lama Wangyal tossed even more when he saw your face."

❧

Despite our shared affection for the old monk, Christine was losing enthusiasm for his planned visit to Canada. During the puja ceremony, Lama Wangyal declared that all four *thanka* must hang side by side in our home, occupying a single room absent of any other furniture. Needless to say, such redecorating was not high on her (or my) agenda, but Lama Wangyal could be bullheaded, and I sensed a standoff.

"I'm burnt out," Christine sighed. "And the last thing I want to do when we get home is spend my days taking care of Lama Wangyal."

I understood what she was getting at. Lama Wangyal's presence in Canada would be an imposition on both of us. I foresaw it tearing me away from book writing, firewood gathering, house maintenance, ski training and all the other things I'd ignored since leaving home.

On the other hand, wasn't the rush of modernity the very thing we were hoping to avoid on our return?

I hoped that the monk's visit might bridge the divide, and carry some whisper of Zanskar's tranquility back home with us. But most fundamentally, I cared for the gruff man, and bringing him to Canada—if that was what he wished for—simply felt like the right thing to do.

Whatever our individual feelings, it was too late to change course.

That afternoon I'd had a tough conversation with Lama Wangyal, explaining that our family's departure from Karsha Gompa was just three weeks away, and if he wanted to return to Canada with us, he needed to submit his visa application to the Canadian consulate in New Delhi—in person, within the week.

Tomorrow we planned to visit Padum together, making a final attempt to complete the application form. If we failed, I'd arranged for a filmmaker in Delhi to help the old monk fill out the forms by hand.

Either way, he needed to begin the long southward journey within days.

❦

Lama Wangyal hollered into a flip phone as we scampered down the steep paths toward Karsha village at dawn. A white jeep waited for us beside the prayer wheel. Five teenage girls in blue school uniforms crammed onto the rear bench beside me, smelling like flowery soap. After six months of wearing the same shirt and pants, I leaned away in embarrassment.

On Padum's busy streets, passersby shouted greetings to Lama Wangyal. Many rushed over and reached for his hand, and he received all with affection. Lama Wangyal barked at a teen, and the youth straightened his sideways baseball cap. Later, an elderly Muslim man approached, and the pair stood close, hands clasped and noses almost touching.

In the Jammu and Kashmir Bank, a crowd was pressed against the wickets, waving white slips of paper overhead, but Lama Wangyal ducked into the bank manager's office. Another crowd had gathered there, pressed around the poor man's desk, waving white slips before his eyes. The manager waved off some, and several customers stormed out in frustration. Others crammed thick wads of cash into sun-bleached backpacks.

When Lama Wangyal was called forward, I explained we required a bank draft for five thousand rupees (one hundred US dollars), payable to the receiver general for Canada. Much head scratching and whispering followed. Eventually we were told it was possible, but would take hours.

To pass the time, we visited a stationery store, printing letters of support for the visa application. One came from me personally, guaranteeing Lama Wangyal all financial assistance, including lodging, food and plane tickets. The second, which I'd drafted, was a message from the Head Lama, confirming that Lama Wangyal was a senior monk in good standing at Karsha Gompa and noting he would assume the prestigious position of Labrang manager upon his return from Canada. I signed my letter, then Lama Wangyal grabbed the pen and prepared to sign the Head Lama's letter. I stopped him.

"It's from the Head Lama. Better if he signs?"

"Same same," Lama Wangyal waved off my concerns. "Buddhist."

It was unclear whether he meant that Buddhists were able to sign for each other, or that no one in the Canadian embassy could tell the difference in the Tibetan script. Either way, I was beginning to suspect no one at the monastery knew of Lama Wangyal's travel plans.

Not surprisingly, the Mont Blanc Cyber Cafe was closed, and my hope of completing the visa application evaporated. After a bowl of chicken curry at a roadside stand, we returned to the bank. The crowd around the manager's desk had dissipated, replaced by a gaggle of tellers. One young man wore a handkerchief tied across his face, bearing amusing resemblance to a cartoon bank robber. A blank draft had been found, but the men were struggling to feed it into a printer. Finally, they just filled the damn thing out by hand.

On the way out of town, I paused at the bakery to buy twenty-five cream-filled horns—a treat for the novices on the final day of class. When I mentioned my Internet frustrations, the baker suggested I visit Lamdon Private School, funded by French philanthropists and sitting on the rocky plains outside Pipiting.

Lama Wangyal caught a ride back to Karsha Gompa while I trudged toward the distant white buildings. Hordes of children milled outside, wearing green and white uniforms. Some danced to American hip hop. Others played cricket. A few lived in Karsha village and shouted "*Jullay*, Mortub!" at my approach.

The principal welcomed me warmly. Unlocking the thick wooden door to the staff room, he flicked on the school's sole computer. With a few keystrokes, the web page for Global Affairs Canada flashed up. Fifteen minutes later, I had completed the five-page visa form. Everything was now set for Lama Wangyal's impending departure.

❧

I was brewing tea in the dark kitchen at dawn when an unusual scratching sound caught my attention. A thousand tiny claws? Mice? Bats? The sound stopped, and then it started again, and as it did, something moved outside the kitchen's opaque skylight.

Scrambling up the ladder, I discovered Lama Wangyal sitting cross-legged on the roof, surrounded by a pile of cream-colored fabric. His hand-cranked sewing machine made a clacking noise as the flywheel spun, remarkably similar to the gnashing of teeth.

"Cold coming soon, Mortub," the old monk said without glancing up. "Me making Tashi and Norbu Zanskari coats."

The previous evening, he had slipped down to the village and bought a roll of heavy piled wool. Working through the night, he had cut an array of panels—arms, shoulders, cuffs, collar, chest and back—for two vastly different-sized boys, all without the aid of a pattern. Now, as scissors flashed and the sewing machine clattered, two robes slowly emerged.

Winter was approaching, and with it came the chance of snow and ferocious cold. In recent weeks, many monks had begun expressing concern about our family's imminent trek over the mountains. So great was Lama Wangyal's unease that he refused to depart for Delhi without first fashioning these thick traditional robes for our boys.

When the sun broke the horizon, Himalayan summits were drenched with merlot and orange. Lama Wangyal grunted and waved for a cup of tea. I brought him a Thermos, along with a plate of flatbread. Then I left him in peace, and the old man sewed without pause through the day.

More than twelve hours later, Christine and I were watching the Milky Way rise when Lama Wangyal finally clambered down from the roof and staggered over to the boulder where we sat, slumping across my lap in exhaustion.

We said nothing for a time, and I watched him as he stared at the stars. Did he feel the same infinite wonder?

After a long silence, he finally asked, "Is there a moon in Canada?"

"Yes," Christine replied.

"The same moon?"

"Yes."

"And mountains?"

"Yes."

Then she added that the mountains in Canada were not as big as these. "The tallest we can see from our house is just ten thousand feet."

Lama Wangyal looked confused. I suspected he'd never encountered the notion of elevation before. I held out my watch, which measured altitude, and showed Lama Wangyal we were currently sitting 12,294 feet above the distant sea. And Zanskar's snowcapped peaks soared to nineteen thousand feet, I told him.

He could hardly believe it, and wanted to know the elevation of everything in the valley: the assembly hall, the guest house, Pipiting Monastery. On impulse I handed him the watch, which had been a trusted companion on many expeditions. The solar-powered device would be perfect in Zanskar, never needing new batteries.

Lama Wangyal appeared genuinely pleased and ambled back toward the house, watch held close to his face, beeping noisily as he pressed buttons. He might inadvertently reprogram the thing, change time zones or turn on all the alarms, but it should last for decades.

❧

Lama Wangyal appeared at our doorway the next morning, holding two cream-colored robes. Both boys leapt from their sleeping bags and slipped on the thick coats, which were adorned with chocolate piping and golden baubles. The old monk wrapped sashes around their waists—blue for Taj, red for Bodi—and warned the pair never to let the fabric touch the ground, for it bore Buddhist scripture, which should never pass underfoot. Then we sat back to admire. They looked magnificent.

Soon afterward, Lama Wangyal departed.

Ahead lay an exhausting journey: overnight bus to Jammu, followed by a forty-eight-hour train ride. In Delhi he would stay in a Tibetan refugee camp, and three weeks later, if all went as planned, he would board an airplane bound for Canada, alongside our family.

I watched as he strode down the trail leading away from Karsha Gompa, dust rising from his feet. All he carried was a small red tote, no bigger than a grocery bag.

18

SKY FISHING

I awoke to a nudge. A steaming cup of instant coffee drifted below my nose.

"Happy anniversary," said Christine, kissing me softly.

Shit! It was September 23. In this land beyond newspapers, cellphones, and calendars, I'd completely forgotten. A wave of guilt washed over me.

"Don't go changing," Christine laughed, unperturbed, cheeks flushed, and golden hair tousled.

The time away had brought forward the best of our bonds, as it always does. Somehow, on the road, instead of staking territory, we operate as one. We need each other and are unquestionably on the same team—or *paspun*. It was a way of being that I hoped to carry home.

Holding a finger to her lips, Christine hauled me from my sleeping bag and we slipped outside, leaving the boys sleeping as we cuddled together on the cliffs, gazing down upon the waking valley that had become our home—and that we would leave in just one week.

This was it. *Finito*. This blessedly simple life was about to evaporate, along with the web of human connections we'd built. While we might return someday—I certainly hoped we would—what we found would never be the same. The novice monks would be gone. The faces in puja would be different. And the great valley itself, soon to be pierced by a highway, would surely have shifted beyond recognition.

It was Sunday, and with no class to teach, we took the boys to the guest house for a final sponge bath. Christine packed a small bag of gifts for Tsomo: hair clips, elastics, pencils, erasers and a pair of warm socks for her baby brother. But the young girl was nowhere to be found, and it was not until we were locking up that she appeared. Christine handed her the bag, and as she dug through the gifts it appeared as though she might cry.

"Thank you, *Aba*; thank you, *Ama*," she whispered. "Bye-bye."

My instinct was to hug her, but I wasn't sure if such physical contact would be welcomed by a girl her age, so I shook her hand instead, feeling ridiculous.

❧

"Hey, big Lego dude," Taj yelled across the room to Bodi. "Can I come to your bed and play?"

"Sure, little Lego dude."

Bodi cleared a space on his pallet, and Taj tumbled across the room.

"I'm a good guy," Taj announced. "I fight bad guys. Kinda like meditating."

Christine wandered over and sat beside me on my pallet. "This is a turning point," she said quietly. "Had we not done this trip, I'm not sure they ever would have played together this way."

Taj had always exhibited affinity for his older brother, but prior to leaving home, Bodi rarely reciprocated. It wasn't that the boys fought or bickered, but they seemed to exist on different planes. Seeing Taj as a disruptive force, Bodi often chose to pass the days alone in his room, where he kept curtains closed (he finds bright light unsettling) and windows open (even in mid-winter, he runs hot).

But the journey to Zanskar had stretched Bodi in unexpected ways. He'd stopped asking Christine for help getting dressed. His social skills were blossoming, and I often spotted him on the trails, gabbing with lamas. If he grew bored in puja, he was happy to walk home alone, something he never would have previously considered. But most staggering was how he'd learned to play with Taj—and truly enjoy his company.

Now, as Christine and I watched, Bodi began creating "superhero gadgets" for Taj: scraps of paper, covered with crude pencil crayon designs. Soon a Spider-Man logo was pinned to his chest, a magic watch was taped around his wrist and Iron Man blasters were taped to the palms of his tiny hands. As Taj ran in circles, beaming as he leapt from bed to bed, Bodi basked in our praise.

"You are growing into such a kind and handsome young man," Christine gushed. "You are going to be a hot commodity."

"Mom! Yesterday you said I was cool. Make up your mind."

"Yeah, well, they kinda mean the same thing."

"No they don't! They are opposites."

Before Christine could explain further, the pair dashed out the hobbit door, shouting in unison, "We stick together in any weather."

"Where on earth did that come from?" I asked.

"No idea," Christine shook her head. "But it's their new anthem. All I can say is thank goodness the iPad battery ran out."

That afternoon we went for a stroll together, following a dirt road being carved into the mountainside that would soon allow bus groups direct access to the upper temples. Modern tourists, it seemed, were either unable or unwilling to climb the steep paths.

Bodi skipped ahead in golden light, tall and lanky. Taj raced after, flaxen hair flying in the sun. He appeared constantly on the verge of a fall, although he was still so short that his tumbles were more of a roll than a collapse. Christine and I walked behind, hand in hand.

We were approaching the village when a pickup truck appeared on the distant plains, racing toward us, raising plumes of dust. As it neared, we saw it was packed with the novice monks from our class. It looked like a scene from *Mad Max*, with some boys leaning from open windows and others perched precariously on running boards. A horde stood in the back, surrounding Wang Chuk. As the pickup bounced past, Bodi and I held out our hands for high-fives and a flurry of tiny hands reached back.

Later, we found the novices milling outside Labrang temple. Wang Chuk told us that *yarne*, the season of seclusion, had ended, and to celebrate, Padum villagers hosted a luncheon for the novices. The monk boys eagerly recounted the day's glories: a buffet of peas, potatoes and lamb, followed by an ice cream cone and topped off with a rare treat—visiting Padum's markets.

They had returned with a bounty of junk plastic: toy airplanes, model cars, bouncy balls and water pistols. Purbu had bought a pair of shiny soccer cleats—but these offered no purchase on the monastery's pathways, and he skittered like a deer on a frozen pond. Sonam the math whiz clutched a poster tube, which I worried might hold a photo of a bikini-clad woman. Instead, he proudly unfurled a pastoral Swiss mountain scene, with a small cabin and snowcapped peaks. It could have been Zanskar—and perhaps that was why he bought it.

Norphal showed me a Che Guevara lighter, and I wondered if he'd taken up smoking, but before I could ask, he explained, "For incense."

"Do you know who that is?" I asked, pointing to Che.

"Bob Marley," he said proudly.

❧

Bodi returned to our room with a mustard-colored ball of yarn, which he had discovered on the rocky slopes below the assembly hall. Now he wanted to take his bounty to the abandoned roof. To play. Could Taj come too? Please?

Christine nodded, and the pair dashed out. After cleaning the dishes, we followed, finding the boys lowering a Lego mini-figure over the parapet on a makeshift yarn climbing rope.

A shout from below caught our attention. It was Purbu, standing on a distant rooftop. We waved. He waved back. Soon he was charging uphill toward us, scrambling over cliff bands. His happy shouts gained the attention of Joray, Lichten and Nawang, who were doing chores nearby, and they too joined us. Shortly after, Tashi Topden appeared, wandering the paths alone, suffering from a raging fever. Next a group of novices came trundling up the winter trail carrying loads of laundry. Upon spotting us, they dropped their clothes and ran to the abandoned rooftop. Within fifteen minutes, all twenty-one boys from our class stood beside us.

As each novice breathlessly arrived, Christine tore a strand of wool from Bodi's tangled ball—he was insistent that everyone get a piece of line—which they accepted with bowed heads. Lined up along the edge of the precipice, the boys coiled up their yarn, then cast it outward, and as the wool unravelled, it billowed aloft, caught in updrafts, drifting in snakes and plumes toward the flame-blue sky.

Everyone wanted us to watch. "Look, Angmo! Look, Mr. Bruce!"

When the lines tangled, as they inevitably did, we tried to separate them, but some had to be torn. Some boys lost their lines altogether, the mustard strands floating upward like spider webs, disappearing into an indigo ocean. But there was always someone else willing to split what remained in their hands.

Then at once, all the boys became Spider-Man. Gripping one end of their yarn with a curled finger—in the universal web-slinging position—strands of mustard wool shot out before them, carried on the breeze. Leaping, screaming, running and vaulting over mud bricks in flimsy sandals, they chased each other with outstretched hands.

All except little Norgay the *tulku,* who stood alone, hands stuffed in the pockets of his brown robes. Was such play foreign to him? Did he too struggle with social cues? Then Nawang accidentally bumped the young incarnate, and it was as if a switch were thrown. Norgay leapt after his classmate, and the two tumbled across the dusty roof, laughing and tussling, entangled in yarn.

Bodi himself was lost in the frenzy, giggling, dancing and striking odd poses, revelling in such unstructured play where language had no role.

An hour later, the monk boys began to drift away.

Only Sonam and Skarma remained, building makeshift kites from the yarn and a sheaf of paper they'd discovered on the slopes. To my amazement, the kites flew extraordinarily well.

When the dinner horns sounded, our family was left alone in silence on the dusty rooftop, as crimson peaks faded to black.

And still the mustard yarn's service was not done.

The next morning I found Bodi and Taj using the dregs as a diving cord, sending their Lego mini-figures deep into the crystalline waters of the rusty barrel outside the hobbit door.

19

THE SHATTERING

Without fanfare, the lamas began departing Karsha Gompa, setting off in groups to perform home pujas in satellite villages. It was an annual ritual from which they wouldn't return for weeks. We would never see most again.

Lama Dorjey Tundup, the jolly monk we called the Manchurian, stopped by our room at sunrise to bid us farewell. I'd grown fond of Lama Tundup, for he treated the novices with compassion and extended the same genuine interest to our own boys. Unable to speak a word of English, he placed *khatas* around each of our necks, then handed Christine a traditional Zanskari women's hat of orange carded wool, with seven turquoise beads sewn to the brim. We stood together for some time, all three of us holding hands and the boys between us, saying, *Jullay, jullay, jullay, jullay.* Finally Lama Tundup pulled himself away and disappeared down the earthen hallway. Christine's eyes were damp as she slumped onto her pallet.

Raising everyone's spirits, Taj grabbed the hat and popped it on his head, holding up a hand in salute. "Reporting for duty, sir!"

By noon, the only adults at the monastery—besides Christine and me—were the cooks, Wang Chuk and a *geshe* who taught Tibetan debate (and bore an uncanny resemblance to Telly Savalas). Even the Nepalis had gone. The assembly hall was padlocked, so the next morning the *geshe* led an informal puja in the classroom, craggy face obscured by shadows, body bowed forward, eyes closed.

The monk boys, sitting in two rows, began a game of out-chanting the other side, and the resulting uproar was deafening, but the *geshe* only smiled and swayed.

Afterward, we gathered on a rooftop. Butter tea arrived from the kitchen. Copper urns of *tsampa* were passed around. The boys joked and laughed.

Abruptly Wang Chuk asked, "When you leave?"

The boys fell silent. Sadness swept over me. I wanted to declare, *Never. We are not going. We are going to stay here with you, eating* tsampa *and drinking tea, watching choughs dive and soar as clouds tumble across the blue sky.*

"Friday," I admitted. It was just five days away.

"Yippee!" Bodi exclaimed, and the monk boys turned to look.

"You'll miss Karsha Gompa once we go," Christine suggested gently.

"No he won't," Taj explained. "Because Lama Wangyal bought us a pressure cooker, and that will help us remember."

❧

Christine and I carefully prepared a series of lessons for our final week of class, but that afternoon, as we stood before the novice boys we'd grown to love so deeply, I was overcome by a sense that the most valuable gift we could leave behind would be encouraging them to continue speaking English. Their progress since our arrival had been phenomenal, but if they stopped now, their comfort with the strange tongue would dissipate.

"Mr. Bruce, Angmo, Norbu and Tashi are leaving Karsha Gompa," I began, and they all stared at me with eyes as deep and still as a mountain lake at dawn. "But you can keep practicing English together."

"Not possible." Norphal shook his head, and the finality of his words winded me.

"What about tourists?" I asked. "Do you ever talk to tourists?"

The entire class laughed and shook their heads. No. Never.

"If you want to learn English, the most important thing you can do is keep talking. So from now on, you should talk to every tourist you see."

They looked confused, and knowing none of the novices would approach a foreigner without guidance, I scribbled a list of ice-breaking questions on the blackboard. They dutifully copied these queries into their notebooks: *What is your name? What country do you come from? How long are you staying in Zanskar? Did you go to puja? Do you like butter tea?*

The last question amused the class greatly. No tourist liked butter tea, they declared. It amused Wang Chuk too, who had arrived early and was listening from the back corner as he brewed tea.

Christine slipped out and raced down to Lama Wangyal's, returning with the box of cream-filled pastries I'd bought in Padum. The monk boys scuttled to their places on the carpet in anticipation. Bodi distributed the treats one by one, and then we ate in silence, the only sound that of slurping tea and dipping pastries.

Christine had purchased farewell gifts for all the novices, which she now presented: a pair of plastic sandals and a T-shirt (in their favorite color, bearing their favorite cartoon character) for each boy. The novices were ecstatic and compared wares.

"I couldn't help myself," Christine whispered as she plopped down beside me. "They have so little. Not even a mother to take care of them."

When the pastries were done, Norphal asked, "Mr. Bruce, Angmo, when will you come back?"

"I don't know," I stammered, my uncertainty feeling like a betrayal.

I stumbled out of the classroom forlornly, but the air was dizzyingly clear, and before me spread the great valley, ice-capped summits and blazing blue sky, and I paused, trying to imprint the scene upon my mind—for I knew I'd need its sustenance in seasons ahead.

❧

Christine and I were sitting in our room, preparing for the final class farewell party, when I became aware that someone was standing over us. Glancing up, I realized it was little Jigmet—not the almond-eyed Jigmet who lived upstairs, but rather a shy twelve-year-old who generally kept to himself.

"*Jullay*, Jigmet! How are you?"

No reply.

Looking up again, I noticed his face was pale. A strip of maroon cloth—torn from robes and cinched around his head like Rambo—was drenched in blood. Jigmet collapsed into my arms.

Christine leapt up, and together we laid the boy on a pallet. Beneath the bloody rag, I discovered a deep gash in his forehead, running from eyebrow to hairline. I delicately probed the wound, and it opened so wide I could see the boy's skull.

A crowd of monk boys appeared in our doorway, looking uncomfortable. "What happened?" I asked. "Did he fall?"

No one answered.

"Big rock," Norphal finally said, and the group shuffled. I suspected someone had kicked a boulder down on Jigmet from above.

Christine retrieved our trauma kit. I yanked out gauze, anaesthetic, antibiotic cream and sutures. Keeping my hands busy gave me a chance to think. Jigmet needed stitches, but getting him to Padum might take hours. And how well equipped was the clinic? Perhaps we should try sewing the gash up ourselves? I'd never actually placed a stitch in a wound, although I once watched seventy-nine go into the smashed face of a fallen Sherpa at Everest base camp, and somewhere in the recesses of my mind remained a vague memory of the double twisting knot used to cinch the thread.

Jigmet moaned. Christine struggled to staunch the bleeding. Better to do it right here and now, I decided.

We rinsed Jigmet's forehead with alcohol, and the young boy writhed, fluttering on the edge of consciousness. After packing antibiotic cream and topical freezing into the wound, there was nothing left to do but get on with it.

I unwrapped a suture, and the monk boys at the doorway gasped. I would have preferred not to have an audience, as I was not confident in what I was about to attempt, but I ignored the whispers and focused on Jigmet.

Christine aligned the edges of the gash. "You can do this, Bruce."

The suture needle was the size and shape of a torn fingernail. Gripping it with a pair of surgical tweezers, I placed the tip on the edge of the wound and pushed. I expected it to slip in easily, like a hypodermic needle, but the skin resisted. I pushed harder, until I was misshaping Jigmet's forehead like a tarpaulin filled with water. Still nothing. Harder. Blood seeped from the wound. Jigmet cried out. I felt sick.

Taking a deep breath, I tried again.

This time, with a mighty shove, the needle punctured the skin, and I guided it through the wound and up the other side. My attempt at a double-wrap knot failed, so I secured it with a clumsy granny. But the stitch held, and the edges of the wound were aligned. I breathed in relief.

Then I tried to put in a second stitch, but no matter how hard I pushed, the needle refused to penetrate the skin.

"Let's take him to the clinic," Christine finally whispered.

I was frustrated, for I'd wanted to fix Jigmet myself, but I knew she was right.

Norphal raced off to find Wang Chuk, and the monk soon came barrelling into our room. He bellowed at Jigmet, unconvinced the poor boy needed medical attention, but I insisted. So Wang Chuk went in search of a car in the village below. After a sip of juice, Jigmet and I followed, limping down the pathway with his arm draped over my shoulder, finding Wang Chuk waiting beside a tiny blue Suzuki.

Forty-five minutes later, the driver dropped us at a steel Quonset hut on the outskirts of Padum, with an immense white and red cross painted on the roof. Two elderly women sat in the shade of a willow, spinning wool. After collecting a two-rupee (three-cent) outpatient fee, they summoned a rake-thin Indian doctor, wearing shorts and T-shirt. He led us past rooms labelled THEATRE, DISPENSARY and WC, to a ceramic-tiled alcove, holding a small bed and steel sink heaped with dirty implements.

Yanking Jigmet's dressing off, the young doctor broke into laughter as he inspected my stitch. He continued to laugh as he scrubbed his hands, doused Jigmet's forehead with water and injected an enormous quantity of local anaesthetic. Finally, when the quivering boy could no longer feel a needle scratching against the surface of his skin, the still-snorting doctor sewed up the wound.

It was a surprisingly crude process. Using a needle suitable for moose hide, he pushed and tugged with the vigour needed to sew a pair of moccasins. Jigmet, I surmised, possessed one seriously tough forehead. When it was done, a strip of gauze was wrapped around Jigmet's head, again and again, until he looked like a war victim—or mummy.

Back in Karsha, village children surrounded our car, besieging Jigmet with questions. He smiled but said nothing. Together we climbed back up to the monastery.

Later I saw Jigmet bounding down a pathway with a pack of other novices. A knit beanie of maroon wool—exactly the same shade as Buddhist robes—covered his bandages.

❧

Shale clouds drifted across a lavender sky. The icy summits rising above Padum flamed orange, like torches. It was our final day at the monastery, and I sat outside the hobbit door, cradling the moment, knowing it would never come again.

For three months, I'd watched as the great rivers sweeping across Zanskar's central plains—the Stod and the Tsarap—shifted colors: tortoise-shell green, slate grey, turquoise, mocha. Now they ran silver, wending eastward.

Running parallel to their banks was a dirt track, twisting and whirling across the undulating gravel flats like a piece of yarn that has been pulled taut and then released. This was the route we would follow tomorrow, toward another world.

❦

A group of novices rushed into our room, inviting us to join them in the classroom at ten o'clock—a final goodbye.

We arrived to find the classroom empty, and I momentarily wondered if they had forgotten about the invitation. Then Wang Chuk waltzed in, carrying an armful of shiny biscuit packages. Slowly novices trickled in behind him, one by one.

While we waited, I wrote our "real" names on the blackboard; Bruce, Bodi, Taj and Christine Kirkby. I also wrote our mailing address and my email, promising if any of the novices ever needed our help in the future, we would do whatever we could. It may have been in vain. None of the boys had ever posted a letter before. And no one knew what email was.

But the monk boys were ecstatic, and insisted we write the contact information ourselves, in each of their notebooks, just to ensure there was no mistake. The process reminded me of signing high school yearbooks—a fleeting memento of a departing friendship that felt so significant in the moment, yet was destined to be forgotten.

When Jigmet arrived, he plopped down on my lap, dark eyes dancing. Peeking under his dressings, I found the wound healing well. I pressed a tube of antibiotic cream into his palm and urged him to use it in the days ahead.

When the debate-teaching *geshe* shuffled in, everyone settled on cushions. The *geshe* said a few words in Zanskari (translated to English by Wang Chuk): "We thank you for coming and teaching at Karsha school. We are embarrassed, for our students and our equipment are very far behind what you know in Canada, and we appreciate every sacrifice you have made. Please, we ask that you will always remember us. And know that anytime in the future, you or your partners will be welcome here, with us, at Karsha Gompa."

Wang Chuk presented us each with school satchels, embroidered with a crest. Mine was addressed to "Mr. Brush." Then he placed *khata* scarves around our necks. Christine and I pressed our hands together and bowed. Bodi and Taj followed suit.

I assumed the ceremony was over, but from the corner of my eye, I caught sight of monk boys yanking *khatas* from satchels. Little Nima approached first, reaching way up to put a scarf around my neck. Next he hung one on Christine, Bodi and finally Taj. Then came big Jigmet. And little Jigmet. Then Thurchin. Sonam. Purbu. It was an avalanche. White scarves filled the air, landing on our necks so quickly I couldn't keep up.

"*Jullay! Jullay! Jullay! Jullay!*"

And these were no ordinary *khatas*. Rather, the boys had given us brilliantly embroidered silk scarves, probably received on special occasions in their own pasts. Taj disappeared beneath a mountain of silk. Amid all those scarves, I glimpsed Christine, tears streaming down her cheeks.

Finally we lined up—students, faculty, family—and took a class photograph— the only one that exists from those three months.

As we walked from the classroom for the last time, little Nima ran after us, tugging at my shirt, asking hopefully, "See you tomorrow, Mr. Bruce?" But even as the words came out, he looked unsure.

"Maybe next year," I croaked.

Purbu's singsong voice followed us down the sunny path. "See you soon."

And Norgay the *tulku*: "See you tomorrow!"

❧

Sonam Dawa had returned to Zanskar to lead our trek out, and was scheduled to pick our family up at noon, so we spent the rest of the morning packing duffels, once again jettisoning anything we could do without.

When shy Tsephal dropped by to say one more final goodbye, I handed him a water bottle, the cheap plastic type similar to those given away at cycling races. His joy was such that you'd think I'd given him the keys to a new car. When I showed him how the nozzle popped up, he clapped.

Christine admitted that she'd given her designer wristwatch to Skarma that morning. "I just couldn't help myself."

Next we cleaned the room, plucking crumbs from the carpets, scrubbing walls, wiping the table and windows. And as we worked, I thought of Tashi Topden, Paljor and Jigmet, taking care of themselves in this ramshackle house, perhaps until the end of winter. I felt guilty for tearing their teacher away. Would it make their lives easier or harder? I suspected a bit of both. Undoubtedly they'd move into this room the moment we left—it would not look the same when Lama Wangyal returned.

"Put some effort into it," Christine chided the boys as they tidied, and Taj turned to stare at her in astonishment.

"Put the F-word into it?"

Eventually Christine shooed us all outside, for it seemed we were creating more mess than we were cleaning.

The three of us loitered in the shade of the rose bushes, waiting for Sonam. Noon came and went. One o'clock passed. Then two. There was still no sign of his pickup. My mind remained on the monk boys, sitting in the quiet classroom somewhere far above, studying English with Wang Chuk. I wondered if their hearts ached too.

At three o'clock, Bodi and I scrambled to the abandoned roof and scanned the central plains, finding no vehicles in sight.

At four o'clock, Christine allowed us back into Lama Wangyal's house and we lazed on the pallets.

At five o'clock, Bodi and I retrieved our journals and sketched the grand valley, sitting side by side on a boulder.

When six o'clock arrived, we climbed back up toward the courtyard for dinner. I was reluctant to relive the painful goodbyes, but we had no other choice. There was no food in Lama Wangyal's house.

The monk boys were eating alone, without an adult in sight, and screams of *Jullay!* greeted us as we emerged from the stone passageway. Skarma dragged us by hand into the dark kitchen, where Chagar heaped our bowls with broth from a blackened cauldron. As we sipped on soup, the monk boys sprinted in circles, shrieking, leaping from walls, smashing into peers.

"I can't imagine this not ending in tears," Christine observed.

Nawang tied his robes around his neck like a superhero. Tsephal proudly carried his new water bottle, and soon a game of catch evolved, as it was thrown back and forth like a football above a throng of thrashing young monks. Christine hoisted Norgay the *tulku* atop her shoulders, and he laughed hysterically as they charged through the fray.

Then silence.

Norphal stood at the courtyard door. "Sonam Dawa here," he announced flatly.

As quickly as the game started, it was over. The monk boys followed us down the pathway, little feet slapping behind us. Together we carried the heavy duffels to the waiting pickup. After more goodbyes, more hugs, more high-fives, we climbed into Sonam's truck.

Seven-year-old Nawang, the tough little boy who I'd watched shake off being pelted by a boiled egg, asked one last time, "See you at puja tomorrow?"

I moved my mouth, but no words came out.

A great chorus of *Jullay! Jullay!* followed the truck as we bounced off down the dirt track. Taj was soon asleep, flushed and sweaty. Bodi's bony hip ground against mine. From across the cab, Christine rested a hand gently on my arm.

I was gasping, every breath an effort. My heart felt heavier than an anchor on the ocean floor, and through damp eyes I looked east, toward a yellow moon rising behind us.

4

IMPERMANENCE

A country at the crossroads between modernization *cum* destruction and an isolation that would preserve its identity has no real choice: others have chosen on its behalf. Businessmen, bankers, experts from international organizations, officials of the UN and half the world's governments are passionate prophets of "development" at all costs. They believe unanimously in a kind of mission not far removed from that of the American general in Vietnam who, after razing a Vietcong-occupied village to the ground, said proudly: "We had to destroy it to save it."

—Tiziano Terzani,
A Fortune-Teller Told Me

20

THROUGH THE BARRICADES

❖

Sonam's truck followed a dirt track into the high peaks. We could have driven right to Leh of course—a jarring two-day journey—but walking seemed the only proper way to relinquish this stillness.

Three months earlier, we had arrived in Zanskar from the south, trekking over the Great Himalaya Range. Now we would depart to the north, a two-week foot journey crossing sparsely inhabited ranges and fourteen soaring mountain passes, en route to the ancient monastery of Lamayuru, on the Leh–Srinagar Highway.

Bodi noticed that the speedometer in Sonam's pickup was broken, which upset him greatly. "I want to know what speed we are going!"

I explained it was more important that Sonam drove safely, and suggested we were probably travelling about fifty kilometers an hour.

"How do you know it's not fifty-one?" Bodi demanded. "Or forty-nine?"

"What type of bozo needs to know the precise speed of the truck?" I joked.

"Me. I'm that type of bozo. OK?" Then Bodi cracked an enormous smile.

The valley narrowed, and slopes of rust, black and sulfurous rock soared above. Winds raised dust devils on the flats. Heat shimmered on the horizon. Many of the glaciers in surrounding peaks had disappeared during recent years, Sonam explained, and without runoff even the scrub brush was dying.

A toothless elder stood by the roadside outside Pishu—a forlorn scattering of homesteads on sun-scorched plains—and I waved as our truck bounced past, but she stared through me, expressionless. Not far beyond, the truck jolted to a stop on the grassy banks of the Zanskar River.

Inside a blue cook tent, we met the three men who would accompany Sonam and our family across the mountains. The cook, Sundup, sat cross-legged behind a kerosene stove, frying rings of battered onion. A cook boy, fourteen-year-old Tsewang, hovered close by, wearing a brown beanie, tattered fleece, britches and knee-high socks. Stretched on the floor was an athletic-looking fellow in black tights and a Gore-Tex jacket: Tundup. All hailed from Sonam's village of Shegar.

After helping Sonam unpack his truck, Christine and I lazed on a riverbank, while Bodi and Taj floated sticks downstream. Wagtails flitted near our feet, and nearby, an extraordinary bridge of woven twigs—more than one hundred meters wide—led across turbulent waters to the village of Zangla.

Sonam's white pickup belched to life and started to drive away. Sensing something amiss, I sprinted after the truck, banging on the tailgate. Sonam stopped and rolled his window down.

"Where are you going?" I asked.

"Me no trek coming," he admitted, looking sheepish.

I was speechless.

Sonam explained that plans had changed, and instead of coming on the trek, he was instead going to join a group of Zanskar businessmen on an economic mission to southern India. Clearly he'd known for days, and I was frustrated that he hadn't told us—almost surely because he didn't want to disappoint. But more than anything, I felt sad, for the quiet man was a good friend, and I valued his insights. Our trek wouldn't be the same without him. Before Christine and the boys could say goodbye, he revved the engine and was gone.

As the sun dropped behind tall peaks, I pulled Lama Wangyal's coats onto the boys. Frigid shadows grew, and the stars beckoned.

❧

Six horses appeared on the dusty flats the next morning, driven by two weary farmers. The pair had been up all night searching for an escaped mare, and collapsed in the kitchen tent, hungrily dipping chunks of bread into milky tea. When I asked which horse Bodi would ride—Sonam had assured us he'd arrange for one—Tundup shuffled uncomfortably.

"Pony Men say riding not possible."

The horses were exhausted from harvest, he explained, and with sparse fodder in the mountains at this time of year, they would only grow weaker. All six were required to carry gear. I wasn't pleased, and nor was Tundup, for the news meant he would have to carry Taj. Once again, Bodi would ride on my back.

Christine glanced at me and then began to laugh. "Oh well. Guess it's time for you to open a can of toughen up."

Bodi and Taj returned to camp dragging poplar branches behind them, which they explained would be their walking sticks. I tried to quash the idea but Christine shot me a sharp look, and I acquiesced. Instead, I snapped the tree limbs into a reasonable length using my knee.

"Ready to go?" Tundup asked, tinny music escaping from his earbuds. I gave the thumbs-up, and our boys raced off along the banks of the Zanskar River—a blur of dust, heels and swinging sticks.

We followed a well-trodden path that once stood among the world's most popular trekking routes. But twenty years earlier, when a road was first carved along the opposite bank—part of the goliath, but as yet uncompleted, Zanskar Highway Project—the backpackers dried up.

As we walked, occasional white pickups raced past on the far shore, heading deeper into the mountains, and I spotted a yellow excavator, half submerged in the river, giving itself a bath with its own bucket, like an elephant. Apart from groves of yellowing aspen and scrubby sea buckthorn laden with orange berries, the land was relentlessly brown. Overhead, the sun floated like a diamond in an unbroken sky.

Not until dusk did we stop, in a clearing on the outskirts of Hanumal village, where sun-bleached chairs and a shack plastered with Godfather Beer posters were reminders of the hordes that once passed this way.

"Spooky spot," Sundup the cook whispered.

A snow leopard had attacked their horses in this clearing, he told us, a year earlier. The great cat managed to tear a mare's stomach open before the men chased it away. Later, it killed fifteen sheep in a nearby stable. "Blood everywhere."

After setting up our tent, Bodi and I sat in the sun-bleached chairs. While I made notes in my journal, he sketched a Ladakhi flag, taking inspiration from a string of plastic versions fluttering overhead. Soon he was kicking his feet in frustration, and tears streaked his cheeks. One of the stripes he'd drawn was too narrow.

"It looks great," I assured him. And I honestly thought it did.

"Maybe it looks okay for you, Dad. But I happen to be an Ass Burger. And that means I like things to be right."

I felt a sharp pang at his mispronunciation of Asperger, worrying the term might hang over him in future schoolyards. But my unease was overshadowed by disbelief that, in just a few weeks, he'd already gained such self-perspective.

❧

A snow leopard didn't materialize during the night. But a domestic cat did, sneaking into the cook tent and stealing our supply of mutton.

"Very smart cat," said Tundup, who had spotted the feline skulking in the bushes before retiring. "She comes slowly, slowly, and then . . ." Tundup made a sudden motion of yanking the bag away. So it would be a vegetarian trek.

We were shouldering packs when a short man in a blue puffy jacket and dark sunglasses dashed up. Bowing low, he introduced himself as Tenzin and offered his services as a porter. A scruffy beard was shaven from his upper lip, like an Amish farmer, and his smile revealed teeth so perfectly white and large they reminded me of piano keys. Tundup pointed to Bodi. Tenzin nodded. And just like that, our party had grown by one.

We set off in single file, navigating a narrow path carved into the edge of a gorge. Vertical layers of black rock soaring overhead were reminiscent of stacked vinyl records.

"Dad! You better get up here," Bodi suddenly yelled. "Bear prints!"

And he was right. Two bears had walked down the trail before us: mother and cub. The animals had passed recently, probably within the last few hours, for their prints were unaffected by winds. The tracks looked remarkably similar to a barefoot human's, Taj observed, apart from the claws. We passed frequent piles of scat, laden with orange buckthorn berries.

I was astounded, for the Himalayan brown bear (a subspecies of the grizzly) is critically endangered, facing precipitous habitat loss, population fragmentation and poaching across its range. But here they were, still in Zanskar.

Our boys were eager to spot the pair and scanned the hillsides, but at some point the prints simply vanished from the trail, and the bears eluded us.

❧

We were grinding up our first pass—a relatively gentle ascent to the Perfi La—when we caught a glimpse of the Zanskar River, languid and green, snaking away into canyonlands to the east. This marked the mouth of the legendary Chadar gorge; sheer cliffs and ferocious whitewater downstream acted as a barricade to Zanskar.

Traditionally, the Chadar was only passable in the depths of winter, when brave Zanskari butter traders tiptoed over uncertain ice. Travelling in *jato* (leather-soled, straw-stuffed woollen boots with upturned toes), the men used walking sticks to sound for thickness. When water flowed over the ice, as it often did, the men walked barefoot. Elsewhere, they inched precariously along ledges on canyon walls. By night they slept in caves, huddled close beneath robes, on their knees.

This extraordinary practice of sleeping balanced on knees—arms laid backward and hands grasping ankles—was once common throughout Zanskar, and children were taught the skill from the earliest age. It was a habit born of necessity, leaving only shins and forehead in contact with the ground, for to lie flat on a cold surface exposes one's entire body to substantial heat loss. And it speaks to a toughness that has since passed from our world.

Today, the Chadar represents the final and most challenging link in the Zanskar Highway project. Road surveys began here in 1971, and dynamiting started soon afterward. But progress has been painfully slow, with annual gains measured in meters, exacting terrible loss of life. Despite legions of foreign laborers and fleets of heavy equipment, completion targets continue to be pushed back, and there still is no end in sight.

But at some point, traffic will flow.

As I stared down at the tiny road carved into the walls of the canyon, I saw a crack in the natural dam protecting Zanskar. When the road is completed, this millennia-old barricade will fail, flooding the hidden valley with modernity. And while undeniable benefits will arrive, including improved education and medical services, other more insidious changes will slip in too, such as real estate speculation, cheap labor, foreign-owned factory farms, poverty and homelessness. Within one generation, Zanskar's co-operative, self-reliant lifestyle will be extinguished.

Buddhists accept impermanence unhesitatingly. Why did I struggle to do the same? Was it just nostalgia? And was it even fair for me, a transient visitor, to mourn such a loss?

These were questions I'd wrestled with all summer.

ॐ

That night we reached a deserted mud-brick hut on the banks of a turquoise creek, bearing a lopsided sign: WELCOME T-STALL, DINK HERE ALL.

Tsewang, the cook boy, forced the lock and Sundup set up the kitchen inside, cooking chapattis while Hindi pop music blared from a phone. Tundup and our new porter, Tenzin, dozed on the steps.

Seeking quiet, Bodi and I leapt naked into the creek's crystal waters, the current whisking us through a marvellous slot canyon. Clambering atop a mid-stream boulder, swirled red and green like a bowling ball, I wrapped an arm around my son's goosebumped shoulders, as we were warmed by sun above and stone below.

Later, I joined the Pony Men, who were sorting halters and ropes. Sixty-three-year-old Phuntsok, the older of the pair, was a giant by Zanksari standards: broad-shouldered and six feet tall. Well-polished *mala* beads hung atop his grubby red fleece jacket. The father of four had worked as a Pony Man for fifteen years, he told me, to supplement his subsistence farming income.

Geyatso—Phuntsok's younger companion—reminded me of Johnny Depp in *Pirates of the Caribbean*, with a sharp chin, wispy beard, long hair and golden hoops in both ears. Across Zanskar he was known as TongTong, a reference to the threadbare stovepipe hat with upturned earflaps that never left his head.

"TongTong even wearing hat in bed," Phuntsok laughed.

"Very good hat," TongTong retorted, explaining he bought it twenty years earlier in Leh. "Good for cold. Good for rain. Good for sun. Good for wind."

As we bantered, Phuntsok unstitched a burlap sack, no larger than a purse, which contained barley. Sifting through the grain, he removed pebbles and twigs, then divided the precious fodder into six equal shares, which TongTong placed in muzzle feeders for the famished horses.

Later the pair crawled beneath a smoke-darkened sheet of plastic and fell asleep, using only saddles for pillows and horse blankets for warmth. They were the same stock of men that once slept upon knees and foreheads.

ॐ

Moonlight cast shadows on the camp. Christine and I lay awake in our tent, discussing the journey ahead.

The current arrangement for carrying our boys was not working. Tenzin and Tundup were struggling terribly: faces ashen, legs shaking, our pace often little more than a crawl. Tomorrow, we would tackle the gruelling Hanuma La (4,720 meters), and even more tortuous passes loomed beyond. In their exhaustion, I worried the porters might injure themselves—or our boys.

The obvious solution was for me to carry Bodi, leaving Tenzin and Tundup free to share Taj between them. But I worried the pair might bristle at such a suggestion.

"Let me try talking to them," Christine said. "I think it will be easier coming from a mother."

So the next morning, as we prepared to leave, I watched as she sat beside Tundup and the pair talked briefly. Suddenly Tundup leapt up, and heaving Taj to his back, set off alone at a blistering pace.

Christine looked at me and shrugged. "He thought I was questioning his strength."

Ten minutes later, with horses loaded, we followed in pursuit. I half-heartedly reached for Bodi's backpack, but Tenzin laughed and wagged a finger at me. But soon he was bent in half, gasping.

We finally caught Tundup, lying beside a stream, a hand-rolled cigarette dangling from his lips. Taj crawled beside him, picking buttercups. After slurping water from cupped hands and nibbling chocolate, I simply scooped up Bodi and set off. No need to make a big deal out of it. Face was saved, and the new arrangement would endure.

Wolf prints littered the mountainside. There were at least five animals, including two tiny pups and an immense male. We passed bleached bones, crushed in powerful jaws, and piles of white scat. I suspected the pack was denning somewhere nearby, but despite scanning the slopes, could spot no entrance.

It took seven excruciating hours to crest the Hanuma La pass, its summit marked by prayer flags strung between rocky spires. In the uncannily dry air, it seemed we could see forever. To our back rose brooding Himalayan summits, plastered with snow and ice. Ahead lay a sea of shattered ochre peaks, seemingly bending away with the curvature of the earth. In all that vast land, I couldn't spot a single sprig of vegetation.

❦

It was two more days before we stumbled upon a sign that people existed amid such desolation.

Nyalo, a native fodder shrub now orange with frost, had been cut and rolled into bundles. Stacked trailside and weighed down with stones, these loads would eventually be carried home by villagers, their homes still ten kilometers distant, in preparation for winter.

An hour later, a distant gathering of homesteads came into view. This was the village of Lingshet, perched in a high mountain bowl. Sheer cliffs soared above, the color of cherry and smoke.

We passed a deep pit on the village outskirts, its walls lined with stone. "Wolf trap," Tundup explained, and it wasn't hard to imagine a canine pacing those depths, lured by sheep entrails. Its howls would rouse villagers and lead to an inescapable fate, delivered by either rock or bullet.

No sooner had we set up camp in the shadow of Lingshet's small monastery than piano-toothed Tenzin announced he was leaving. Construction of a new school was about to commence in his village, and Tenzin needed the work. Minutes later he was running back down the trail.

I was saddened to see the cheery man go. And concerned, for his departure left our party weakened. When Tundup noticed me studying maps, he hinted we might shorten our route by veering northward, toward a new road.

"Snow's coming soon. Maybe boys tired. Maybe road good?"

I wasn't interested in ending our isolation with a soul-crushing trudge on pavement, and I sensed a standoff.

❧

One glorious autumn day rolled into the next. The skies remained clear and electric, the days pleasant, the nights bitingly cool.

Our route traversed highlands sprinkled with orange *nyalo*, where glaciated giants sparkled in the distance. Migratory birds grew common. We disturbed a flock of chiffchaffs, and the small brown birds flowed away like water down the slopes, hundreds of wings flapping in unison.

When the shadow of a tern passed my feet—a familiar friend from my days of raft guiding in the Yukon—I found myself wondering what inner force drove this astonishing creature to fly from the Arctic to the Antarctic, and then back again, year after year. Some instinct of course, but it's an impulse difficult to distill into words. And it reminded me of the query Christine and I so often face: Why take your boys on a trip like this?

Instinct, I suppose.

I watched Bodi as he skipped ahead, head cocked to one side, gusts of wind lashing his hair. He stared out over the shattered peaks leading toward Tibet. How wondrous to know such wildness and freedom as a child.

Many ask if I hope Bodi and Taj will grow up to be adventurers, to follow in our footsteps, but such an outcome seems irrelevant to me. I only want them to be free: free to live the lives they were meant to live—whether carpenters or concert pianists, homebodies or nomads, city slickers or country bumpkins.

And the only way I know to teach freedom is to live it myself.

As I gazed at Bodi's freckles and clear eyes, a wave of love swept across me, the immensity of which I suspect only a parent knows. Then, on its heels, came a shadow. I'd felt it before: that inescapable reality that something bad, even tragic, could happen to my precious boys someday—no matter what I did.

To love is to risk loss. One cannot exist without the other.

❧

It began to snow on the sixth day.

At the base of the notorious Sengge La (Lion Pass), the boys fenced with walking sticks while Christine snoozed in our tent. Under the Pony Men's plastic tarp, I found Phuntsok hunched over a kerosene stove, cooking peas. His grey whiskers had grown long, and he looked tired. TongTong handed me a bowl of *tsampa*, splashing tea on top. Too poor to afford butter, the Pony Men's brew carried only salt. I stirred the scalding mixture with a finger and we ate in silence.

"Horses very weak," TongTong finally said.

Fodder was sparse in these hills, and he worried less would be found ahead.

Phuntsok wanted more tea, but the water jug was empty. I sprang up to fill it, but TongTong seized my wrist. It was not my work, he insisted. After much bickering, he yielded.

Thin ice covered the black waters of a nearby spring. Plunging the jug in, I filled it to the brim, then slid it under the Pony Men's tarp. Hearing nothing, I peered inside. Both men were sound asleep on the rocky ground, mouths open.

❧

Overnight, fantastical ice formations sprouted from the rubble. They looked like tulips, with delicate petals of ice, and I'd never seen anything remotely similar. My guess was warm vapor escaping from the glacial till had frozen, forming these superb structures.

It was a sign that winter was coming, Tundup said. We passed hundreds of such ice flowers as we climbed. When sunlight finally hit the slopes, the wondrous creations didn't melt, but rather in a final act of magic, they sublimated, vanishing before our eyes.

It was bitingly cold on the summit of the Sengge La. This marked the geographic border of Zanskar: rain falling on the slopes ahead would flow toward the Indus River, and not the enchanted vale behind us. I gazed south one final time. Tucked somewhere amid those craggy peaks was Karsha Gompa. I hadn't found a guru during our months there. Nor had I learned any Buddhist theory. And my meditative efforts remained inconsistent at best. Nonetheless, the ancient way of life we'd glimpsed felt vitally important.

Could anything I'd learned during those precious months be carried forward, to lives lived in thicker air?

❧

Snow sloughed off our tent fly all night. Morning revealed a landscape painted white. Christine pulled Zanskari coats onto the boys, then they dashed from the tent to greedily eat snowballs. I found TongTong and Tundup huddled around a small fire, leaden fingers over orange embers, listening as Phuntsok read Tibetan scripture aloud. We packed quickly.

"Taj, you'll be tired if you run around all day," Christine warned as we prepared to set off.

"Yes, but then I'll regroup and be like two of me," he laughed. Then his short legs carried him off in pursuit of Bodi, leaving us wondering where such ideas came from.

A pair of choughs followed us most of the morning, and marmots whistled from sandy dens at our passing. The blood-red stones underfoot—damp with melting snow and embedded with veins of quartz—were so reminiscent of steak that I sank into an extended food daydream. When a wolf turd appeared on the trail, I explained to Bodi how carnivore excrement could be recognized by its white, chalky shade.

"Then why isn't our poop white?" he asked. I had no answer.

Clouds swirled and the snow thickened.

"Look, look!" Bodi shouted. "Orange elephants!"

And indeed odd creatures were staggering through the storm. Finally I surmised they were donkeys, buried beneath immense loads of *nyalo*, headed toward the village of Photaksar.

That night, temperatures plummeted and vicious winds scoured the peaks. Christine warned, "No more laundry on this trek, boys. It's officially time to turn your underwear inside out and backward."

❧

The spring outside our tents was frozen solid the next morning, and our boys delighted in playing hockey with walking sticks on the glistening surface, whacking at pucks of ice.

Thank goodness I had listened to Christine and had not forbidden them from bringing the heavy sticks on our journey, for they provided endless diversion and joy. The pair used the sticks to play golf and hockey, and as javelins and spears. They'd stuffed boots on the ends and pretended to lift barbells. They'd tied strings to them and gone fishing. More than once, I'd run back down the trail to retrieve a stick left behind at a snack break.

As we packed camp, Tundup again beseeched the Pony Men to surrender one of their steeds for Bodi to ride.

Reluctantly Phuntsok dragged over a thin, grey mare. A grapefruit-sized lump protruded from the horse's belly, and Phuntsok explained she'd been gored by a yak as a filly. He had pushed her guts back inside, then sewn her crudely up. When she survived the trauma, she earned the name Toe-Luke, meaning "yak attack."

Bodi leapt aboard and Tundup yanked on the halter. As they clattered away, I raced to stay close behind. But I needn't have worried. Bodi remained an amazingly natural rider. When the horse faltered on steep slopes, as it routinely did, he never flinched and instead leaned casually forward. Christine reminded him to grip the mare's belly with his knees, but he brushed her off. "Yes, Mom, I'm fine." Then he continued babbling to himself.

A vast collection of prayer flags and *khata* scarves adorned the summit of the Sisar La (4,760 meters). Beyond lay a moonscape as bleak as I had ever seen: a barren land of ochre spires, dappled with sand, iron, rock and clay. This marked a critical decision point. I expected Tundup to urge us northward, toward the new road that was being constructed, but he was distracted with his earbuds. So the Pony Men pushed straight on.

Snow fell in squalls, and clouds tumbled across an azure sky, tattered—like us—by their journey across the high peaks.

"How far do we have to go, Dada?" Taj asked from my back.

"Three more days," I admitted.

"Oh good. That's not far," he clapped.

Hours later, TongTong dropped to his knees on a parched stream bed. Putting an ear to the ground, he listened for the tinkle of water somewhere beneath the rubble. Clearing tent spots, we set up camp. The ravenous horses nibbled at the dirt. Darkness brought with it a violent cold.

❧

We were climbing again at dawn, for moving was the only way to stay warm. The horses broke trail through fresh snow, weaving upward between fins of orange rock. Wind tore at our clothes. On the summit of the Nigutse La (5,130 meters), the air held half as much oxygen as it did at sea level. We paused for a hurried photograph. This marked the highest point on our route. From here, everything was downhill.

I descended the slopes cautiously, kicking steps in an icy crust, aware of both Taj on my back and the drop at my feet. When Bodi's feet grew agonizingly cold, Christine tore off his boots and rubbed bare feet in waxen hands. We passed the mummified remains of a horse, legs broken from a fall, lips pulled back in an eternal scream.

Three more hours of walking brought us to the mouth of the Shilla Gorge.

❧

I awoke in darkness. In a sleeping bag beside me, Taj snuggled close.

"Dada," he whispered. "There's a problem with my water bottle."

The water had frozen into a solid puck, which amused Taj greatly, and he began shaking the bottle like a rattle. Bodi was soon awake, shaking his own frozen bottle. By the time we'd packed camp, everyone was shivering. With chattering teeth, we all completed fifty jumping jacks. Then we entered the gorge.

Catastrophic flooding had recently scoured the abyss, leaving behind a mess of unstable boulders, so we moved cautiously, leaping from one rock to the next, crossing the frigid creek again and again. Before long, everyone had soakers. A rainbow of pebbles spread underfoot.

"I could collect an entire suitcase," Christine sighed.

But we had imposed a strict limit of five stones per person on the flight home; otherwise overweight charges might bankrupt us.

We saw no sign of previous visitors: no footprints, no rubbish, no fire scars or tent rings. But wolves had been here before, wandering the silty shorelines. And a family of weasels.

As the walls of rock pressed closer, the sky faded to a memory above. Parts of the gorge never received direct sunlight, Tundup explained, and here frozen waterfalls hung like chandeliers from overhanging faces. Bodi delighted in knocking down the delicate structures with his walking stick. Taj stuck his own stick in the back of his pants and ran in circles shouting, "Look! I'm a scorpion!"

After eight hours, I began to sense the end was near. Tundup raced ahead. Even lazy Toe-Luke started trotting. Rounding a bend, we met an incongruous sight—a straight line. A concrete wall.

We'd reached hot springs popular with Muslim families from Kargil. Several veiled women were cleaning laundry by hand in the outflow, and they scattered upon our approach, crouching behind boulders, sneaking curious glances at our boys as they passed. The sulphurous waters nourished a swath of dandelions, and the blooming flowers shocked me with their simple beauty.

Beyond lay a parking lot full of cars. And a tarmac road.

A ninety-minute trudge led toward Wanla village, where we would camp on the edge of town. But the mountains had released us. The spell was broken. Already, Tundup was on his phone.

21

GOING, GOING . . .

I awoke before dawn, feeling haunted. Our tent was pitch-black, and I slipped out, careful not to disturb Christine or the boys. The Pony Men had already left, leading their horses away toward Zanskar in darkness. Cold gusts snatched the remaining leaves from tall poplars.

How do we hold on to the things we love most, knowing seasons are always changing?

With silver shading the eastern sky, I wandered the empty streets, past rows of concrete buildings, their storefronts hidden behind steel garage doors. Red Coke flags streamed from fences, and a plastic bag bounced down the center of the road like a tumbleweed.

The silhouette of a monastery beckoned from a ridge above town, and I climbed to it. Passing through a stooped doorway, so narrow my shoulders could barely fit sideways, I found myself before a golden statue of Avalokiteshvara, at least nine meters tall.

At its feet sat an elderly monk, chanting alone beside a candle. I lowered myself beside him.

Of all the deities in Tibetan Buddhism's dizzying pantheon, it was Avalokiteshvara, the bodhisattva of compassion, who spoke most powerfully to me: the one who had forsaken nirvana in the hope of aiding others on their own quests for enlightenment. For some time I thought only of my breath, swaying with the monk's chant, admiring the golden figure before me—its own peaceful eyes gazing toward the infinite. Eventually I rose to leave. But first I rummaged through my pockets and placed a handful of rupees at Avalokiteshvara's feet, adding to drifts of bills.

Then I bowed, ever so slightly.

I bowed to the monk, chanting alone by a flickering yak-butter candle. I bowed to all the men and women chanting in all the musty temples still dotting the Himalaya, perched on the precipice of extinction. I bowed to the scholars, lamas and mystics who created this vibrant expression of humanity. I bowed to the idea of compassion itself, something the world could use much more of. I bowed to the statue towering above me, the incarnation of compassion itself, the first in an ancient lineage leading all the way to today's Dalai Lama. I bowed to my son, who seemed a bodhisattva himself, sent to strip away my ego and clear my illusions. And I bowed to the Avalokiteshvara in all of us.

Then I slipped out, toward a brightening day.

❧

Three soapy-smelling men had arrived in camp while I was away, wearing blue jeans and puffy jackets. Their shiny minivans would carry us, and all the trekking gear, back to Leh, some one hundred kilometers distant. All three hailed from Zanskar. And all three were neighbors of Sonam Dawa. The ageless system of the *paspun* endured, even here.

As we awaited breakfast in the cook tent, I squeezed onto a crate beside one of them. With bookish glasses and carefully coiffed hair, twenty-five-year-old Norbu was an excellent English speaker who would not have appeared out of place on the streets of New York. A programmer with India's Department of Defense, he had taken a day off work to help his friends, Tundup, Sundup and Tsewang.

That trio was now almost unrecognizable, having scrubbed themselves in an irrigation ditch, run gel through their hair, put on collared shirts and splashed themselves with aftershave. (I surmised there was a fair chance of encountering young women in the hours ahead.) By contrast, still wearing Lama Wangyal's Zanskari robe, I remained scruffy and unshaven, my hair tangled like a Nick Nolte mug shot.

"Isn't it silly?" Norbu laughed as we gulped down chapatti and eggs smothered in chili sauce. "We are all dressed up like Americans. And you are dressed up like a Zanskari."

When I asked his thoughts on the changes sweeping through his homeland, Norbu paused.

"We have a new tradition in Zanskar," he finally began. "When a child reaches fourteen or fifteen years old, they leave their village, usually without telling their parents. They travel to Leh, where they work for some months, in a shop or doing construction. They can make quick money, and it is an easy life. Maybe they rest for some weeks between jobs, if they like. Of course, they eventually return to Zanskar to visit their family, but when they do, they have changed. They dress differently. They talk differently. They think differently. And these changes seem very attractive to other village kids. So they too soon leave their farm and travel to the city. Every year the cycle grows. I know, because that was what happened to me."

I asked about the highway project.

"When that road reaches Zanskar, it will bring money. And medicine. And better education. And those things are important. But it will also bring bad things. Maybe some very bad things. But I don't think people in Zanskar see this, because they are all hungry for easy money."

"What bad things?" I asked.

"Today, there are no rich people in Zanskar. But there are no poor people either. This is a concept we don't understand. Everyone is the same, more or less. The families owning the best land live side by side with families holding the worst. They socialize together. They help each other. They harvest together. They go to weddings together. And funerals. But in Leh, life is different. The rich form clubs. They drive fancy cars. They eat together. They go to each other's weddings. But they don't live close together.

"And the poor? They have nothing. You'll see them sleeping on the streets. Begging. No one is helping them. Such a thing could never, ever happen in Zanskar. At least not now. But it is coming."

We talked about Zanskar's traditional lifestyle, and Norbu mourned the vanishing knowledge.

"A good example is Tundup's father," he said, pointing to the young man who had crossed the mountains with us, now wearing dark sunglasses and listening intently. "I visited him in Zanskar just last month. I've known him since I was a baby, because he is my neighbor. Some in the city might say he is *just* a farmer. But think about how much he knows. He can shoe a horse and birth a yak, so you might say he is an animal doctor. He knows when to plant his barley, based on the arrival of a bird or the length of the sun's shadows. So he is a biologist and astronomer too. He designed his own house and built it by hand. He is an architect and carpenter. He forges iron, repairs ploughs and constructs irrigation ditches, so he's an engineer too. But that's not everything. He knows his family history going back for generations. And he knows all the legends of his village, so he is a historian. He can read and write in Tibetan, so he is a scholar too. And he can sing. Not just one song, but hundreds. At a party last month, he sang from the start of the evening to the very end. He is an entertainer. He is an amazing man. But the important point is, in Zanskar, he is not unusual."

There was a long pause. Everyone in the tent was listening.

"And us? The next generation?" He pointed at the circle of shiny-shoed men huddled around the kerosene stove, wearing pleated pants and doused in cologne. "We can speak English and use a computer. So what? It makes me so sad to see all that lost in one generation. But what can we do? Nothing. So we just sit and watch."

❧

We stopped at the famous Lamayuru monastery, a tangle of white and ochre temples perched atop a high knoll beside the Leh–Srinagar Highway. The paved parking lot was chock full of tour buses. Inside, altars and treasures were hidden behind Plexiglas. Large signs in English, French and German explained the site's history. In the former home of four hundred monks, we saw just one, and he scurried away quickly.

"Something about this place feels so inauthentic," Christine moaned. "It's like they are just trying to make money from tourists."

Lamayuru was no longer a monastery, but rather a museum. And in it, I saw Karsha Gompa's future.

At a roadside stand, we ordered bottled water and chicken curry. After four months of isolation, Bodi and Taj had forgotten the perils of traffic, and we had to constantly remind them of the heavy trucks roaring past. Then we climbed back into the minivan and purred off toward Leh.

Christine and the boys drifted to sleep, but I remained restless and alert, watching as the rocky plains turned to industrial wastelands, strewn with scrap metal, tires, rusting vehicles and abandoned shells of concrete buildings. An interminable line of trucks was parked along the highway shoulder, surrounded by men wearing undershirts and velour track suits. Next came the military bases, fuel depots, vehicle compounds, target ranges, field hospitals, airfields, hangars and camouflaged barracks.

By the time the fabled city spread below us, I was numb.

✢

Winter was approaching, and the tourists had fled.

Our minivan zipped down streets lined with shuttered shops: Dreamland Cyber Cafe, Apple Tree German Bakery, Himalayan Magic Carpets, Hotel Yak Tail, Shangri-La Restaurant. A few ambitious vendors still lingered, selling the same trinkets found in Varanasi and Kathmandu: fake turquoise necklaces and little Buddha statues, blackened in the pit fires of Manali.

Our family were the only guests at the Padma Guest House. Surrounded by tall poplars and vegetable gardens, it was owned by a young Zanskari couple—friends of Sonam, of course. Opening the padlock on our small room, we found two beds and a stale pile of electric blankets inside. Christine immediately leapt into a warm shower. The boys plopped down in front of the television, and I plugged in the iPad with a forgotten feeling of anticipation surging through me.

Opening email for the first time in six months, I discovered 3,800 new messages. The majority were spam. A few came from friends and colleagues, and what struck me most was the curtness of these interactions, the sparseness of human connection. Most contained only a few sentences—it was all business. Rarely did the sender sign off with "cheers," "thanks" or even "regards." Most of the messages weren't even signed. Normally, I appreciated such brevity, but now it spoke of a breathless existence.

Wandering into the bathroom, I passed a mirror. The reflection looking back was almost unrecognizable: hollow eyes, unkempt hair, gaunt cheeks peppered with stubble.

"We're going outside to play, Dada," Taj yelled.

Despite a satellite dish offering countless channels, they had lost interest, and through a window, I watched the pair chasing yellow leaves on a chilly wind.

✢

In the years ahead, the bond between Bodi and Taj would continue to flourish. Despite a three-year age difference, the pair still play together today: building Lego scenes, bouncing on our trampoline, waiting patiently for the other to return from school before enjoying their half-hour allotment of "screen time," side by side, in a shared *Minecraft* world.

"This never would have happened if we hadn't gone away," Christine remarked recently. Then, with the awareness of a parent who knows she will someday be gone, she added, "My greatest hope is that they'll always have each other."

Several months after our family's return to Kimberley, we were visiting a local swimming pool when I noticed Bodi surrounded by a pack of grade seven boys on the slippery deck. The larger boys seemed to be jostling him, and I wondered what on earth was going on. Was he being bullied? Only as I raced to intercede did I realize that the boys were actually high-fiving Bodi, who grinned hesitantly.

"Saw you on TV," one toothy tween gushed. "That was so awesome."

The television series itself was a dismal failure, bumped from prime time after just three weeks and replaced by a far safer ratings bet: *Bikinis & Boardwalks*.

In the intervening years, I visited Wes (now a father of three) in Los Angeles and have stayed loosely in touch with the other television crew members, mostly via social media. Heartfelt emails occasionally arrive from viewers who have found *Big Crazy Family Adventure* on some obscure channel—usually parents or children whose lives have been touched by ASD—and for these alone, I am grateful we documented our travels.

But the greatest reward of the television project remains watching Bodi and Taj together, as they watch the show—which they love to do. I suspect their memories of those events have been cemented by the recording, and they often parody their favorite lines. Taj: "I do not like meatballs." Bodi: "Peking duck kinda tastes like, well, Peking duck."

On the rare occasions Christine and I actually sit down to watch *Big Crazy Family Adventure* with them—seeing oneself on television is as unsettling as listening to oneself on the answering machine—we both cringe whenever my narration broaches Bodi's autism spectrum diagnosis. So great is our discomfort that we tend to talk over such moments. But our boys appear completely unfazed. So why do we flinch?

While we don't second-guess our disclosure of Bodi's diagnosis, I suspect a part of our hearts will always waver.

Mercifully, the decision appears to have done him no harm, yet. To the contrary, it seems an understanding of Bodi's challenges has led many in our small community to support and encourage him, even those with whom he only crosses paths tangentially.

Indeed our journey marked a shift in the tides of Bodi's life.

Before leaving home, most days were a battle—both for him and us. In the years since, he has flourished with unexpected vigor: developing and expanding a circle of friends, learning to paint and play flute, joining speed skating and drama clubs, enjoying the challenges of French immersion. As Bodi's resistance to change and social interactions ebb, a sharp wit and unexpected joie de vivre have emerged. Now budding with confidence, he appears to understand himself with enviable clarity.

Such leaps in his development may have been coming all along, and only by a fluke coincided with our journey to Zanskar, but I don't think so. Rather, I suspect our immersion in that ancient community—with its abundance of time, stillness and attention—somehow invigorated such advances.

I suspect it invigorated my parenting as well.

Being the parent of a child on the spectrum has always felt like a delicate balance to me, a search for the right mix of both acceptance and support. And while it has never been our objective to "cure" Bodi of the unique thinking and wonderful eccentricities that make him who he is, it also goes without saying that we want to provide him with every tool we can, in order that his true nature might shine through.

I think we are not alone in this approach to navigating autism's tangled challenges.

Yet in my experience it's easy to pay lip service to "acceptance," while focusing fiercely on the interventions, therapies, and training: the "cure." My own internal balance likely tilted this way before our trip.

It seems ironic that children on the spectrum are routinely accused of *lacking empathy*, when perhaps it's the rest of us neurotypicals that are lacking.

Even years after our visit to Karsha Gompa, the most enduring gift of that time remains my newfound ability to slow down, to quietly watch and listen, and actually meet Bodi where he is—rather than trying to bend him to where I feel he should be.

If there *is* a secret sauce for me, that's it.

❧

The morning after our arrival in Leh, we shared a breakfast of toast and milky tea in the guest house courtyard, then set off to explore the city's historic bazaar. A wearisome barrage assaulted us: horns, flashing billboards, blank stares and jostling crowds. I felt as if I'd been peeled raw.

The streets themselves were a shambles, torn up by excavators. In deep trenches, shirtless men built viaducts by hand, while crews of sari-clad women mixed cement and carried drums of gravel on wooden yokes. Christine and I gripped the boys' hands fearfully, lest in a moment of inattention they tumbled into one of these pits. Overhead, a billboard announced, LEH BEAUTIFICATION PROJECT UNDERWAY.

The barley fields that once spread across these slopes had been paved over, but the irrigation channels remained. Running alongside the streets, they were now clogged with leaves, cardboard, plastic and paper refuse. Teams of men cleaned these aqueducts by rake, piling the muck by the side of the road and leaving it to dry. It would later be burned.

At a deserted pizzeria, Christine picked at her food. "I don't want to sound all holier-than-thou about it, but I think I'd rather just have a bowl of dal."

What unsettled her—at least in part—was the cost. After three months of spending almost nothing, money was again flowing from our pockets. There were tourist maps to buy and trinkets to investigate. Bodi wanted to expand his collection of gemstones. Taj had spotted a *Tintin* in the front window of a used bookshop. Christine herself wondered about trying to ship home a hand-woven carpet. In a single day, we were on track to spend more than a local family earns all year.

Like all Western tourists visiting Ladakh, we probably appeared, to local residents, to be successful and happy. And I suspected it was difficult for Ladakhis—especially those living in rural regions—to weigh the hidden costs that come with such material wealth: the desk-bound hours, the unfamiliar neighbors, the parents without time for their own children, the fast-food diets, emails and loneliness.

Meanwhile, for a Westerner visiting Ladakh, it is easy to assume that money plays a similar role here as it does at home, and thus feel horrified by the meager wages and rudimentary living conditions. But what we do not see is the peace of mind many villagers still possess: the co-operative living, the *paspun*, the abundance of time, the contentment—all things that a modern economy cannot measure, and thus does not value.

Helena Norberg-Hodge, noted critic of globalization and among the earliest outsiders to visit Ladakh, recorded a rural farmer's reaction upon first visiting Leh: "I can't understand it. My sister in the capital, she now has all these things that do the work faster. She just buys her clothes in a shop, she has a jeep, a telephone, a gas cooker. All of these things save so much time, and yet when I go to visit her, she doesn't have time to talk with me."

Outside the restaurant window, I watched farmers and gaunt laborers shuffle slowly past. None would likely ever sit in the seats we occupied. Instead, they would become flotsam, caught up in a modern flood that would soon sweep across the high peaks and into Zanskar.

22

GONE

❖

Then we flew south, to India's steaming, teeming plains.

In a posh Delhi neighborhood, uniformed guards saluted our taxi as it pulled up to the wrought iron gates of a colonial hotel. After circling the car, using mirrors on hand-held sticks to ensure no bombs were mounted on the undercarriage, they waved us on.

Beyond lay manicured lawns shaded by frangipani, palm and eucalyptus. Fountains sprayed, peacocks strutted and flocks of lime-green parakeets zipped between treetops. A bellboy in tux and top hat welcomed us to the opulent world of Maidens, part of the luxurious Oberoi Group.

Sonam had booked our rooms in advance, never mentioning where. Now, upon seeing the hotel, Christine was mortified. "It's too much, Bruce. He knows us better than this!"

But the humidity was crushing, and we didn't have the energy to look elsewhere. So I handed my credit card to a murmuring, sari-clad woman behind a mahogany desk.

While the marble hallways, turquoise pool, terraces and balustrades were all gorgeous, what struck me was the pervasively sour mood. No one smiled. Not those milling in the lobby. Not those lying on poolside chairs, sipping cocktails. And for the first time in months, no one acknowledged our boys—except when they disrupted the serenity, which brought darkened glances.

On any other visit, at any other time, I don't think I would have noticed. But there exists a fleeting cusp as one emerges from a journey, when the world is seen with unusual clarity. When attitudes and assumptions generally invisible—the simple beauties, the jarring inequities—come into sharper focus. This likely seems self-evident, even facile, but as I gazed around that glassy lobby, the impression was overwhelming.

We'd only just dragged the heavy duffels into our tennis court–sized suite—the boys were already jumping from one king bed to the next as if on trampolines—when the phone purred. It was Lama Wangyal. He was waiting downstairs.

I had been planning on calling his mobile after we'd settled in, but there was no need: the wide-reaching Zanskari web had apprised him of our whereabouts.

"Come on up!" I told him, giving our room number.

But he couldn't. He was being held at the front doors, he explained, not allowed to enter the colonial hotel until I appeared to vouch for him.

Throughout Zanskar, Buddhist monks are held in highest esteem, shorn skulls and maroon robes symbolizing sacrifices made on behalf of all. As the former head of the largest monastery in the valley, Lama Wangyal's prestige and influence remained immense. But here in modern Delhi, such attributes were meaningless. I, on the other hand, possessed light skin and a credit card, which could open almost any door.

I hustled down, and there he was, silhouetted against the window.

The instant I saw his familiar fatherly figure, I was flooded with unexpected joy. I'd missed the stern man. The bellhop saluted theatrically and waved Lama Wangyal inside. I wrapped my arms around him.

"This very happy day," the Lama said softly, kissing my cheeks over and over.

He carried the same red canvas bag he'd departed with from Karsha Gompa. Clearly he was moving in with us, which was no problem, for our suite was ridiculously large and held plenty of spare couches.

"This *very* big hotel," he whispered as we walked down the carpeted hallway. Then he pointed to the vaulted ceilings. "Mortub, why so tall?"

I could offer no sensible answer.

"Very difficult to heat in winter," he declared, thinking pragmatically as always.

When I tried to explain that there was no winter here, at least not in the way he knew, and that the hotel was heated by oil that arrived in trucks, rather than firewood, Lama Wangyal just shook his head, as if he'd rather not know. I didn't say that the people staying here couldn't care less about the expense of heating such a grand palace; that we'd slipped beyond the world where such warmth demanded a physical toll.

After a happy reunion with Christine and the boys, we sat on a sofa together, eating fruit and cheese from a platter, talking of the trek, of our final days at the monastery and of Lama Wangyal's journey to Delhi. He had stayed in a Tibetan refugee settlement, initially renting a dormitory room for five dollars a night. But when the costs began adding up, he moved into a monastery, sleeping on the floor beside a snoring monk.

Then Lama Wangyal got down to business.

"No visa," he said, confirming rumors I'd heard from Sonam. "But Mortub, you can fix?"

He showed me the letter he had received from the Canadian embassy. It was a pile of bureaucratic jargon, almost unintelligible, even to a native English speaker. After quoting at length from Parliamentary Acts, the missive ended with a list of possible reasons why any application could be refused. In Lama Wangyal's case, just one box had been checked: *Insufficient funds*.

The letter came unsigned and carried no return address. It was the universal administrative obfuscation: faceless and cowardly.

And the decision seemed fundamentally flawed, for Lama Wangyal's application carried with it a signed guarantee that I would cover all his expenses, and included bank statements and tax returns to verify my capability. Submitting a new application was out of the question at this late date. So I set off with Lama Wangyal to visit the visa center, despite a warning not to on the letter.

In bustling streets, we flagged down a tuk-tuk, and the blinding disparity of modern India rolled past. At every intersection, children with wild hair and fetid clothes emerged from cardboard boxes, begging at the tinted windows of BMWs and Jaguars. Rake-thin men pushed bicycles carrying staggering collections of mustard oil tins, which they'd gathered from restaurant trash bins, eventually to be sold to the poor as cooking pots. Others carried stacks of flattened cardboard boxes, which they flogged as beds.

For many Zanskaris, Delhi represented the promised land, but whose dream was this?

Midday traffic moved at a crawl. Horns honked frantically. Cars pressed frighteningly close, but never hit. Overhead, the sky was filled with thunderheads, and my shirt was sodden in the humidity. Crammed closely on the tuk-tuk's rear bench, hip bones ground.

"Visa application center close," Lama Wangyal promised after we'd been driving an hour.

Two and a half hours later, the tuk-tuk spluttered to a stop before the glassy high skyscraper. My watch read 3:52 P.M. The visa centre closed at 4:00 P.M. Sprinting up escalators, we found security guards barring the entrance.

"Come back tomorrow," they instructed. I showed them my watch, which read 3:57, but they shook their heads.

Sitting on the marble floor, overcome with frustration, I watched as men in business suits continued to whisk in and out of the office, carrying armfuls of passports. They were travel agents, the guards explained. Then, inexplicably, one of the uniformed men whistled and waved me in.

I joined a long queue and eventually arrived before a pane of bulletproof glass, where I made my case to a young man in an immaculate blue suit.

"This application was refused because of lack of funds, but that can't be correct, because I've guaranteed return tickets, food and lodging."

"We don't make the decisions here," the man explained, his voice coming through an unseen speaker.

"Can I talk to the person who made this decision?"

"No."

"How can I appeal?"

"You can't."

"Do you have a phone number for the embassy?"

"No."

After much badgering, he eventually pushed a confetti-like slip of paper beneath the glass. "Contact," he said, then waved me off.

I was filled with hope—until I got outside and glanced at the paper, which held the generic email for Canadian Consular Services in Ottawa.

That evening I composed a lengthy email, summarizing the situation and noting the urgency. Minutes after hitting send, my email pinged. My hopes soared again. I'd received a reply. Maybe someone out there actually cared.

But it was only an autoreply, pages of bafflegab that essentially said: *You are shit out of luck, because we won't reply to any query, ever.*

The most frustrating part was that Lama Wangyal met all the requirements. He was legitimate. Yet he had been caught by some invisible trap. He would never possess the simple freedoms I took for granted.

Lama Wangyal sat beside me, watching me type. "You fixing, Mortub? You very good fixing man!"

I promised him I wouldn't give up.

❧

I awoke unsure of the time. Thick drapes blocked the windows. Only the hum of the air conditioner and the click of the coffee machine broke the unnatural silence. The hotel room, in its utter uniformity, could have been anywhere: Vancouver, Toronto, New York. This was the world I knew, and to which I was returning.

Bodi wanted to go shopping in Delhi's busy markets; he'd been carefully saving rupees for the occasion. Christine was happy to accompany him. She wanted new pillowcases for home. But the thought of shopping was more than I could bear.

So instead, I took Lama Wangyal and Taj to visit Humayun's Tomb, the lavish mausoleum of India's second Mughal emperor—reminiscent of the Taj Mahal. As we shuffled across marble courtyards, assaulted by heat and crowds, little Taj tugged my hand.

"Dad, I'm hungry. Do you have any *tsampa*?"

Sadly I told him I didn't have any *tsampa* balls in my pants pockets. The Himalaya seemed a distant memory.

Just then, a foghorn blew: the deep, rumbling sound of an ocean-going vessel or lighthouse. But there was no harbor nearby, and I wondered aloud what the sound could be.

"Dad!" Taj looked at me like I was crazy. "It was the puja horn."

❧

We are not Buddhists, nor are we trying to be, but years after our return to Canada, I continue to meditate, or at least I try to.

And when life rears up, as it often does—waiting in queues, stuck in traffic, dealing with crashed computers, cramming luggage into overhead airline containers—I catch myself instinctively shifting focus to my breath. One breath in. One breath out. It's astonishingly effective.

Bodi meditates too, as part of his bedtime routine. Every night we listen to a guided practice on the cracked and outdated iPad, and while I'm not convinced

Bodi always pays attention, the ritual of breathing undeniably calms our agitated son. And as a stickler for statistics, he remains highly motivated to extend his "run streak," which now sits at over a year.

Occasionally I catch Taj muttering *om mani padme heung* while he fiddles with Lego on his bedroom floor. Even more touching for me, as his father, is discovering him watching documentaries about endangered animals or threatened ecosystems as part of his precious screen time. The Buddhist compassion for *all sentient beings* certainly exists within him—whether that is in part due to our journey is much harder to say.

For her part, Christine tends to view spirituality through a gentler lens. "Formal practice feels less important now," she admitted recently. "What matters to me is finding ways to make those ideals a part of daily life."

Lama Wangyal's four *thankas* hang in a row above our kitchen table. Tea lights and incense often burn below. We eat barley on occasion, though *tsampa* is hard to come by in Canada. I still spice my tea with a mixture of cardamom, cinnamon and cloves. (Christine, not so much.) And my aging mother, after a lifetime of living in Toronto, recently bought a nearby house in our tiny mountain town and joined (or rejoined) our *paspun*.

On a deeper level, my relationship with time has shifted. I pause more frequently, just to breathe or watch light in the clouds, and engage more often with friends, neighbors and strangers, instead of rushing past. Christine and I seem to have found more space for each other as well. We sit together each morning, coffee in hand, and watch the sun rise—over the Rockies instead of the Himalaya. And we frequently stroll through our neighborhood, just for the heck of it: something I would have never considered before.

We both turn work aside as soon as the boys are home from school, not out of obligation, but because it's how we want to spend our hours. Phones never come to the dinner table, and we always read to the boys for an hour before bed.

Taken individually, these may seem like token efforts, but together I believe they are making a difference.

While Zanskar changed us, in small but enduring ways, it too is changing, now caught in an accelerating vortex of decay. Tragically, much of what we saw is already gone. The yellow digger crossed the Shingo La not long after we departed. Cars, motorbikes and trucks followed the next year. The Chadar will be breached soon. Massive highway tunnels are planned. What will be left a decade from now? Or a century?

In much the same manner that an overburdened society unconsciously tries to bend those on the spectrum (or anyone else who stands out) toward its own mould, so too does it try to bend remote and ancient cultures, and it has for centuries. As the advances of modernity pour in, most everyone is too damn busy to slow down and pay attention, and anything that stands out gets paved over or hammered into place. As homogeneity spreads, we all suffer the loss: of diversity, of ideas, of possibilities.

But still, some opaque hope remains.

In eerily prescient words, the great Buddhist reformer Guru Rinpoche predicted a millennium ago that, "when the iron bird flies and horses run on wheels, the Tibetan people will be scattered like ants across the face of the earth."

I like to imagine we are now part of that scattering, carrying in our own humble way a tiny sliver of Zanskar's ancient knowledge—a seed of difference.

❦

Diwali, the great Hindu festival of lights, was approaching, and with five days until our flights to Canada, we escaped the noise and crowds of Delhi and headed to Rajasthan, a day's drive southwest of the capital.

The six-lane highway was crowded with holidaymakers. Tuk-tuks screamed past like lawn mowers, overflowing with passengers, others perched precariously on rear bumpers. Entire families travelled by moped: two or three youngsters between Dad's arms, Mom riding behind, sidesaddle. Bony cows ambled the wrong way through traffic. Gigantic trucks followed, sending cars spilling into the ditch. No one seemed concerned.

On the outskirts of Jaipur, camels and elephants wandered amongst tent cities. Cows and pigs—stained with festive purple dye for the holidays—rooted through smouldering piles of garbage.

We'd reserved two rooms at the glassy new Fortune hotel: one for Christine and Bodi, the other for Lama Wangyal, Taj and me. Lama Wangyal gasped when I swiped our plastic room card.

"Key?" he asked, trying it himself several times, marvelling as the lock clicked.

The room offered endless discoveries. Curtains could be raised and lowered with a remote control. A miniature fridge full of booze. Light switches responded to touch.

"This bigger money than Delhi hotel?" Lama Wangyal asked, but I shook my head.

The old monk hopped on a digital scale in the bathroom, registering seventy kilograms—remarkably svelte for his towering height. Afterward, I weighed myself and stared at the results in disbelief. I'd lost ten kilos at Karsha Gompa and weighed less than I had in high school.

When I tossed a cloth bag that once carried apples into the garbage, Lama Wangyal retrieved it and deftly fashioned an odd-looking red hat. Nothing went to waste, even here.

The boys splashed with Christine and me in a rooftop pool, but we couldn't persuade Lama Wangyal to join us. He had never swum before. Instead he sat on a deck chair under a green and white umbrella, wearing monk's robes and his new red hat. When a pigeon crashed headfirst into a nearby window, flapping uselessly across the deck with wings askew, Lama Wangyal corralled the bird and carefully carried it to the chair beside him, where despite his ongoing care, it died.

As the sun set, fireworks shattered the evening.

"Jaipur very good city," Lama Wangyal smiled, leaning against the railings.

"Why?" I asked.

He pointed toward distant hills. "Delhi too flat. This reminding me of Zanskar."

❧

"Mortub, what is that light?" Lama Wangyal asked as we lay awake in the king bed. It was the smoke alarm, blinking on the ceiling above us, and I explained its purpose to him.

Silence.

Then Lama Wangyal spoke again. "Mortub, I no lucky man."

I'd tried everything I could to turn the tide on his visa application. I'd canvassed friends in Canada to write letters of support. I'd dispatched email after email to Consular Services. Left voice mail after voice mail. I'd submitted further proof of my finances. But there had been no reply. And in my heart, I knew one would never come.

In the meantime, Lama Wangyal had grown progressively withdrawn. I sensed a storm brewing.

❧

I awoke sometime later to the sound of chanting.

Lama Wangyal sat silhouetted before the hotel window, and I was overcome with profound grief. I knew he was retreating to the clear blue skies of his home. Our farewell was approaching.

It was now a national holiday. There was no way a visa would be issued in time for Lama Wangyal to board our flight tomorrow. Instead, his ticket to Canada would go unused, and I would buy him a seat on a plane bound for Leh.

Making matters worse, he had declared that if he couldn't come to Canada now, with us, then he never wanted to come. Travelling alone, halfway around the world, was more than the old monk was willing to contemplate.

Quietly I tiptoed over and sat beside him, struggling to bridge the divide. Lama Wangyal continued chanting, refusing to look at me, only breaking his rhythm to occasionally dispute my words, then returning to scripture.

He was angry. Angry at me and other foreign friends for not trying hard enough. I imagined how powerless he must feel, playing a game he didn't understand, on a tilted field with opaque rules, his ambitions thwarted by a system he couldn't recognize.

For the first time, he called me Bruce instead of Mortub, and something broke inside me. I stood to leave, but he called me back, arms open. We stood silently together, both in tears, the old man holding my cheek.

❧

We returned to the Maidens in Delhi and packed our duffels one final time.

I felt guilty: guilty that I'd failed to get Lama Wangyal a visa; guilty for my excitement at returning home; guilty for the comforts I would soon enjoy.

Earlier that afternoon, Lama Wangyal had picked up a white envelope that slid under the door. It was the bill for our one-night stay: more than the average Zanskari would earn in a year. Now the old monk asked for money, to pay for this and that, which we gave. He suggested we sponsor the Labrang temple, and we promised to wire more money. He demanded we ask friends at home to sponsor the temple as well. I just wanted to fly away.

Our flight departed after midnight so, following dinner, we tucked the boys in for a short sleep. Then Christine and I collapsed in our king bed. She cuddled close, an arm draped across my shoulders, and drifted off. I lay awake, watching the blinking smoke alarm.

Lama Wangyal sat on a sofa nearby, chanting.

Earlier that day, I'd booked his ticket home. He would come to the airport with us, where we'd drop him at Domestic Departures before checking in for our international flight. Christine had prepared a pullout bed for the lama to sleep in, but instead he crawled into the king bed beside me.

"What time we leave hotel, Mortub?"

"Eleven," I told him. Carefully, he set the alarm on his watch.

"*Om mani padme heung, om mani padme heung,*" he whispered over and over.

Then he rolled to face me. If someone had looked down on us at that moment, we would have appeared like a pair of brackets—open and closed—with a void between us. And across the expanse of that white sheet, Lama Wangyal reached for my hand.

Do not try to use what you learn from Buddhism to be a
Buddhist;
    Use it to be a better whatever-you-already-are.
                          —His Holiness Tenzin Gyatso,
                            the Fourteenth Dalai Lama

NOTES ON LANGUAGE AND SPELLING

Zanskari is a dialect of Ladakhi, a language of Tibetic origins. While parallels exist between Ladakhi, modern Tibetan (speech) and classical Tibetan (Buddhist scripture), the three are not mutually intelligible, and are considered distinct languages.

In this book, I have rendered Zanskari words phonetically and identified them using italics (*khata, tsampa*) except for familiar terms, such as lama or yak. While more accurate romanized representations of Zanskari words can be accomplished through Wylie transliteration—a standardized scheme for rendering Tibetan script, created in 1959 by American scholar Turrell V. Wylie—the shortcoming of the Wylie system is that it does not reflect pronunciation, which is essential for readers. For example, the men's name Tenzing (phonetically rendered) would be unintelligible to most in its Wylie form, *bsTan.'Dzin*.

One drawback of phonetic renderings is the significant number of spelling discrepancies that arise. For example, the common Zanskar greeting *Jullay* may also be seen as *Ju-Le, Juley* or *Julley*. In this text, I have attempted to employ the most common phonetic forms found in literature, or lacking that, I have rendered the words as they sounded to me. But be warned: travellers to the Himalaya may be familiar with wildly alternative spellings.

288 ❧ NOTES ON LANGUAGE AND SPELLING

Names can be particularly troublesome. The previously mentioned Tenzing can also be found phonetically rendered as *Tenzin*, *Stenzin* or *Stenzing*. Yet all refer to the same Tibetan name, *bsTan.'Dzin*.

Geographic place names are equally confusing. Every village, river, mountain and pass mentioned in this text will have alternative phonetic renderings. The village of Karsha can also be found in both popular literature and academic papers as *Kurscha* and *Karscha*. There is no correct answer to the question: *Pipiting* or *Pibiting*? The ancient Shingo La pass was recently signposted by the Indian Government as *Shinkola*.

Even the name Zanskar itself presents uncertainties, being variously recorded throughout history as *Zansgar* and *Zaskar*. John Crook, a University of Bristol professor of anthropology with deep roots in the region, argues that *Zangskar* is the most accurate rendition. But because the majority of modern maps and writers have adopted *Zanskar*, I do the same in this text.

The name Zanskar itself has been widely translated as "land of bright copper," but no entirely convincing etymology exists. Other theories include *Zan* (food) *mKhar* (palace), and *bZang* (good) *dKar* (white), in which "good" refers to the auspicious triangular shape of the valley and "white" describes the innate religious inclination of the local people.

JULLAYS

My deepest appreciation goes first and foremost to the people of Zanskar and their unflinching generosity, warmth and support. May your ancient ways light a path forward for us all.

Of special note is Lama Tsering Wangyal, to whom this book is dedicated, and without whom none of this would have been possible. *Jullay, jullay meme.*

The novice boys of Karsha Jhamling Monastery School will always hold a place in our family's hearts, and we send much love to Stenzin Purbu of Pidmo, Stenzin RamJam of Rantasha, Skarma Eshay of Phay, Stenzin Jigmet of Zangla, Sonam Tsephal of Hanamor, Stenzin Nima of Abran, Stenzin Norgay of Sendo, Stenzin Lakdan of Tahan, Stenzin Joray of Zangla, Lobsang Changchup of Karsha, Sonam Chospel of Pishu, Tashi Tundup of Sang Pha Lay, Stenzin Thurchin of Phay, Stenzin Phuntsok of Pishu, Stenzin Nawang of Lungmur, Stenzin Tsewang of Tsazar, Jigmet Rinchen of Shamuling, Tsering Paljor of Tungri and Stenzin Norphal of Taman.

Our deepest gratitude goes also to the monks of Karsha Gompa, who opened their doors to four Canadian strangers and welcomed us in their midst. I trust it is clear that the affectionate nicknames we bestowed upon them were born of our own linguistic limitations. Heartfelt *jullays* to all present during the summer of 2014, including Meme Khampo Purbu, Lama Tsering Wang Chuk, Lama Jimba Sonam, Lama Tsering Norbu, Lama Ishay Sundup, Lama Dorjey Tundup, Lama Lobsang Mortub, Lama Tham Chouy, Lama Yarsal Thakpa, Lama Tsering

Sundup, Lama Kachen Tenzin Chosang, Lama Stenzin Ta'han, Lama Stenzin Jamyoung, Lama Lobsang Strab, Lama Sonam Wangchuk, Lama Tashi Gyaltsen, Lama Lobsang Khedup and Lama Thukstan Chosphel. Immense *jullays* also to the monastery cooks, Tashi Tsering and Chagar, as well as the delightful crew of Nepali workers who welcomed us in their midst.

Although we spent just five days with Jamyang Lamo and Ringzin Dorjey of Tungri, in that short time it felt our families intertwined, and for their golden hearts, so many *jullays*. Deepest thanks also to Sonam Dawa, who guided us into Zanskar and became a close friend during our stay. *Jullay* also to his wonderful wife Tolma of Shegar.

Last but not least, *jullay* to Lobsang Tsering, Lama Wangyal's nephew, who launched our journey with his prophetic words: *Most generously. Problems are none.* Now a student in France, his guidance during the writing of this book expanded my understanding of Zanskari culture and Buddhism at large.

I am often asked if traveling with the television crew was a pain in the butt, for many suspect I'm underplaying the challenges. But in truth, it wasn't that bad. Of course tensions bubbled up from time to time, but by the time we arrived in Zanskar, the crew felt more like friends than co-workers, and for that, I owe a heartfelt thanks to all who shared in that wondrous journey. There are too many to name—more than eighty by my reckoning—but in the trenches the entire way, we send the biggest of hugs to Austin, Brock, Buzz, Dave, Shauna, Jeff, Jonathon, Caitlin, Gurmeet and Dustin.

An extra-special thanks to Wes Dening, whose vision launched the project, and whose hard work, across continents and oceans, brought it to the finish line. Wes was a wonderful companion on the road, and now has become an even better friend. Cheers, mate.

On this journey and many others, I have been lucky to receive the support of Mountain Equipment Co-op, for whom I am a proud Ambassador. *Jullay,* MEC, for everything you do to get more Canadians outside, more often.

Also, special thanks to Speakers' Spotlight, my speaking agency and close friends, whose decades-long faith in my work has provided me the freedom to tackle projects like this.

The writing of a book can be a lonely journey—five years in this case—but along the way I've been blessed to receive the support and encouragement of many literary-minded friends, who offered valuable feedback on early drafts, including Kate Harris, Nadine Sander-Green, Jordan Zinovich, Jeff Pew,

Dave Quinn, Kelly Comishin, Ace Kvale, Mary McIntyre, Helen Sander, Don Gillmor, Barbara Pulling, Pegg Davidson, Nima Dorjee, Pat Morrow and my wonderful mother, Joan Kirkby, who has proofed every book I've written—several times!

At Simon Fraser University, Scott Steedman's Master of Publishing editing class dissected an early version of my manuscript as a term project, the students offering deft and timely insights. Thank you.

It was the unshakable confidence of my literary agents, John Pearce and Chris Casuccio of Westwood Creative Artists, that propelled me through valleys of doubt. And it was their unflagging efforts that landed the manuscript with the perfect pair of publishing partners. *Jullay, jullay.*

Which brings me to this book. While my name stands alone on the cover, it takes a team to bring any manuscript to life, and I am forever endebted to all who toiled behind the scenes. First and foremost, the dynamic and warm-hearted duo who championed this book from the moment it landed on their respective desks: Anna Comfort O'Keeffe, publisher at Douglas & McIntyre (Canada) and Jessica Case, deputy publisher at Pegasus (USA). On their teams, my deepest gratitude goes to Derek Thornton for his gorgeous cover design, Maria Fernandez for the graceful layout, Nicola Goshulak for the uncanny proofreading, Rebecca Pruitt MacKenney for shepherding the multinational production, and my indefatigable publicists, Annie Boyer, Corina Eberle and Andrea Córdova, for connecting the words to new readers. Finally, an especially fond hug to my editors—Anna, Jessica, Derek Fairbridge, and Emma Skagen—whose gentle touch and clear instincts carried the story much further than I ever could have alone.

It was a particular delight to count Bodi among the proofreaders on this project. He reviewed the manuscript diligently during a sea kayak expedition, sitting by the fire each night and rooting out factual errors. Afterward he declared it "very good, but unlikely to ever be a *New York Times* bestseller."

An invaluable teammate on this literary journey, and so many journeys beyond: no words can suffice for Christine's unending support and encouragement. For her, and our beautiful sons, I save the last and very biggest *jullay* of all.

SELECTED BIBLIOGRAPHY

On Zanskar and the Greater Himalaya

Boyden, Mark. *Travels in Zanskar: A Journey to a Closed Kingdom.* Dublin: Liffey Press, 2014.

Conover, Ted. *The Routes of Man: How Roads Are Changing the World and the Way We Live Today.* New York: Alfred A. Knopf, 2010.

Crook, John, and Henry Osmaston, eds. *Himalayan Buddhist Villages: Environment, Resources, Society and Religious Life in Zangskar, Ladakh.* Delhi: Motilal Banarsdass, 1994.

Crook, John, and James Low. *The Yogins of Ladakh: A Pilgrimage Among the Hermits of the Buddhist Himalayas.* Delhi: Motilal Banarsdass, 1997.

Crowden, James. "The Road to Padum: Its Effect on Zangskar," *Recent Research on Ladakh 6, Proceedings of the Sixth International Colloquium on Ladakh.* Henry Osmaston and Nawang Tsering, eds. Delhi: Motilal Banarsidass, 1997.

Demenge, Jonathan. "The Political Ecology of Road Construction in Ladakh." Doctoral thesis, University of Sussex, 2012.

Diamond, Jared. *The World Until Yesterday: What Can We Learn from Traditional Societies?* New York: Penguin Books, 2012

Gokhale, Sandhya. "Man Environment Interaction and Problems of Socio-Economic Development in Zanskar (Ladakh)." Doctoral thesis, Jawaharlal Nehru University, 1986.

Gutschow, Kim. *Being a Buddhist Nun: The Struggle for Enlightenment in the Himalayas.* Cambridge: Harvard University Press, 2004.

Handa, O.C. *Buddhist Western Himalaya, Part 1: A Politico-Religious History*. New Delhi: M.L. Gidwani, 2001.

Harvey, Andrew. *A Journey in Ladakh: Encounters With Buddhism*. New York: Houghton Mifflin Company, 1983.

Hopkirk, Peter. *The Great Game: On Secret Service in High Asia*. London: John Murray Press, 2006.

Hopkirk, Peter. *Trespassers on the Roof of the World: The Race for Lhasa*. London: John Murray Press, 2012.

Matthiessen, Peter. *The Snow Leopard*. New York: Viking Press, 1978.

Meredith, Robyn. *The Elephant and the Dragon: The Rise of India and China and What It Means for All of Us*. New York: W.W. Norton, 2007.

Mingle, Jonathan. *Fire and Ice: Soot, Solidarity, and Survival on the Roof of the World*. New York: St. Martin's Press, 2015.

Norberg-Hodge, Helena. *Ancient Futures: Learning from Ladakh*. New Delhi: Oxford University Press, 1991.

Norman, Rebecca. *Getting Started in Ladakhi: A Phrasebook for Learning Ladakhi*. Leh: Melong, 2001.

Peissel, Michel. *Zanskar: The Hidden Kingdom*. New York: E.P. Dutton, 1979.

Rizvi, Janet. *Ladakh: Crossroads of High Asia*. New Delhi: Oxford University Press, 1983.

On Buddhism and Meditation

Harris, Dan. *10% Happier: How I Tamed the Voice in My Head, Reduced Stress Without Losing My Edge, and Found Self-Help That Actually Works*. New York: Dey Street Books, 2014.

Iyer, Pico. *The Open Road: The Global Journey of the Fourteenth Dalai Lama*. New York: Alfred A. Knopf, 2008.

Revel, Jean-François, and Matthieu Ricard. *The Monk and the Philosopher: A Father and Son Discuss the Meaning of Life*. New York: Schocken, 1999.

Ward, Tim. *What the Buddha Never Taught*. Toronto: Thomas Allen Publishers, 2010.

Wilson Ross, Nancy. *Buddhism: A Way of Life and Thought*. New York: Alfred A. Knopf, 1980.

On Autism

Attwood, Tony. *The Complete Guide to Asperger's Syndrome*. London: Jessica Kingsley Publishers, 2007.

Robison, John Elder. *Be Different: Adventures of a Free-Range Aspergian*. Toronto: Doubleday Canada, 2011.

Robison, John Elder. *Look Me in the Eye: My Life with Asperger's*. New York: Crown, 2007.

Silberman, Steve. *Neurotribes: The Legacy of Autism and the Future of Neurodiversity*. New York: Penguin Random House, 2015

Suskind, Ron. *Life, Animated: A Story of Sidekicks, Heroes, and Autism*. New York: Kingswell, 2014.

Venables, Stephen. *Ollie: The True Story of a Brief and Courageous Life*. London: Arrow Books, 2007.

On Distraction

Carr, Nicholas. *The Shallows: What the Internet Is Doing to Our Brains*. New York: W. W. Norton, 2010.

Harris, Michael. *The End of Absence: Reclaiming What We've Lost in a World of Constant Connection*. Toronto: HarperCollins, 2014.

Iyer, Pico. *The Art of Stillness: Adventures in Going Nowhere*. New York: Simon & Schuster, 2014.